BECOMING A

....

NEW MAN

Daily Spiritual Workouts

COMPILED BY
THE EDITORS OF *NEW MAN*
MAGAZINE

WRITTEN BY
J. NELSON BLACK, PH.D.

BECOMING A

NEW MAN

Daily
Spiritual
Workouts

COMPILED BY
THE EDITORS OF *NEW MAN*
MAGAZINE

WRITTEN BY
J. NELSON BLACK, PH.D.

CREATION
HOUSE
Orlando, FL

BECOMING A NEW MAN DEVOTIONAL by J. Nelson Black
Published by Creation House
Strang Communications Company
600 Rinehart Road, Lake Mary, Florida 32746
Web site: http://www.creationhouse.com

Unless otherwise noted, all Scripture quotations are from the New King James Version of the Bible. Copyright © 1979, 1980, 1982 by Thomas Nelson Inc., publishers. Used by permission.

Scripture quotations marked TLB are from The Living Bible. Copyright © 1971. Used by permission of Tyndale House Publishers Inc., Wheaton, IL 60189. All rights reserved.

Scripture quotations marked NIV are from the Holy Bible, New International Version. Copyright © 1973, 1978, 1984, International Bible Society. Used by permission.

Scripture quotations marked AMP are from the Amplified Bible. Old Testament copyright © 1965, 1987 by the Zondervan Corporation. The Amplified New Testament copyright © 1954, 1958, 1987 by the Lockman Foundation. Used by permission.

Scripture quotations marked NAS are from the New American Standard Bible. Copyright © 1960, 1962, 1963, 1968, 1971, 1972, 1973, 1975, 1977 by the Lockman Foundation. Used by permission.

Scripture quotations marked RSV are from the Revised Standard Version of the Bible. Copyright © 1946, 1952, 1971 by the Division of Christian Education of the National Council of the Churches of Christ in the USA. Used by permission.

Scripture quotations marked NLT are from the Holy Bible, New Living Translation, copyright © 1996. Used by permission of Tyndale House Publishers, Inc., Wheaton, IL 60189. All rights reserved.

Scripture quotations marked KJV are from the King James Version of the Bible.

Interior design by Lillian L. McAnally

Library of Congress Cataloging-in-Publication Data:
Becoming a New Man devotional (pbk.)/J. Nelson Black, general editor.
1. Men—Prayer—books and devotions—English.   2. Promise Keepers
   (Organization—Prayer—books and devotions—English. 3. Devotional calendars.
I. Black, Jim Nelson.   ISBN: 0-88419-577-5
BV4843.B43   1997   97-30929
242'.642—dc21   CIP

89012345 RP 87654321

Printed in the United States of America

CONTENTS

Foreword. . . . . *vii*
Introduction. . . . . *ix*

☰ FIRST QUARTER ☰

WEEK　1 Leadership 1
WEEK　2 Accountability. 7
WEEK　3 Being a Giver 13
WEEK　4 Faith 18
WEEK　5 Honor 24
WEEK　6 Friendship. 30
WEEK　7 Unity. 36
WEEK　8 Humility 42
WEEK　9 Contentment 48
WEEK 10 Encouragement. 54
WEEK 11 Discernment 60
WEEK 12 Being a Peacemaker . 66
WEEK 13 Longsuffering 72

☰ SECOND QUARTER ☰

WEEK　1 Love 79
WEEK　2 Vision 85
WEEK　3 Ambition. 91
WEEK　4 Forgiveness. 97
WEEK　5 Nurturing 103
WEEK　6 Strength 109
WEEK　7 Diligence. 115
WEEK　8 Faithfulness. 121
WEEK　9 Reconciliation. 127
WEEK 10 Submission 133

WEEK 11 Self-Control 139
WEEK 12 Respect 145
WEEK 13 Courage. 151

≡ THIRD QUARTER ≡

WEEK 1 Wisdom. 158
WEEK 2 Purity 164
WEEK 3 Patience. 170
WEEK 4 Commitment. 176
WEEK 5 Mercy 182
WEEK 6 Freedom 188
WEEK 7 Honesty. 194
WEEK 8 Creativity 200
WEEK 9 Gratefulness 206
WEEK 10 Dependability 212
WEEK 11 Servanthood 218
WEEK 12 Flexibility 224
WEEK 13 Persistence 230

≡ FOURTH QUARTER ≡

WEEK 1 Worship. 238
WEEK 2 Sensitivity 244
WEEK 3 Focus. 250
WEEK 4 Passion 256
WEEK 5 Gentleness. 262
WEEK 6 Steadfastness. 268
WEEK 7 Praise 274
WEEK 8 Caution 280
WEEK 9 Security. 286
WEEK 10 Fun 292
WEEK 11 Acceptance 298
WEEK 12 Hope 304
WEEK 13 Watchfulness. 310

Foreword

"Come, let us worship and bow down,
Let us kneel before our Lord, our God, our Maker."

THESE LYRICS DESCRIBE the perfect posture for a godly man—on his knees in adoration of his Creator. When men take this position, the whole nation will reap the blessing of almighty God. We will see children healed and marriages saved. The needs of the widows and orphans will be met. And the unbelieving world will see a genuine demonstration of God's incredible love for the entire human race.

We believed this when we founded *New Man* magazine in 1994—and we believe it with greater intensity today. Every week we get letters, many from women and children, who have been touched by God through a man who decided to yield his life to Christ. We have also been amazed that God can use a simple magazine as a spark for changes that have eternal rewards.

With God's help, we will continue to publish *New Man* magazine for many years to come. But we also want as many men as possible to benefit from the articles we have already published. In this book, you will find excerpts from some of the classic articles—timeless truths in a devotional format. In the course of one year, you can study fifty-two traits of a godly man—one for each week—along with a short thought for each day.

Keep this book near your Bible, and pull it out each morning. As you go through the day, think about what you read. We believe you will gain a greater knowledge and a greater love for Jesus—the one true companion who never fails. He has so much He wants to give to you.

We hope this book will help you receive His very best.

—THE EDITORS OF *NEW MAN*

TIME ALONE WITH GOD

*So now, brethren, I commend you to God and to
the word of His grace, which is able to build you
up and give you an inheritance among all those
who are sanctified.*

—ACTS 20:32

IF YOU COULD SPEND one hour each morning
doing the most important thing in the world,
what would it be? Would you write your congressman?
Would you spend the time admiring great masterpieces
of literature or music or art? Would you spend it on the
golf course working on your handicap? Or would you,
perhaps, play with a child? No doubt all those things
are important, and each offers some valuable benefits.
But what if you could spend an hour every day alone
with God?

It's not an unrealistic thought. In fact, throughout the
Bible God challenges His people to seek Him out and
to have dialogue with Him. "Come now, let us reason
together," He says in Isaiah 1:18. And in Jeremiah He
says, "For I know the thoughts that I think toward
you . . . thoughts of peace and not of evil, to give you a
future and a hope . . . And you will seek Me and find
Me, when you search for Me with all your heart" (Jer.
29:11, 13).

The very idea is so compelling—that God would
implore each of us to seek Him, to call upon Him, to
search for Him with our hearts, so that He can teach us
from His Word. What an awesome invitation! The
opportunity to find a special, quiet place to be alone in

the presence of the most high God, and then to meditate on His Word, to grow in the grace and knowledge of our Lord and Savior Jesus Christ, is a privilege no man of God should ever miss.

This volume has been designed as a fast-paced, concentrated workout for growing Christians, focusing on the virtues of a godly man. Each quarter is divided into thirteen parts, and each part includes a short reading excerpted from articles that have appeared in the pages of *New Man* magazine. Following each reading are six daily workouts, labeled Monday through Weekend, dealing with important aspects of the issues and the devotional focus for that week. Daily entries also include suggestions for prayer and praise.

The work is meant to be suitable for Bible study groups, prayer groups, and Sunday school classes, as well as personal devotions. Each section covers a thirteen-week study cycle, compatible with the educational programs of many churches. The material can be used in a seasonal manner, or as a twelve-month daily devotional, whichever seems most appropriate for your application. Those who use it in group settings may also want to prepare three or four questions to stimulate conversation over the material.

The volume contains fifty-two topics for fifty-two weeks. Each issue, in turn, touches on several related topics and practical concerns of Christian men. The guiding principle and purpose of the work is that you may be drawn into the wonder and joy of your one-on-one relationship with Jesus Christ, and that you may be strengthened and built up in the faith, as a new man and a citizen of the kingdom.

There has never been a time when the influence of godly men has been so badly needed. Modern culture has made a mockery of common decency and turned moral values upside down. Our cities are in decline, neighborhoods are unsafe, and families are being shattered by dangerous illusions and lies. Our only hope for restoration is to return to the faith of our fathers.

We always seem to find time for the things we enjoy, whether it's jogging or watching football. But if we expect to see revival and renewal in the land, it will only come when the men of God begin putting the things of God first in their lives.

I hope you'll accept this invitation to spend some time with God. Charles Spurgeon once said that if we truly understood the majesty of life we'd be more careful how we start the day. The God who made us has a plan for our lives, but we can only know it if we make ourselves available to His will. If we hope to spend eternity with the Lord, shouldn't we get into the habit now of spending time alone with Him each day?

—J. NELSON BLACK, PH.D.
DALLAS, TEXAS

FIRST

←·····················→

QUARTER

....
LEADERSHIP

■■■■ ON A COLD October morning in 1992, five bleary-
■■■■ eyed men gathered in a pastor's overcrowded
office in north Atlanta to form a men's ministry leadership team. One of them thought: *It's 6 A.M., and here I
am trying to figure out how to motivate guys to be
involved in a men's ministry. I'm probably more a part
of the problem than the solution. Besides, I have never
seen men get excited about breakfast meetings, retreats,
or small groups.*

The men knew what to do: They prayed. That morning,
their hearts melded as they talked about getting men
excited about growing in their Christian faith, breaking
down barriers, and building meaningful relationships.
That same autumn, another pastor was meeting with
four other men. His desire was to reach pastors. He had
heard about the changed lives of men who attended
Promise Keepers, but would his guys go with him to
some conference in a football stadium—fifteen hundred miles away?

When they left the sold-out Promise Keepers conference the following July, they couldn't believe their
eyes. Some fifty thousand men from every ethnicity
and denomination were singing and praying and crying
and pouring their hearts out to each other and to their
Lord, Jesus Christ.

What is happening to men? Coach Bill McCartney
says it best: "When we gather in His name, He becomes
our standard. And when we rub elbows with each other,
with Christ as our focus, almighty God raises the standard for what it means to be a godly man, a promise

....

keeper, in our marriages and families, in our churches and communities, and in our friendships."

At Promise Keepers conferences, each man can expect to be challenged in a different way. As praise and worship music sets the tone for the conference, one feels the presence of the Spirit of God. Men break down walls of prejudice and pride as they embrace in moments of prayer. Gifted men of God deliver tough messages about family, sexual and moral purity, accountability to each other, and what it means to be a godly man.

The leadership principles of Promises Keepers are expressed in these seven promises. A Promise Keeper is committed to:

1. Honoring Jesus Christ through worship, prayer, and obedience to God's Word through the power of the Holy Spirit.

2. Pursuing vital relationships with a few other men, understanding that he needs brothers to help him keep his promises.

3. Practicing spiritual, moral, ethical, and sexual purity.

4. Building strong marriages and families through love, protection, and biblical values.

5. Supporting the mission of his church by honoring and praying for his pastor and by actively giving of his time and resources.

6. Reaching beyond any racial and denominational barriers to demonstrate the power of biblical unity.

7. Influencing his world, being obedient to the Great Commandment (Mark 12:30–31) and the Great Commission (Matt. 28:19–20).

These are the commitments that help Promise Keepers to build the vital relationships that allow them to be a godly influence in their world.

—PROMISE KEEPERS

MONDAY

IN ONE WAY or another, we're all leaders. Even if we're not leaders at work, we all set standards for ourselves and our families to live by. But real leadership is not based on wishful thinking: It's based on a personal commitment to seek out the goals and priorities that God would have us follow. If you think about the example of that remarkable prayer meeting in England, or of Coach Bill McCartney calling men to a higher standard, you soon discover that real leaders are men of prayer—men who depend on God for their strength.

As you begin this time of study and devotion, it's important that you find a special hour and a special place to be alone with God. How can you hear the voice of the Spirit and the Word of God speaking to your heart unless you give Him your undivided attention?

Pray that God will prepare your heart to hear His gentle voice. ▤

TUESDAY

PAUL WRITES, "For by grace you have been saved through faith, and that not of yourselves; it is the gift of God, not of works, lest anyone should boast" (Eph. 2:8–9). Faith is another essential trait of leaders; men who expect to accomplish great things know that they can accomplish nothing unless God prepares the way. That's why the pastors and the Promise Keepers in Atlanta made prayer their first priority. Real leaders strive for success, but they also recognize their dependence upon Christ's leadership.

The writer of Hebrews says, "Let us run with endurance the race that is set before us, looking unto Jesus, the author and finisher of our faith" (Heb.

12:1–2). Yes, the prize goes to the winner; but the winner is the one who learns the rules, practices them tirelessly, then runs with endurance.

Do you want to be a better leader? Ask God to build your faith. ◼

WEDNESDAY

PRAY WITH EXPECTATION. What an important lesson for a new man. On the road to Jerusalem one day, Jesus paused to pick a fig but found no fruit on the tree. He cursed the tree: "Let no one eat fruit from you ever again." Peter didn't say much until they returned later and saw what had happened. "Wow!" he must have said. "Jesus, look, the tree you cursed is all shriveled up!"

Now here was a *teachable moment!* Suddenly He had Peter's full attention, so Jesus said, "This is the absolute truth—you can say to this Mount of Olives, 'Rise up and fall into the Mediterranean,' and your command will be obeyed. All that's required is that you really believe and have no doubt!" Looking Peter in the eye, He said, "Listen to me! You can pray for anything, and if you believe, you have it; it's yours!" (Mark 11:23–24, TLB).

Do you want to be a man of God? Then pray that He will make you fruitful and obedient to His will. And if you truly believe, it's yours! ◼

THURSDAY

IT STARTED with small bands, praying that God would move in men's hearts. Then God stirred a few leaders to challenge a few others to pray, to seek His face, and to trust Him for a miracle. Today, millions of men all over the world have accepted the challenge to live godly lives and to repent of sin, anger, and indifference in order to be men of godly character. Do we need good leaders? You bet. Challenging messages? Of course. But the most essential requirement for building this or any movement is the power of prayer.

Every leader needs a plan. How can you expect to reach your goals if you don't know where you're headed? But no plan will prosper unless it's the plan God has laid on your heart, nourished through His Word, and brought to fruition through dedicated prayer.

Pray today that God will fulfill His individual plan for your life. ▤

Friday

THE SEVEN PROMISES of Promise Keepers focus on several key principles that can help make us well-rounded men of God. Worship, relationships, purity, strong families, giving of our time and resources, racial and denominational reconciliation, and being bold servant leaders: These are characteristics of men who have been redeemed and fully transformed by Jesus Christ.

When these personal commitments become a regular part of your life, you find that people will be curious: They want to know what makes you tick. Why are you so different? Why are you at peace when others are constantly under such intense stress? Answering their questions may provide some *teachable moments* when you can share the Source of your hope.

Pray that you may be built up and fully transformed for Christ's service. ▤

Weekend

ARE YOU BOLD enough to stand up for Christ in a world that often sneers at faith? Jesus' challenge to "Let your light so shine before men, that they may see your good works and glorify your Father in heaven" (Matt. 5:16) can seem frightening at times. If you worry about such things, remember this: Jesus meets us halfway, but He leads us all the way. Even the desire to be a man of character was instilled in your heart by the Lord.

When Timothy was shy, nervous, afraid to take his role as a leader, Paul assured him, "For God has not given us a spirit of fear, but of power and of love and of a sound mind. Therefore do not be ashamed of the testimony of our Lord" (2 Tim. 1:7–8). When we kneel in prayer, seeking courage and wisdom, we are given access to the power of God, "Who has saved us and called us with a holy calling, not according to our works, but according to His own purpose and grace which was given to us in Christ Jesus before time began" (2 Tim 1:9).

Will you take the first step of a real leader and meet the Savior halfway? ▤

Week 2
ACCOUNTABILITY

My BALANCING ACT of trying to maintain a family, a job, and a full-time doctoral program took its toll on my loved ones. That became clear when my daughter showed me a picture she had drawn of our family. *I wasn't in it.* My daughters, my wife, and the family dog were in the picture. "Where is your dad?" I asked.

"You're at the library," she said.

Sarah's words hit me in the gut like a two-by-four. In my effort to succeed in the marketplace, I had failed at home. When I set out to make things right, I realized I needed to be accountable to a few other men. "A three-fold cord is not quickly broken" (4:12), says the author of Ecclesiastes. We can't walk through life solo: being a man of God is a "team sport."

Through my church, I teamed up with other men in "A-teams" (accountability groups). In the past I tended to say things were okay at home when they really weren't. I was too scared to admit it. When I finally told my group what I needed, they responded: "Hey we're not counselors, but we'll do all we can to help restore you to your family." That was just what I needed to hear.

Our weekly meetings took on a deeper level. We asked each other about our thought lives, finances, physical temptations, our prayer lives, and Bible study, as well as relationships with the wife and kids. And then the final one: "Are you shooting straight with me or blowing smoke?"

What started as a twelve-week trial run for four guys turned into a weekly meeting of about four hundred men. Today, more than one thousand in Des Moines and hundreds more in eighteen other cities call themselves "CrossTrainers." That is, men who meet for crosstraining in their roles as believers, husbands, dads, friends, and members of their churches and communities.

Our weekly meetings usually involve Bible study and discussing the books for men we have read. If you're interested in starting a similar group, let me share our six foundations for a healthy small group. *Acceptance* means allowing the other guy to be who he is and accepting him, "warts and all." *Authenticity* means committing to be fully honest with each other. We all need brothers to whom we can say anything and still feel safe.

Confidentiality means that whatever we discuss stays within the group. Risk builds relationship; relationship builds trust; trust strengthens character. *Encouragement* means being uplifting. If you need encouragement, be encouraging with a brother. The fifth foundation, *Accountability,* means surrounding yourself with men who love you enough to challenge you. Accountability is like a guard rail on a mountain road that keeps you from going over. *Obedience,* the final foundation, means being obedient to the Father and helping others to do the same.

Today, I'm back in my family picture, and you can be in yours. But you need the support of other men. Let's finish well—together.

—GARY ROSBERG

MONDAY

SOMETIME BEFORE our teen years, we reach the age of accountability. This means we become accountable to God for knowing right from wrong, and are fully responsible for our sins. But there is another kind of accountability: answering to others for our daily behavior. When Gary Rosberg saw the portrait his young daughter had drawn, he was shocked to see that he was not a factor in the lives of his family. He let other pressing matters take him away from those he loved, and, in the process, he had let them down.

James tells us, "Confess your trespasses to one another, and pray for one another, that you may be healed." And then he adds, "The effective, fervent prayer of a righteous man avails much" (James 5:16). When we fail, we need to be confess to God first; but being accountable to others, combined with fervent prayer, can help turn us around.

As you consider Gary's example, pray for God's guidance in this area of your life. ▤

Tuesday

"Two heads are better than one." That's a wise old proverb, but the writer of Ecclesiastes understood the concept even better. He said, "Two can accomplish more than twice as much as one, for the results can be much better. If one falls, the other pulls him up; but if a man falls when he is alone, he's in trouble. Also, on a cold night, two under the same blanket gain warmth from each other, but how can one be warm alone? And one standing alone can be attacked and defeated, but two can stand back-to-back and conquer; three is even better, for a triple-braided cord is not easily broken" (Eccles. 4:9–12, TLB).

Gary Rosberg got serious about accountability in a hurry. His desire to be faithful to his family led to the formation of an accountability group, then A-teams in his church, and eventually a national CrossTrainers program. Are you accountable? Do you want to be? Why not pray that God will help you to be a godly man who is truly accountable? ▤

WEDNESDAY

BEFORE WE CAN get right with God, we have to admit we have a problem. The whole basis of forgiveness is heartfelt confession of wrongdoing, and that calls for honesty with ourselves, with God, and with others. When we ask other men to hold us accountable, we set up a relationship that demands honesty and sincerity at every level. We give each of them the right to ask if we're being faithful stewards of our resources, if we have kept our tempers in check, if we have avoided the appearance and the substance of evil and lust, if we're walking with God every day, and if we're behaving like men of God at home. We also know that they have the right to ask us, "Are you shooting straight with me, or are you just blowing smoke?"

Proverbs 19:1 says it's better to be poor and honest than rich and dishonest. Have you got your priorities straight? Are you just blowing smoke? Why not pray about it. ▤

THURSDAY

WHEN OUR HEARTS are right with God, good things happen. Consider these words of King David in Psalm 1: "Blessed is the man who walks not in the counsel of the ungodly, nor stands in the path of sinners, nor sits in the seat of the scornful; but his delight is in the law of the Lord, and in His law he meditates day and night. He shall be like a tree planted by the rivers of water, that brings forth its fruit in its season, whose leaf also shall not wither; and whatever he does shall prosper. The ungodly are not so, but are like the chaff which the wind drives away" (Ps. 1:1–4).

What a vivid portrait of the choices we each must make. The ungodly man will perish; even his best-laid plans will go wrong. Solomon says, "The way of the wicked is like darkness; they do not know what makes them stumble" (Prov. 4:19). But the man who is honest and accountable will flourish like a fruit tree in season.

Ask God to help you to grow deep roots, to be a man who delights in Him. ▤

FRIDAY

ONE OF THE FRUITS of Gary Rosberg's ministry is his list of six foundations of healthy small groups. They include *Acceptance* of others as they are, *Authenticity* and complete honesty, *Confidentiality* with what you know of other men's struggles, *Encouragement* of others, *Accountability* to them along with a willingness to challenge each other, and, finally, *Obedience* to God the Father, plus helping your brothers to obey.

Too much to take on? Hear Paul's words to Timothy: "Even when we are too weak to have any faith left, [Jesus] remains faithful to us and will help us, for he cannot disown us who are part of himself, and he will always carry out his promises to us. Remind your people of these great facts. . . . Work hard so God can say to you, 'Well done.' Be a good workman, one who does not need to be ashamed when God examines your work. Know what his Word says and means" (2 Tim. 2:13–15, TLB).

Today, pray that God will help you to understand these principles of accountability. ▤

WEEKEND

FINISH WELL, TOGETHER. That's what it comes down to. The challenge of this week's devotional is not just to think about being men of integrity who are responsible and accountable to others, but to live out each day the kind of godly example we want to model. If Promise Keepers, or your local men's group, or your church groups aren't helping you to be a more loving husband, a better father, and a true friend to your extended family and friends, then something's not working. Being accountable is not a short-term project but the vehicle we employ to make sure that we look, act, and think like men of God—all the time.

The writer of Hebrews offers this word: "Let us hold fast the confession of our hope without wavering, for He who promised is faithful. And let us consider one another in order to stir up love and good works" (Heb. 10:23–24).

As you remain in the Word of God, and seek Him in prayer, you become an instrument of His love in the lives of others. Pray that He will draw you closer. ■

BEING A GIVER

▰▰▰ FOR THE FIRST fifteen years of our marriage, I did
▰▰▰ not help Diane make our house a home. I had
determined that housework was women's work. Diane
was my personal secretary and mom to our two daughters. She waited on me hand and foot and never
demanded that I help her.

I really loved my wife, but I had not learned to show
my love. Like a cave man, I made brutish sexual
advances believing that was how a real man expressed
love. No wonder our love life had cooled. Oaf that I
was, I couldn't figure out the problem with her. Wasn't
she grateful? Of all the women I could have married, I
chose her.

And now, God was ready to use a vacuum cleaner to
teach me a lesson. Looking up from my crossword
puzzle, I saw the door to the storage closet was slightly
ajar. Standing in the dim interior was . . . the vacuum
cleaner. I had paid more than three hundred for that
vacuum cleaner, but it never did suck dirt, according to
my wife. I stared at the rug-sucker from my armchair
and decided to give it a spin. Sure enough, the machine
would not pick up important things like toothpicks or
burrs. It would fling rubber bands across the room, and
it would hold lint for an indiscriminate period of time
and spit it back out.

The trash I fed it was snatched from my fingers, dis-
appearing into the bowels of the hissing monster. That's
when I discovered the stripes. As I vacuumed in one
direction, a stripe would appear. Going in the opposite
direction would create a stripe of a different shade.

Fascinated, I striped the whole room. I got so carried away that I dusted the furniture, waxed, and straightened the entire house.

I was reunited with my easy chair when Diane came home. She struggled through the door, clutching a bag of groceries under each arm, kicked the door shut with one foot and then saw the house. Her mouth dropped open. "Who did this?" she gasped.

"I did," I said. Then she attacked me.

Diving on me before I could stand up, she smothered me with kisses and thanked me over and over. The kisses grew more passionate. We broke the chair. It was wonderful!

The vacuum cleaner taught me a lesson that day. Love is more than just words. When a husband shares the burdens of homemaking, it shouts "I love you" to any woman. After thirty years of marriage, I still have a lot to learn, but I could never treat my wife as I did back then.

Now I say "I love you" with a variety of actions. An unexpected card or bouquet of flowers. Picking up after myself. Cooking. Squeezing toothpaste from the bottom of the tube. And the physical passion has returned to our marriage with intensity I have not experienced in years.

I have learned my lesson. I keep a Dust Buster with me everywhere we go!

—KEN DAVIS

MONDAY

TOOLS ARE SUCH basic things. Most men know something about them; we know how to fix objects, but we often seem lost in space when it comes to keeping our personal relationships in good repair. You may think it's funny that it took a cantankerous old vacuum to get this guy's attention, but think how often we all fail to consider the needs of those around us.

In his article, Ken Davis describes, in an amusing

way, the learning process many new husbands go through in the early days of marriage. Sharing household duties with your wife may have some tangible benefits, as in Ken's case; but you also gain a sense of self-respect when you learn to give in this way.

As you reflect on your own relationships, ask yourself if you're doing enough.

Pray that the Lord will show you how you can give more freely. ▤

TUESDAY

JESUS SAID, "'You shall love the Lord your God with all your heart, with all your soul, and with all your mind.' This is the first and great commandment. And the second is like it: 'You shall love your neighbor as yourself.' On these two commandments hang all the Law and the Prophets" (Matt. 22:37–40).

What a remarkable statement! The Jewish law includes more than 613 precepts and commandments that were to be taken seriously by committed believers of the day, yet Jesus declared that when we love our God and love our neighbors as ourselves, we have fulfilled the entire purpose and intent of the law. How can that be? Have you ever thought about what that statement really means?

Think about it. What would it take for you to love your *God,* your *family,* and your *neighbors* in this way? ▤

WEDNESDAY

AT ONE POINT near the end of Jesus' ministry on earth, James and John came to the Master and asked if He would allow them to sit next to Him in the kingdom of heaven, one on the left and one on the right. No doubt Jesus shook His head at their naïve question, for they didn't have a clue what they were asking.

But in answering the question, Jesus taught them an important lesson about giving, saying, "Whoever desires to become great among you shall be your servant. And whoever of you desires to be first shall be slave of all" (Mark 10:43–44). Even His disciples knew how to take—but they had to be taught how to give.

When Paul reminded the early Christians of Jesus' words, that "it is more blessed to give than to receive" (Acts 20:35), they were deeply humbled. Like us, they struggled with the idea of giving. Pray that Christ will teach you how to serve and to give more freely. ■

THURSDAY

WE GET A marvelous insight into the giving spirit in Paul's letter to the Romans, where he writes:

> Be kindly affectionate to one another with brotherly love, in honor giving preference to one another; not lagging in diligence, fervent in spirit, serving the Lord; rejoicing in hope, patient in tribulation, continuing steadfastly in prayer; distributing to the needs of the saints, given to hospitality. Bless those who persecute you; bless and do not curse.
>
> Rejoice with those who rejoice, and weep with those who weep. Be of the same mind toward one another. Do not set your mind on high things, but associate with the humble. Do not be wise in your own opinion. Repay no one evil for evil. Have regard for good things in the sight of all men. If it is possible, as much as depends on you, live peaceably with all men.
>
> —ROMANS 12:10–18

What would it take for you to live and to love like this? Why not pray about it? ■

FRIDAY

MORE THAN just a good idea, the challenge to love your wife, to honor her, and to treat her with respect is a strict biblical admonition. Peter tells us, "Husbands, likewise, dwell with them with understanding, giving honor to the wife, as to the weaker vessel, and as being heirs together of the grace of life, that your prayers may not be hindered" (1 Pet. 3:7). As the stronger sex, men sometimes have to be reminded that superior size and strength does not mean we are superior in any other way. For husband and wife are one flesh in the eyes of God, and, when both are believers, both receive the gift of eternal life equally. Peter warns that when we fail to honor our wives, our prayers will have no punch, because our bad behavior demonstrates that we are not truly sons and heirs of the kingdom.

Whether or not you're married, the same spirit of grace should abide in you. Pray that your heart will be sensitized to show honor and respect for others. ▤

WEEKEND

WHEN JESUS SAID, "Inasmuch as you did it to one of the least of these My brethren, you did it to Me" (Matt. 25:40), surely He included the members of our own families. As you reflect on each of your relationships, think about the importance of giving to others. How can you bless your wife?

Are there ways you can think of that your actions or conversation could strengthen and encourage her? Are there any tasks that you could take over that would make her life a little easier and more enjoyable? And how about all the other people in your life? Are there ways you could demonstrate a new spirit of giving to them?

Review the scriptures in this week's workouts, then pray that God will show you how you can be more of a blessing to those you love. ▤

Week 4
FAITH

MOST PEOPLE don't realize how big a part faith plays in everyday affairs. It takes faith to get married because marriage vows are basically promises. It takes faith to send children off to school. It takes faith to get a prescription filled and to take the medicine when we get it. It takes faith to eat in a restaurant, deposit money in a bank, sign a contract, drive on a highway, or get on an airplane or an elevator. Faith isn't some kind of religious experience; it's the glue that helps hold people's lives together.

But remember, faith is only as good as its object. If we trust people, we get what people can do; if we trust money, we get what money can do; if we trust ourselves, we get what we can do; if we trust God, we get what God can do. But what does it mean to "trust God"? When you read Hebrews 11, the great faith chapter, you discover four basic facts.

1. *Faith begins with a revelation from God.* What these "heroes of faith" did was in response to what God said to them. Faith isn't psyching ourselves up so that we're confident God is on our side. Faith is listening to what God says in His Word and acting on it.

2. *Faith grows out of a relationship with God.* Trust is a relationship that can be built only over time. To loan five hundred to a stranger and expect to get it back isn't faith; it's presumption. The people described in Hebrews 11 were people who walked with God and had a relationship with Him. They knew His character

was such that His word could be trusted.

3. *Faith motivates us to do the will of God.* True faith isn't feeling good about what God says; it's *doing* what God says. Faith isn't discussing the will of God; it's *obeying* the will of God. James told us that "faith without works is dead."

4. *Faith, when acted upon, gives us the witness of God.* True faith rests on the *objective* Word of God, but it is witnessed to *subjectively* by the Spirit of God. Faith is "the evidence of things not seen" (Heb. 11:1), and the word *evidence* means "conviction." When we have true biblical faith, it produces the inner conviction that God will do what He says.

Christians with little faith are fearful people who doubt God's Word and do a great deal of worrying. Consequently, they can't really minister to others or give a strong witness to the lost. Instead of walking by faith and claiming their inheritance in Christ, they're wandering in the wilderness of unbelief and missing God's best for their lives.

Let's pray that our faith will be one that will draw us—and others—not away from but closer to the living God. We should heed Jesus' words: "According to your faith let it be to you" (Matt. 9:29).

—WARREN WIERSBE

MONDAY

WE DON'T OFTEN think about just how big a role faith plays in our lives. As Warren Wiersbe points out, it takes faith to sign a contract, educate your kids, purchase medication or other items from the store, ride an elevator or an airplane, and even to eat in a restaurant. How ironic that we are willing to put our trust in those things so quickly but sometimes act as if faith in God is a mystery.

David went through many hardships in his life and

suffered many wounds, some of which were self-inflicted. But he learned to trust God. After many trials and temptations, David became king of Israel and, through David's line, God brought forth the Messiah, Jesus. David sang, "The Lord is my rock and my fortress and my deliverer; my God, my strength, in whom I will trust; my shield and the horn of my salvation, my stronghold" (Ps. 18:2). Faith in God isn't just a good idea; it's the best idea of all.

Would you praise Him now for His goodness and faithfulness to you? ◼

TUESDAY

FAITH, AS THIS week's reading points out, is only as good as its objects. People can let you down, gold and silver surely can't be trusted, and even the best of contracts can be broken. The one sure thing in this world—as well as the next—is faith in God.

Hebrews 11:6 says, "But without faith it is impossible to please Him, for he who comes to God must believe that He is, and that He is a rewarder of those who diligently seek Him." That's a loaded verse. It says that God expects all His children to have faith in Him, and He is disappointed when they don't. Although some people have tried, you can't discover God with a telescope or a calculator. It takes a diligent act of faith. But when you learn to trust Him, you'll begin to enjoy the rewards He reserves for His own. Have you experienced those rewards?

Pray today that God will build you up in the faith and teach you to trust Him in all things. ◼

WEDNESDAY

THE FIRST OF Warren Wiersbe's four principles is that *faith always begins with a revelation from God.* You can't hype yourself into faith. It isn't some kind of mind game. Faith is the natural response of a person who has found God dependable because he has witnessed His handiwork. Hebrews 11 offers many examples: "By faith Abraham obeyed when he was called . . .," "By faith Abraham, when he was tested, offered up Isaac. . . ." But also remember that scene of Peter stepping out on the sea of Galilee, the centurion whose servant was healed because he trusted Jesus, and the faithful at Pentecost who waited for a sign from heaven and were touched by tongues of fire and filled with the Holy Spirit.

Have you witnessed the faithfulness of God? Have you experienced His touch on your heart and life? Then praise Him, and thank Him for His faithfulness. ▰

THURSDAY

THE SECOND fact of faith, according to Mr. Wiersbe, is that *faith grows out of a relationship with God.* In his letter to the Romans, Paul offers a marvelous statement of this truth, saying, "Therefore, having been justified by faith, we have peace with God through our Lord Jesus Christ, through whom also we have access by faith into this grace in which we stand, and rejoice in hope of the glory of God. And not only that, but we also glory in tribulations, knowing that tribulation produces perseverance; and perseverance, character; and character, hope. Now hope does not disappoint, because the love of God has been poured out in our hearts by the Holy Spirit who was given to us" (Rom. 5:1–5).

Notice that faith is the first step—the doorway to peace, grace, hope, character, and the love of God. No one wants to endure difficulties; but through faith, even persecution can draw us closer to the glory of God.

Are you glad to know that God is always faithful? ▰

Friday

THE THIRD fact of faith is that *faith motivates us to do the will of God*. Sometimes we act as if faith is just some sort of warm fuzzy feeling, that God's in His heaven and all's right with the world. We have trusted Jesus, got our fire insurance, so now we can just go on with life as usual. But it doesn't work that way for two reasons. First, being transformed by the renewing of our minds, as Paul says in Romans 12:2, means that we're no longer conformed to this world but we have become new creations in Christ! We have a new identity and new responsibilities. James says, "For as the body without the spirit is dead, so faith without works is dead also" (James 2:26). But, second, the joy of our salvation provokes us to seek out ways to serve. We should be overwhelmed by the reality of Christ's gift of eternal life!

We talk a lot about motivation these days. But if we truly serve the risen Lord we shouldn't need a pep talk.

Pray today that Jesus will renew your spirit with His motivation. ▤

Weekend

PERHAPS THE BEST description of faith in the Scriptures is the first verse of this great faith chapter in Hebrews, which says, "Now faith is the substance of things hoped for, the evidence of things not seen" (Heb. 11:1). Faith is not some wispy intangible as we often think, it's a powerful force. It is the very substance of what we hope for; it is evidence of the things we pray for but cannot see just yet. The fourth of Wiersbe's facts of faith is that *faith, when acted upon, gives us the witness of God*. In other words, we find God in His most certain reality when we do those things that require us to act on faith.

When we hesitate in fear, thinking that God will not act or that He will let us down in a crunch, we get what we expect. Faith comes in inverse proportion to your fears. The more you let fear control your actions, the less faith you have. But when you step out in faith, trusting God, your fear melts away because God is as good as His word.

Pray that God will demonstrate that kind of faith in your life. ▤

Week 5
HONOR

I REMEMBER the story told by Father Richard Rohr about a friend, a Catholic nun, who was working with prison inmates. Early one spring, an inmate asked if she could get him a Mother's Day card to send to his mom. She brought him a card, and pretty soon word got out, and several other inmates asked her for cards. Wisely the nun contacted a company that donated whole boxes of Mother's Day cards, and she distributed all of them to the inmates.

Then she realized that Father's Day was approaching, and again the company sent her plenty of cards. To her surprise, Father's Day came and passed, and not one inmate asked for a card to honor his father. The reason was clear: How can we honor someone we don't respect? But my response may surprise you: It can, and must, be done.

Honoring fathers means that we place value on the role of fathers in our society. We are not merely *called* to honor fathers, we are *commanded* to honor fathers. The commandment says nothing about whether they were involved, reliable, nurturing parents. The command is unconditional.

One woman said, "I was abused by my father, and I could not respect him in any way until I began to deal with the condition of my heart and ask for healing. Then over the years I was able to visit him. I took time to sit with him, to talk to him, call him on the phone, and I even wrote him a note. Then in time I realized the love and respect I was showing him was coming from another Father who was helping me work through my own pain. Finally I even helped him financially until he died last year."

This story is being lived out by scores of men and women. When another Father has showered His love upon you, it empowers you to forgive and extend grace to your fathers. It's a difficult step for many, because it may mean you have to forgive your father for his behavior toward you. If your dad did a pretty good job, applaud and honor him. Doing so will honor God. But even if you have nothing but negative feelings toward your dad, we have a mandate to look for the good in our fathers. Think of ways you can help your father. If all else fails, ponder this inescapable truth—without your father, you wouldn't be here.

Remember, fathers need respect. When a father is given respect, it endows him with a fresh sense of responsibility, compassion, and humility. Here's how one older dad responded: "I never expected to receive this in my life. After my son called and thanked me for being his dad, I wept for days, and I get tears in my eyes when I think about it now."

Men, we have the power to give that overwhelming respect and honor to our dads and other men in our lives.

—KEN R. CANFIELD

MONDAY

THE FIRST FOUR of the Ten Commandments focus on the righteousness and authority of God. We are instructed to love God and honor Him first; we are told to shun idols, to show reverence for the name of God, and to keep His day of worship holy. Then, the next commandment says: "Honor your father and mother, that your days may be long in the earth." Paul observes that this is the first commandment with promise (Eph. 6:2). We honor God because it's right and good; but we honor our fathers and mothers so that it may be well with us, and so that we may live long and prosperous lives.

Because our earthly fathers are human and fallible, sometimes it is hard to honor them. Ken Canfield's story about the inmates' disinterest in Fathers' Day cards is a telling illustration. But God gives us little choice in the matter: if we want to obey Him, we must honor our dads.

Pray that God will teach you how to do that. ■

TUESDAY

JESUS REFERRED to the importance of honoring our fathers and mothers on several occasions, and even told the Pharisees that withholding financial support from their parents in order to give it to the temple was a sin. He reminded them that Moses had said, "He who curses his father or his mother shall surely be put to death" (Exod. 21:17). Yet they found it easier to dishonor their parents than to keep God's commandments.

Can we honor someone we don't respect? Yes, we do it because God *commands* it; but we also do it because society *needs* it. In fact, one reason we may find it hard to honor dads is because society has made an institution of mocking fathers. Instead of *Father Knows Best,* the new generation laughs at male authority, scorns the role of father, and often acts as if we'd be better off without them. Turning these attitudes around will be a long-term project, but the first step is to become honorable men, and then to demonstrate honor for dads and other men.

Let your prayer be that you will always be an honorable man. ■

WEDNESDAY

WHEN WE FIND it hard to obey God on the basis of reason alone, we should do it by faith. Like the woman in this week's reading, we honor our parents because we know God expects it; then, as we examine the condition of our hearts, we find that God uses these situations to transform us into the kind of person He wants us to be.

The key word is obedience. God doesn't ask that we understand; He asks that we honor Him by obeying His commands. "Observe and obey all these words which I command you, that it may go well with you and your children after you forever, when you do what is good and right in the sight of the Lord your God" (Deut. 12:28). Failure to obey God leads to catastrophe; but the blessing for doing what is right flows onward from us to our children and to all those around us.

What better reason could you have to give Him praise? ▤

THURSDAY

FORGIVENESS for past wrongs unleashes a remarkable power. Not only does it free the other person from the guilt they may bear for having wronged you, but, more importantly, it frees you as well. In the model prayer Jesus used to teach His disciples to pray, He made forgiveness a big part of it, praying that God would forgive us to the degree that we forgive others. But then, in the very next sentence, He says: "But if you do not forgive men their trespasses, neither will your Father forgive your trespasses" (Matt. 6:15).

That should be motivation enough for us to practice forgiveness. But can we move from forgiveness to actually honoring others? Yes, if we understand that we are all children of God, our heavenly Father, who has extended His grace to us. Through no merit of our own, He has honored us with eternal life. Of course, we can never match God's great gift of love, but we should be able to honor others freely, without expecting anything in return. That is one of the distinguishing marks of a godly man.

Ask Him to help you do that. ▤

FRIDAY

A REMARKABLE THING happens to others as they perceive that we're honoring them: They begin to behave more like honorable people. It's not manipulation but simply a human characteristic. Except in the hardest cases where there is a history of abuse, giving honor to others produces a sense of responsibility and self-respect. Treat others with respect, and they become more respectable.

If we understood the difficulty and disrespect our dads and granddads may have lived with, we would be more patient of their failings and more grateful for their strengths. If they behave badly, you have the capacity to love them anyway. If they love you and treat you well, then you have the capacity to express your gratitude. Remember Jesus' words? "There is a saying, 'Love your friends and hate your enemies.' But I say: Love your enemies! Pray for those who persecute you! In that way you will be acting as true sons of your Father in heaven" (Matt. 5:43–45, TLB).

Pray for the strength to live this way each day. ▰

WEEKEND

IT IS IMPORTANT to understand that giving honor to others is a sign of strength and personal courage—traits that God wants to build in us. When Moses led the Israelites out of bondage in Egypt, they had to do battle against the people of Canaan; but Moses encouraged them, saying: "Be strong and of good courage, do not fear nor be afraid of them; for the Lord your God, He is the One who goes with you. He will not leave you nor forsake you" (Deut. 31:6). Later, Joshua said the same thing to his troops at Jericho.

When we truly understand that God is with us, that He goes before us not only to prepare the way for change in others but to renew our hearts from the inside

out, we should fall on our knees in praise and thanksgiving. What kind of God would honor us in this way?
And what kind of men should we be in response?

Thank Him today for His en*courage*ment, for His love
for you, and for the way He is working in your life. ▤

FRIENDSHIP

IN THE EARLY YEARS of marriage, it's just the two of you. Waking up with bad-hair days and asking your spouse not to kiss you until you swished Listerine. Remember? In the child-rearing years, kids fill your life with scores of Kodak moments. But kids also increase the pace of life. You're busy building a career, trying to keep in shape, doctor visits, car pools, sports, music, and homework.

Maybe you haven't had a meaningful conversation with your spouse in a week. But you know that's to be expected because kids are high maintenance items these days. Looking ahead, the golden season of marriage begins the day the last child leaves for college. If you're afraid your mind will blare, *This isn't what I expected marriage to be!* Good. This is a healthy fear. But what are you going to do about it?

Work is important, spending time with your children is essential, serving at church is needed, but these are secondary to two other priorities: 1) Keeping God central to everything, and 2) Doing everything within your power to make sure your wife is the strongest, most important priority among all the rest. Nothing should come between you and your "first love." However, I have talked to dozens of men who read their Bibles and pray almost every day, but they have grown weary of pursuing a relationship with their wife. And men who do not persevere in pursuing their wives on a more intimate level than sex *will* eventually self-destruct.

Attaining a solid friendship with your wife will make the picture of your life come into focus. Here are some practical steps to consider:

1. *Decide to do it.* There's nothing better for you than a close friendship with your wife, and nothing worse than living separately under the same roof.

2. *Enlist your wife's support.* Let her know you're ready to make some changes. Begin by deciding on some things you'd enjoy doing together.

3. *Find snippets of time each day to be alone together, to talk, take a walk, or just unwind after a long day.* Teach the kids to respect these private times.

4. *Schedule time away.* It may be a date night each week, an overnighter each quarter, or a second vacation for the two of you, without the kids.

5. *Talk about everything.* Don't wait until the kids are gone to learn how; start today.

6. *Develop hobbies you can do together—games, crafts, sports, or church activities.*

7. *Connect spiritually.* The closer you grow to God, the closer you will grow to each other.

8. *Get on automatic pilot.* When a plane veers off course, the auto pilot guides it back. In a marriage, auto pilot is giving each other permission to say, "It feels like we're heading off course. How can we get back on track?"

Make a commitment to these action steps, then watch your marriage take a turn in the right direction.

—GREG JOHNSON

MONDAY

THE BIBLE teaches the value of friendship in many

ways. Friendship creates a special bond between men: "A friend loves at all times, and a brother is born for adversity" (Prov. 17:17). But it also says that friendship is a two-way street: "A man who has friends must himself be friendly," and adds, "But there is a friend who sticks closer than a brother" (Prov. 18:24). Jesus said, "Greater love has no one than this, than to lay down one's life for his friends" (John 15:13). And that's precisely what our Best Friend did for us on the cross.

Friendship is one of the most important relationships we can have. Jesus is the Friend who sticks closer than a brother, but we have also had boyhood friends, school chums, military, or golfing buddies—and others: These are all important relationships, and they can teach us a lot. But we should never forget that our best friends should be those closest to us. Is Jesus your friend? How about your wife, or fiancée, or family members?

Ask God to show you how to be best friends with those closest to you. ▤

TUESDAY

THE MOST COMMON words for "friend" in the New Testament, *philos* and *philia,* are common Greek words for love. Jesus told His disciples He called them "friends" rather than "servants" because He loved them and had entrusted them with the secrets of the kingdom (John 15:15). It's helpful for us to remember that love and friendship are closely related, since this relationship does create a special bond of affection.

Paul says, "Love suffers long and is kind; love does not envy; love does not parade itself, is not puffed up; does not behave rudely, does not seek its own, is not provoked, thinks no evil; does not rejoice in iniquity, but rejoices in the truth; bears all things, believes all things, hopes all things, endures all things. Love never fails" (1 Cor. 13:4–8). Can you imagine what would happen to our friendships if we demonstrated this kind of love for our wife, children, family, and coworkers?

Pray that your ability to love like this might grow. ▤

WEDNESDAY

SOME MEN TEND to think of marriage as a sort of duty, and friendship as something they enjoy outside the home. How unfortunate, for God expects us not only to love our wives and be responsible husbands, but to share our lives with them in every way. Solomon offers some sage advice when he says: "Be happy, yes, rejoice in the wife of your youth. Let her breasts and tender embrace satisfy you. Let her love alone fill you with delight. Why delight yourself with prostitutes, embracing what isn't yours? For God is closely watching you, and he weighs carefully everything you do" (Prov. 5:18–21, TLB).

If we're not careful, we can let relationships at the office, on the job, or through our hobbies and amusements take us away from our family, and that can have many damaging consequences.

Would you pray today that God will help you to keep your priorities straight regarding your wife, your loved ones, and each of your other friends? ▤

THURSDAY

WHEN A MAN has a solid friendship with his wife, his whole life comes into sharper focus. If that's a new concept to you, then why not think about how you can put Greg Johnson's eight principles to work in your life? First, decide to do it; second, tell your wife you want to be a better friend; third, put some muscle behind your commitment and start finding ways the two of you can spend time together, doing stuff you enjoy.

The fourth step is to schedule time alone with your

wife. Fifth, get in the habit of talking everything over with her. Sixth, find some things you enjoy doing together—games, sports, travel, group activities—and seventh, grow together in your relationship with Christ and the church. Finally, commit to be honest and open with each other about your problems. Put these steps into action and just watch what happens in your marriage!

Pray that you will be more sensitive to your wife, so that you can be best friends. ≣

FRIDAY

WHEN TWO PEOPLE live together for a long time they either grow closer together or they can grow apart. Have you ever known two people who lived in the same house with each other for years but, for all practical purposes, they were really strangers? It's tragic, of course, but it does happen, and more often than you might suspect.

Whatever your situation, you need to find ways to keep your loved ones the number two priority in your life—that is, right after your relationship with Jesus Christ. Consider John's words when he says, "Let us stop just saying we love people; let us really love them, and show it by our actions. Then we will know for sure, by our actions, that we are on God's side, and our consciences will be clear, even when we stand before the Lord" (1 John 3:18–19, TLB).

Is your marriage at risk? Don't wait until it is. Make this vital friendship a priority, and begin praying with and for your wife every day. ≣

WEEKEND

SENECA, WHO LIVED at the time of Christ, said: "What is more delightful than to have a friend to whom you can tell everything as you would to yourself? No pains therefore must be spared to preserve what is so rarely found, a true friend, for he is a second self." The Roman philosopher knew how important it is to have a friend, but like many men of his day, he tended to see the relationship from his own side, and for his own benefit.

The Bible teaches that true friendship focuses not on ourselves but on the other person. Paul says, "Be kindly affectionate to one another with brotherly love, in honor giving preference to one another; not lagging in diligence, fervent in spirit, serving the Lord; rejoicing in hope, patient in tribulation, continuing steadfastly in prayer" (Rom. 12:10–12). When we grow to the point that such affections are truly on "auto pilot," we're close to becoming the men of God we all strive to be.

Pray that God will make you a friend who demonstrates this kind of love. ▤

Week 7
UNITY

SOMETHING UNIQUE is occurring today in the body of Christ. Men of varied backgrounds are uniting in outreach, discipleship, and corporate worship as never before. While this is unprecedented in our culture, it is not so in biblical history where the Lord raised up twelve tribes of Israel to show unity in diversity.

One might conclude that God took a "calculated risk" with this fascinating initiative. Though Israel eventually divided, it was always God's intention that His people rise above tribal differences and embrace their destiny as a nation chosen to glorify Him.

Paul wrote, "But now in Christ Jesus you who once were far off have been made near by the blood of Christ. For He Himself is our peace, who has made both one, and has broken down the middle wall of separation" (Eph. 2:13–14). Consistently, then, the Bible reinforces God's ideal and desire for a united body.

Unfortunately, the church still wrestles with "tribal tensions." Psalm 133 says, "How good and pleasant it is when brothers live together in unity," adding that, "there the Lord bestows His blessing" (Ps. 133:1, 5, NIV). Blessings are given when brothers really *dwell* with each other, not just when they attend a Promise Keepers conference.

When brothers of different denominational and ethnic backgrounds are involved with each other in meaningful ways, they bear witness to the love of God—and *that* awakens the world! Following Pentecost, the disciples went from house to house breaking bread ". . . and the Lord added to the church daily those who were being saved" (Acts 2:47). Clearly, solidarity in the church bears witness to Christ and to the supernatural love of God.

It's also plain that God's grace flows unhindered from a unified church, bringing the unsaved to repentance. Where the net is strong, He knows it is safe to send a school of fish, but where it is torn He knows fish will "fall through." God has ordained that only a unified body will fully glorify Him—and be most effective in saving the lost.

Christ alone is the source of our unity, and as we humble ourselves at the foot of the cross, we believe the walls of pride, fear, and prejudice—and anything else that divides us—will come crumbling down. If that is our posture, oneness will be the result, and revival will follow.

As godly men within the church, we are called to exhibit such focused purpose, unity of spirit, and love for each other that the lost can only conclude that God alone is responsible. Let's strive to model this depth of commitment and show the world the unmistakable power, authority, and grace of Jesus Christ.

For the Lord's sake, I challenge you today to start reaching out to your brothers in Christ of a different color, race, or denomination. Ask Him to show you where to begin, then obey His voice. And finally, be encouraged: we're all in this together.

—RANDY T. PHILLIPS

MONDAY

PERHAPS NO movement of modern times has done so much to bring unity to the nation as Promise Keepers' "Break Down the Walls" events of 1996. In twenty-two gatherings in stadiums all across America, men were asked to focus on the risks of denominational and racial division, and to start living by Christ's commandment to love one another. If the unity experienced in those meetings goes no further, however, there's no guarantee the nation can avoid further strife. A million changed lives is a great start, but for a nation of 250 million to be transformed, every one of us must become a messenger of hope.

But do you remember the parable of the mustard seed? Jesus said, "The kingdom of heaven is like a mustard seed, which a man took and sowed in his field, which indeed is the least of all the seeds; but when it is grown it is greater than the herbs and becomes a tree, so that the birds of the air come and nest in its branches" (Matt. 13:31–32). Could the message of unity grow like that? It can, and it must.

Will you pray for an great outbreak of unity? ▰

TUESDAY

IT'S NOT JUST the general public that has a unity problem; Randy Phillips says the church also wrestles with "tribal tensions." Too often we talk a good fight but do little to change the ways things are. Satan would love to keep us apart, out of fellowship and out of patience with each other. But we have greater weapons, and now is the time to use them.

Paul says, "It is true that I am an ordinary, weak human being, but I don't use human plans and methods to win my battles. I use God's mighty weapons, not those made by men, to knock down the devil's strongholds. These weapons can break down every proud argument against God and every wall that can be built to keep men from finding him. With these weapons I can capture rebels and bring them back to God and change them into men whose hearts' desire is obedience to Christ" (2 Cor. 10:3–5, TLB). What a great image! As someone said, Jesus didn't come to take sides; He came to take over! And we have the privilege of serving Him.

Pray that God will make you a skilled warrior in this campaign. ▤

WEDNESDAY

JESUS TOLD the disciples to remain together until Pentecost, when they were to receive a new manifestation. When the Holy Spirit came upon them, they had an encounter that transformed their lives and produced an awesome sense of unity. We read, "Now all who believed were together, and had all things in common . . . So continuing daily with one accord in the temple, and breaking bread from house to house, they ate their food with gladness and simplicity of heart, praising God and having favor with all the people. And the Lord added to the church daily those who were being saved" (Acts 2:44, 46–47).

What took place was not some communal experiment or some act of fear. It was the spirit of unity inspired by the outpouring of God's gift of love. From the early believers' example of love, thousands came to Christ. Do you see the connection? When the Holy Spirit lives in us, we love one another as never before, and the kingdom will thrive.

Pray that God will manifest His love in you and give you the spirit of unity. ▤

THURSDAY

DIVISIONS BETWEEN JEWS and Gentiles have a long history, and during the early life of the church disunity and distrust were at epic proportions. But the gospel was not for any one group or race or brand of believer—it was for everyone who believed on the name of Jesus. For that reason, Paul's message to the church at Ephesus about our unity in Christ should have special meaning for us. He said: "For He Himself is our peace, who has made both one, and has broken down the middle wall of separation, having abolished in His flesh the enmity . . . so as to create in Himself one new man from the two, thus making peace, and that He might reconcile them both to God in one body through the cross, thereby putting to death the enmity" (Eph. 2:14–16).

What better explanation of government's failure to heal ethnic tensions by social means! Programs don't create unity, people do—people empowered by the love of Christ.

Pray that God will heal our land and bring a new sense of unity through His grace. ■

FRIDAY

THE SIXTH PROMISE of a Promise Keeper says, "A Promise Keeper is committed to reaching beyond any racial and denominational barriers to demonstrate the power of biblical unity." There are many foundations for this commitment. John says, "If someone says, 'I love God,' and hates his brother, he is a liar; for he who does not love his brother whom he has seen, how can he love God whom he has not seen? And this command-ment we have from Him: that he who loves God must love his brother also" (1 John 4:20–21).

The Bible word for *prejudice* is "partiality." Showing partiality for one person over another is not godly behavior. Peter said, "I perceive that God shows no par-tiality. But in every nation whoever fears Him and works righteousness is accepted by Him" (Acts 10:34–35). God is impartial and judges each man, not by his group, but by his heart. Shouldn't we do the same?

Pray that God will keep you in unity with your brothers. ■

WEEKEND

THE CHALLENGE PROMISE Keepers President Randy Phillips offers in this week's meditation reaches beyond this or any movement. He says that nonbelievers will judge the church and the power of salvation to renew men's hearts by the example they see in us. Have you and I turned onlookers away from God by our bad example?

The world knows only too well the provocations for disunity; hatred, distrust, and prejudice because of race or color or the groups men belong to is the natural way. We all have this tendency, so if men of God show that they love one another and consider all men equal in the eyes of God, as they are, then the world will have to conclude that only God could have changed our hearts.

Paul writes, "I charge you before God and the Lord Jesus Christ and the elect angels that you observe these things without prejudice, doing nothing with partiality" (1 Tim. 5:21).

Pray that you may always live in the spirit of unity, whatever the risks. ▤

Week 8
HUMILITY

FIFTEEN YEARS AGO when gospel singer John P. Kee decided to live completely for Christ, he began a journey that has shown him that singing and writing music about the love of Christ are just two of the talents God has given him. Today Kee knows he is also called to preach the gospel and to reach the unsaved in places that others will not go.

"When you really get into who God is," he says, "you realize He is more than a song . . . It's not about the Grammy nominations or the Stellar awards. It's not about who I am. It's about *whose* I am." Gospel music lovers are aware of the tremendous success that has rained down on Kee, but what many don't know is that his spiritual life required major surgery before he was able to shine in Christian music.

As a four-year-old, Kee sang old-time gospel favorites at church, and by age thirteen he had formed a one-hundred-voice gospel choir. From there, Kee's ability took him from coast to coast, performing with the R&B group, Cameo, working with the Miss Black Universe pageant as music director, and as choir director at a large church in Charlotte. Unbeknown to his family, however, Kee had allowed pride and greed to entice him into a double life.

On Sunday mornings he masqueraded as a choir director. But by night, he sold cocaine and marijuana. He became a spiritual impostor. "I was just a straight ol' hustler," he remembers. "I did so many terrible things that year." Despite all the singing in church and the careful upbringing his parents gave him, Kee had never genuinely developed a personal relationship with Jesus Christ. But one night in 1994 he saw something he will never forget.

"I witnessed a close friend of mine get gunned down during a bad drug deal—right in front of my face." That's when the words of his father, the man he admired so much, finally rang clear. "He told me I was my own man. He reminded me that the wages of sin were still death and that I needed to make a decision for myself . . . It came down to being honest with myself and God."

That tug on Kee's heart proved to be a calling. God began to show him that his ministry included the gift of preaching. "I thank God for the music," he says, "but I also want to be known as one who preached a message of Calvary. Jesus did die, not just for me, but for you." Kee recently has begun pulling back on his hectic traveling schedule with New Life Community Choir to become a full-time minister. His focus now is on reaching out personally with the same good news he has long sung about.

"I think a lot of people in this life measure their success by where they go," he says, "but I believe your success happens when you go back to where you came from and make it a better place."

—LYNETTE BLAIR MITCHEL

MONDAY

WHEN WE GIVE our lives to Christ, anything can happen. Some people fear that accepting Jesus as Savior and letting God take charge would be a first-class ticket to a life of suffering on the mission field. But how do you explain the fact that some people, like John P. Kee, become popular entertainers, celebrities, and still serve the Lord? The fact is, Christ only wants our best. He doesn't put people where they have no gifts or interests; we serve Him best where we can do it with joy and genuine ability.

If we resist His call on our lives, insisting on doing things our own way, Jesus can't use us. David says, "The sacrifices of God are a broken spirit, a broken and a contrite heart; These, O God, You will not despise" (Ps. 51:17). And James says, "Humble yourselves in the sight of the Lord, and He will lift you up" (James 4:10). If you give yourself completely, you may be surprised what God can do through you.

Let that be your prayer today. ▤

TUESDAY

HUMILITY MEANS RECOGNIZING that God is greater than your hopes. Humility in action means letting God take the controls and guide your life each day; whereas, pride in action leads to disappointment in this world and damnation in the next. This is a difficult lesson to grasp for those who have experienced success in this world. They see the fruits of their own labor, and they much prefer a life of comfort and ease to what they perceive as a life of toil and self-sacrifice. But don't be fooled: when we resist the Lord's call on our hearts, we always settle for second best.

Paul says, "For the message of the cross is foolishness to those who are perishing, but to us who are being saved it is the power of God. For it is written: 'I will destroy the wisdom of the wise, and bring to nothing the understanding of the prudent.' Where is the wise? Where is the scribe? Where is the disputer of this age? Has not God made foolish the wisdom of this world?" (1 Cor. 1:18–20).

Pray that you may live each day in God's wisdom. ▤

WEDNESDAY

WHETHER YOU'RE A recording star or just a regular guy on the job, it's all too easy to slip into a double life. The temptations are certainly there, and the secular world not only doesn't condemn immoral behavior—they applaud it. Because John P. Kee had trusted his childhood understanding of faith without taking the next step to a more mature relationship with Christ, consequently he slipped gradually away from his commitment to righteousness and faithfulness and became what he called a "spiritual impostor."

How could a gospel singer fall so far? How could he become "a straight ol' hustler" pushing cocaine like a street junkie? Because he had allowed "the lust of the flesh, the lust of the eyes, and the pride of life" (1 John 2:16) to take control. The lights and music turned his head, and his glamorous career became a corrupting influence. Thousands have fallen just that way, but we can learn from Kee's example. Today he is a new man, spreading the Word.

Pray that God will strengthen your defenses against the allurements of this life. ▤

THURSDAY

> Do not be deceived, God is not mocked; for whatever a man sows, that he will also reap. For he who sows to his flesh will of the flesh reap corruption, but he who sows to the Spirit will of the Spirit reap everlasting life. And let us not grow weary while doing good, for in due season we shall reap if we do not lose heart. Therefore, as we have opportunity, let us do good to all, especially to those who are of the household of faith.
>
> —GALATIANS 6:7–10

These words of Paul to the churches in the Roman province of Galatia shine a bright light on the wickedness of pride and selfishness. When those who live according to the flesh scorn the Christian life, they may feel superior. And sometimes even Christians may look longingly at the life of sin, wondering what they're missing. But John P. Kee can vouch for Paul's words: He who sows to the flesh will only reap corruption. The harvest of peace, joy, and life eternal comes in due time to those who sow to the Spirit.

Let your prayer be that you may grow in faith, humility, and the love of God. ▤

FRIDAY

TRAGEDY CHANGES EVERYTHING. For some people, a tragic loss can shatter all their hopes and drive them away from God. "How could God allow my loved one to be taken?" they cry. Somehow the realities of cause-and-effect don't seem to apply, and whether they have suffered from an accident, a fatal disease, or some other circumstance, there's a tendency to blame God when things go wrong.

For John P. Kee, however, a fatal shooting may have been the only thing that could wake him up to the terrible life he was leading. Suddenly, his father's words rang clear, and he understood his predicament. People complain about inflation and how the value of things has changed, but one thing hasn't changed: *The wages of sin is still death.* Paul says in Romans 6:23, "For the wages of sin is death, but the gift of God is eternal life in Christ Jesus our Lord." Kee got the message, and that started his journey home.

Is Christ Lord of your life today? Praise Him. Thank Him for the gift of eternal life. ▤

WEEKEND

"IT'S NOT *WHO* I am but *whose* I am." As the gospel singer let the words of his songs begin to work in his heart, he knew he had to get his priorities straight. Once that happened, he realized the spotlight wasn't what he really wanted anyway. He experienced God's love and forgiveness in a way he had never known, and suddenly John P. Kee felt the call, not just to sing, but to preach the Word of God.

Sometimes we have to give up a lot to serve the Lord. We give up guilt, fear, lying, hangovers, nausea, apologizing for our late nights and bad behavior, running from the truth and fighting with our mates and closest friends. We give up an eternity in hell and eternal separation from God in order to gain everlasting life and peace with both God and man. The fact is, the sin of pride blinds us to the reality that, without Christ, we're just losers; but falling on our faces in humility before a pure and holy God teaches us the right way to live.

Ask God to strip away any pride that is hindering your walk of faith, so that you can give yourself completely to Him. ▤

Week 9
CONTENTMENT

IF YOU HAVE ENOUGH food, decent clothes, live in a home that shields you from the weather, and own some kind of reliable transportation, you are in the top 15 percent of the world's wealthy. Add some savings, a hobby like hunting or fishing that requires equipment, two cars (in any condition), a variety of clothing, and your own house, and you have reached the top 5 percent.

You may not feel wealthy, but that's because you're comparing yourself with someone who owns even more. To get a better handle on reality, consider that more than 1.1 billion people in the world live on less than one dollar per day. About five hundred million are so poor they don't get enough food to be fully productive. Every day nearly seventy-five thousand people, most of them children, die because of dirty drinking water, disease, or malnutrition.

Much of the world lives with an even worse shortage—the Good News that Jesus died for our sins and is the way to eternal life. Ninety-five percent of these unreached groups live in an area from West Africa to China known as the 10/40 Window. Of these 3.1 billion people, two-thirds have never heard of Jesus, at least not as Savior. I don't share these statistics to heap guilt on you or because I advocate taking a vow of poverty. But when it comes to investments, too few Christians consider the importance of investing in eternity.

Each of us needs to ask himself what we are doing with our money that will make a difference a million years from now. Loosening the grip of materialism is a good reason to live more simply. There are a thousand ways to do this. We can buy used cars instead of new, choose a modest home over an expensive one, shop at thrift stores, and own a bicycle instead of a second car.

What's the point? Paul explained in Ephesians 4:28 that the reason for productive work was so we could "have something to share with those in need." When we earn more, we should use those resources to help others. God doesn't call us to increase our standard of living, but our standard of giving. As Christians, we must always be concerned with spreading the gospel through missions work. But we also need relief and development agencies to provide food and medicine. You can't convert a man who is so hungry he can't sit up. How do you feed a billion hungry people? One at a time.

Finally, don't forget the personal payoff for investing in eternity. In Matthew 6:20, Jesus says, "Lay up for yourselves treasures in heaven." If your treasures are on earth, each day you are moving away from them. If your treasures are in heaven, each day you are moving toward them. He who spends his life moving away from his treasures has reason to despair. He who spends his life moving toward his treasures has reason to rejoice.

—RANDY ALCORN

MONDAY

WHAT IS SUCCESS? What does it mean to achieve your dreams? If retirement comes along and you have got a couple of million dollars in assets and a solid portfolio of stocks and annuities, would that be enough? How about a vacation home in the mountains or a place at the beach? When is it enough? Each year the newsmagazines report on the best mutual funds, stocks, bonds, and investment options, and millions of Americans go racing after the hottest new revenue producers. Does that include you?

We all need a certain level of material comfort and we owe it to our families to care for their needs; but it's amazing how quickly things get out of hand. We fill our lives with things and sometimes miss the most important thing. What would the money you'd spend on a luxury car mean to the mission families of Ecuador? What would your spare change mean to a father earning just five dollars a week in the Philippines?

As you speak to God about your needs today, ask how you can be a blessing to someone else in His kingdom. ■

TUESDAY

WHAT IS POVERTY? What does it mean to hit the bottom? The headlines tell of starvation, malnutrition, and genocide in the nations of Africa and Asia, and we hear of wars where families and even whole villages have lost everything. But how much worse when millions enter eternity never having heard the lifesaving message of salvation through Jesus Christ.

Randy Alcorn's message is a hard one; it's a world we'd rather not think about. But surely this is the real "bottom line." In the Beatitudes, Jesus blessed those who hunger and thirst after righteousness; but what about the other side of His message? Remember that? He said, "Woe to you who are rich, for you have received your consolation. Woe to you who are full, for you shall hunger. Woe to you who laugh now, for you shall mourn and weep. Woe to you when all men speak well of you, for so did their fathers to the false prophets" (Luke 6:24–26). The sin isn't having possessions but in turning our backs on those who have so little of the treasure of this world or the next. If we don't care for them, who will?

Pray that your eyes may be opened to the needs of

those Christ wants you to feed. ▤

WEDNESDAY

SAUL OF TARSUS worked hard all his life. As a tent-maker, he worked with his hands. He was a zealous student of Scripture, and even after his conversion he continued working for his bread so that other believers would see from his example that Christians are to be industrious. But success for Paul the apostle wasn't wealth but contentment in Christ.

"Now godliness with contentment is great gain," he wrote to Timothy. "For we brought nothing into this world, and it is certain we can carry nothing out. And having food and clothing, with these we shall be content. But those who desire to be rich fall into temptation and a snare, and into many foolish and harmful lusts which drown men in destruction and perdition. For the love of money is a root of all kinds of evil, for which some have strayed from the faith in their greediness, and pierced themselves through with many sorrows. But you, O man of God, flee these things and pursue righteousness, godliness, faith, love, patience, gentleness" (1 Tim. 6:6–11).

How are you doing by Paul's standards? Why not pray about it today? ▤

THURSDAY

THE WORK IS intimidating. Within the 10/40 window—that band of tropical and subtropical lands where the bulk of the world's population lives—more than three billion people have yet to hear the good news of salvation. They are among the most destitute, despised, and exploited peoples on the planet. But how on earth can you or I have any impact in such places?

Randy Alcorn asks the question even more simply: "How do you feed a billion hungry people?" Just like you feed your family—one at a time. If we focus on the size of the problem, we may say, "Oh, well, it's just too big! What can one person do?" and leave it to others. But in God's eyes, *we are* the others. He doesn't ask us to solve the whole problem by ourselves but to do whatever we can with the resources we have been given. Look around you; chances are there are men, women, and children near you who are hungry for the Word of God. Chances are some need food and clothing, too. Can you give? Could you help?

Ask God to show you how wealthy you truly are, and how you can bless others. ▤

FRIDAY

AUTHOR AND SPEAKER Steve Brown tells the story of the Polish king who disappeared one day, and after several days his counselors found him working as a common porter in the market. "Your majesty!" they exclaimed. "What are you doing here?!"

"This load is far lighter than the one I carried as king," he replied, "and I have slept better here than I ever did in the palace. I'd have to be crazy to go back to that job, so go find yourselves another king!" Compare that to the story of John D. Rockefeller, the richest man in the world. Near the end of his life, doctors restricted him to "a drop of coffee, a spoonful of cereal, a fork full of egg, and a bit of chop the size of a pea." He wasted away, to less than one hundred pounds, and grew bitter and resentful of his lot in life. Do such stories tell you anything about the things that matter most?

The best long-term investment isn't mutual funds, but a personal relationship with the Prince of Peace, who says, "If you love Me, keep My commandments" (John 14:15). ▤

WEEKEND

"YOU CAN'T TAKE it with you." We know the phrase, but anyone looking at the way we live would have to wonder if we really believe it. We spend our lives accumulating stuff as if this world's goods were the most important things in our lives. But are they?

Randy Alcorn says we can either move toward our treasure or move away from it. If we spend all the days of our working life gathering and accumulating material possessions, then we are moving toward a treasure we will soon leave behind. On the other hand, if we spend our days gaining treasure in heaven, then we can enjoy our reward forever. Jesus said it simply: "Do not lay up for yourselves treasures on earth, where moth and rust destroy and where thieves break in and steal; but lay up for yourselves treasures in heaven, where neither moth nor rust destroys and where thieves do not break in and steal. For where your treasure is, there your heart will be also" (Matt. 6:19–21).

Ask the Lord to help you balance your need for security and contentment. ▤

Week 10

ENCOURAGEMENT

EVERY PERSON GOD created has nearly limitless potential. It's God gift to us. What we do with it is our gift to God. So no matter where your children are—whether they're newborn babies, straight-A students getting ready to go off to college, or gang members serving time in juvenile detention—they have great potential that they haven't even touched.

Helping them unlock that potential should be one of our main goals. In the end, it's the greatest gift we can give them—to help them become the people God created them to be. When they don't develop toward their potential, it's a tragedy. Becoming a parent who sees his children not as they are but as they could be takes time and deliberate effort. The key to making it happen is focusing on their potential.

Here are six principles to help you do that:

1. *Develop a potential mind-set.* If we have the mind-set that everything around us has potential, including ourselves, then we are more likely to see it in our children. God did not create us to fail. He created us to "win the race." God will do His part if we do ours. Neither you nor I, nor our children can be all that God intends for us to be until we begin to focus on what we can become.

2. *Model growth as a parent.* Parents who are continually working to develop their own potential—by growing themselves mentally, spiritually, emotionally, and physically—have children who will see that process as "normal."

Look at each day as an opportunity to develop yourself. Make your home a growth environment. You can do that by praising your children anytime they show a desire to learn. Show them that you value growth.

3. *Expect great things to happen.* To give this idea a jump-start, remember what it says in Philippians 1:6, "He who began a good work in you will carry it on to completion" (NIV). That's not only true for you, but also for your children.

4. *Help your children to like themselves.* If you are in the habit of making negative or critical comments about them, start praying for God to change you, and start holding your tongue. Find something positive to say about your children every day, and help them to like themselves when they're with you.

5. *Look beyond your own life . . . invest in the future.* Abraham Lincoln wrote, "A child is a person who is going to carry on what you have started. He is going to sit where you are sitting, and when you are gone, attend to those things which you think are important. . . . He will assume control of your cities, states and nations. He is going to move in and take over your churches, schools and corporations . . . The fate of humanity is in his hands."

6. *Finally, no matter how old your children, dedicate them to God.* When you do, you give God room to work in their lives.

—John C. Maxwell

Monday

A SURVEY OF American teens reported by Associated Press in 1997 states that young people in this country are five times more likely to die violently than children in twenty-five other industrialized nations, and twice as likely to commit suicide. Since 1950 both the homicide rate and the suicide rate have tripled among young people. Why is this happening? What's going on with our kids? Interviews with troubled teens suggest that millions of America's kids have lost hope. They have little relationship with their parents, they have grown up in day care centers and liberal public schools. The lifestyles glamorized by TV, the media, and rock music are materialistic and self-destructive, and they get almost no encouragement from anyone. Consequently, many have decided that life is simply not worth living.

How should we react to such news? Leave it to somebody else? Not if we want to be men of God. You can start with your own kids and those you see on a regular basis.

Pray that God will help you to encourage and demonstrate Christ's love to those you know. ▓

TUESDAY

WHENEVER ANYONE mentions gifts, people have a tendency to start making excuses. Their gifts are so small, they say. That's one reason Paul spent so much time encouraging the early Christians to develop their gifts and find ways to minister to those in need. After all, spiritual gifts are given to each believer by the Holy Spirit for the benefit of everyone. "There are diversities of gifts," Paul says, "but the same Spirit. There are differences of ministries, but the same Lord. And there are diversities of activities, but it is the same God who works all in all." Then he gave the clincher, saying, "The manifestation of the Spirit is given to each one for the profit of all" (1 Cor. 12:4–7).

No one can claim to be useless in Christ's kingdom: great or small, we all have gifts of some kind. The Holy Spirit prepares us for the work He has called us to do. And as John Maxwell points out, what you do with your gift is your gift to God.

Pray that you may be encouraged in using your gifts to help build the kingdom. 📖

WEDNESDAY

WHEN YOU BEGIN unlocking your gifts, you will also be unlocking the gifts of others. That's why Pastor Maxwell encourages men to begin developing their "potential mind-set." If we believe in ourselves, then we will find it easier to believe in others and to encourage them in their works of service. Paul assured Timothy, "For God has not given us a spirit of fear, but of power and of love and of a sound mind" (2 Tim. 1:7). God designed us to be winners, to run the race, to fight the fight. It's important that we see the potential in all of God's children. In his second principle, Maxwell suggests that we begin modeling the kind of values and behaviors we want our kids to exhibit. Even when they seem unimpressed by their parents—more interested in what's happening on the sitcoms or with friends at school—what they see in us does make a difference. If you are courteous, loving, sincere, and able to forgive, your family will notice. Count on it.

Pray for wisdom to model the love that Jesus has placed in your heart. 📖

THURSDAY

LIFE CAN BE HARD, especially for men who have decided to resist the dishonesty and seediness of modern life. The cost of standing up for your principles and denying the seductions of modern society and the lusts of the flesh can be high; but the rewards are so much higher. Remember what Christ had to say about it? As He was nearing the end of His ministry on earth, Jesus warned His followers that choosing the pleasures of this life would be a serious mistake. "He who loves his life will lose it," He said, "and he who hates his life in this world will keep it for eternal life. If anyone serves Me, let him follow Me; and where I am, there My servant will be also. If anyone serves Me, him My Father will honor" (John 12:25–26).

When you're feeling down and discouraged, remember these words: Giving up the dead-end pleasures of this life is nothing compared to the glory to come.

Pray that Christ will encourage and strengthen you as you follow Him. ▤

FRIDAY

WHEN THEY LEARNED that the church in Asia Minor was growing and that many were coming to Christ, the apostles were thrilled. When news came to the ears of the church in Jerusalem, they sent Joses of Cyprus to go to Antioch. Luke says, "When he came and had seen the grace of God, he was glad, and *encouraged* them all that with purpose of heart they should continue with the Lord. For he was a good man, full of the Holy Spirit and of faith. And a great many people were added to the Lord" (Acts 11:22–24, italics added).

A short time later, Joses was sent to find Saul of Tarsus who had been converted through a vision on the road to Damascus. Despite Saul's bad record as a persecutor of Christians, Joses welcomed him with open arms. And what a gift it was, for Saul would soon become known as Paul, the apostle of Jesus Christ; and Joses would be remembered as Barnabas, a name that means "son of encouragement."

As you pray, think about how the gift of encouragement might flourish in your life. ▤

WEEKEND

IT'S NOT ALWAYS easy to be an encourager. There's more than enough trouble in the world to bring us down and for discouragement to be a constant threat. But the Bible challenges us to hang tough in the face of adversity. The writer of Hebrews says, "For God is not unjust to forget your work and labor of love which you have shown toward His name, in that you have ministered to the saints, and do minister. And we desire that each one of you show the same diligence to the full assurance of hope until the end, that you do not become sluggish, but imitate those who through faith and patience inherit the promises" (Heb. 6:10–12). In his reflections on these words, William Barclay says, "One of the highest of human duties is the duty of encouragement. It is easy to pour cold water on their enthusiasm; it is easy to discourage others. The world is full of discouragers. We have a Christian duty to encourage one another."

Pray today that you may encourage others even as you are being encouraged. ▤

DISCERNMENT

THE JUDGE looked down from his bench and declared, "Mr. Wilson, this is your day of reckoning!" He sentenced the man to seven-and-a-half years in federal prison. Wilson was one of four California men convicted of financial fraud. Five were investigated, but the fifth, Mark Jacobs, wasn't charged. Jacobs had been invited to join the financial scheme with four friends in a weekly Bible study. They assured him it was legal, but something inside said it wasn't right.

Defense lawyers argued that their clients had simply used poor judgment in a "gray area," crossing a line that wasn't clear. The judge disagreed: "The guy who drew the line is Mark Jacobs. He knew what was right and what was wrong, and he didn't hesitate." This case is just one example of the moral crisis sweeping our nation. We are a generation that isn't sure where the line is drawn between right and wrong. Many godly men have yielded to the world's values because they failed to discern the subtle changes occurring around them.

Here are seven steps to help you move beyond good intentions:

1. *Make a decision.* When King Nebuchadnezzar conquered Judah, he ordered thousands of Jewish men to be taken as captives. His goal was to immerse them in the seductive culture of Babylon and remake their character. But Daniel was one of those men. He chose to stand for what was right. Being God's man was everything to him.

2. *Choose to put first things first.* We can only reap a harvest of purity and integrity by planting the good seed of God's Word into our lives. To be effective, truth must be planted in our hearts daily.

3. *Determine where the line is, then stay a safe distance behind it.* Moral failure is rarely the result of a blowout; it's usually the result of a slow leak. If something is not clearly spelled out in Scripture, pray about it and seek the counsel of wise friends. Don't see how close you can get to the line without going over.

4. *Guard your heart.* Jesus made it clear that we can't serve two masters. A growing affection for our Lord is the only antidote for the kind of apathy that leads down the primrose path to compromise.

5. *Guard your mind.* The seemingly simple choice of what we set our minds on can determine the outcome of our spiritual warfare. Just a small deviation from God's standard can put us at risk.

6. *Guard your eyes.* King David lingered too long, stared too much. He didn't guard his eyes and ended up committing adultery with Bathsheba and murdering her husband. Guard your eyes.

7. *Guard the little things.* Jesus said "Whoever can be trusted with very little can also be trusted with much" (Luke 16:10, NIV). Beware of the temptation to justify or rationalize. Ask yourself, "Is this more likely to move me closer to or further from my goal of being a Promise Keeper?"

—GARY J. OLIVER

MONDAY

"THERE'S NO SUCH thing as right and wrong." That's

what we have been told for the past three decades. "You must decide for yourself what you believe; everybody has their own morality." In schoolrooms and university lecture halls all across America, such words have led millions of young people into experimenting with sex, drugs, materialistic lifestyles, New Age, and even Satan worship—all in the name of a "value-neutral culture." The consequences of such sloppy thinking, however, show up on the nightly news and in the morning headlines as today's liberalized values clash with the realities of civilized behavior.

Never before has such a sophisticated culture self-destructed in such a profound and heartbreaking way. But as Christians, we know better, don't we? Surely, men of God who know the truth will stand up for God's standards of right and wrong! Won't they? Sadly, rather than standing tall, too many of us have wimped out.

Would you pray that men of conviction and discernment will rise up to help restore the moral fabric of this nation? ▤

TUESDAY

FIVE MEN, five Christians, five decisions: four were convicted and given jail terms up to seven-and-a-half years; only one was exonerated. What happened? Four of the men called it a financial loophole; their defense lawyers called it a gray area; but the court called it fraud. By any other name, the Word of God calls what happened moral failure.

The early church wrestled with such problems, too. In Hebrews we read, "You have been Christians a long time now, and you ought to be teaching others, but instead you have dropped back to the place where you need someone to teach you all over again the very first principles in God's Word. You are like babies who can drink only milk, not old enough for solid food. And when a person is still living on milk it shows he isn't very far along in the Christian life, and doesn't know much about the difference between right and wrong. He is still a baby Christian!" (Heb. 5:12–14, TLB).

Pray that God will mature you in your walk of faith, with honesty and discernment. ■

WEDNESDAY

MOST OF US have good intentions, but that's not enough; we need Christ in our lives to help transform our good intentions into good behavior. Gary Oliver says we have to make a conscious decision to do what's right. Evil is at war with good, offering seductive allurements, constantly muttering Satan's taunt that God only wants to keep us from having "a good time." A second principle is that we have to choose to put first things first. David says, "Your word I have hidden in my heart, that I might not sin against You!" (Ps. 119:11). Are you hiding God's Word in your heart each day? Only prayer, fellowship, and daily meditation on the Word can keep your spiritual ramparts well fortified and your ammunition always at the ready to fend off Satan's evil schemes.

With David, pray, "Blessed are You, O Lord! Teach me Your statutes!" (Ps. 119:12). ■

THURSDAY

TO AVOID STEPPING over the line into moral failure, you have to know where the line is. Gary Oliver says falling into sin is usually a slow leak, not a blowout. Some men move closer and closer to the line until they either stumble or step over it. That's why godly friends and Bible reading are so important. Steve Green's song, "Guard Your Heart," really teaches an important principle: Don't think you can window shop at Satan's sin market and walk away uncontaminated. Oliver's next point, then, is to guard your mind. Entertaining sin can mean simply letting dangerous thoughts roll around in your mind occasionally, so that what starts out as a passing thought eventually becomes an evil deed.

Gary Oliver says next to guard your eyes. All these are doorways to the soul—your heart, your mind, your eyes. What goes in those doors will influence your behavior. The devil knows it, and he's looking for the slightest opportunity to break in.

Pray that in Christ you will be armed and dangerous when Satan comes prowling. ≡

FRIDAY

GARY OLIVER'S last point is to guard the little things. "Little words, not eloquent speeches or sermons; little deeds, not miracles or battles, or one great heroic effort or martyrdom, make up the true Christian life," says Horatius Bonar. Paul says, "These things I have told you are all true. Insist on them so that Christians will be careful to do good deeds all the time, for this is not only right, but it brings results" (Titus 3:8, TLB). We have a tendency to think of faith in macro terms; after all, faith in Jesus Christ is an enormous, life-changing experience. But more often it's the micro stuff that gets us into trouble—the little things, the passing thought, that little detail on the expense report, the casual word, a look that lingers too long, or the subtle suggestion that something is true when you know very well it isn't. Only God may know what's really going on, but that's more than enough.

Temptation is not sin, but giving in to it can cost you a lot. Pray that God will give you a discerning heart and eyes that turn away from every appearance of evil. ≡

WEEKEND

Sin lurks deep in the hearts of the wicked, forever urging them on to evil deeds. They have no fear of God to hold them back. Instead, in their conceit, they think they can hide their evil deeds and not get caught. Everything they say is crooked and deceitful; they are no longer wise and good. They lie awake at night to hatch their evil plots instead of planning how to keep away from wrong.

Your steadfast love, O Lord, is as great as all the heavens. Your faithfulness reaches beyond the clouds. Your justice is as solid as God's mountains. Your decisions are as full of wisdom as the oceans are with water. You are concerned for men and animals alike. How precious is your constant love, O God! All humanity takes refuge in the shadow of your wings.

—PSALM 36:1–7, TLB

Pray for discernment. Pray that you may truly be a man of God. ≣

PEACEMAKER

WHAT IS THE KEY to healing the rifts that divide us in the workplace? When a conflict arises, people often assume there isn't any real dispute, only poor communication. We believe that if we can get the other person to see our perspective, we can work things out. When we get nowhere, the instinct is to *talk more.* But more of the same only makes things worse.

As a mediator, time and again I observe that when there is a true disagreement, we walk into a meeting with the assumption that we are right. We are not exactly in a humble frame of mind. We are intent on pushing our point of view, convinced that we can get the other side to give in. This is an argumentative approach, not one born of respect and love for our fellowman. In 2 Corinthians 5:14, Paul speaks of Christ's love compelling us, giving us the ministry of reconciliation. How can we become reconciled to the other while we are fighting that person?

Arguing with someone is one of the hardest ways to resolve a problem. So what's the answer? Romans 15:7 teaches, "Accept one another, then, just as Christ accepted you, in order to bring praise to God" (NIV). Don't fight the other person's thinking. Accept it. Adapt your approach accordingly. If the other person is saying no to your present request, change it. You don't have to insist, "It's my way or no way!" As a peacemaker, your task is to find a way that works for the other person and solves the problem as well.

A lot of managers try to manipulate others to a predetermined solution. That's one of the worst mistakes you can make. The other person feels you're trying to control them, instead of working with them. That's when they really dig in. So don't try to come up with the solution on your own. Work with the other person to develop it. If each person is sensitive to the other's perspective and each approaches the other with a sense of respect and humility, you'll make progress faster.

Your approach to resolving conflict should be based on *the other person's* perceptions, not your own. The other person's beliefs should dictate your approach. Conventional wisdom says the reverse—that your approach should dictate another's beliefs. After all, the logic goes, the whole point of approaching that person is to get him or her to change.

The way we have been taught to resolve our differences is backwards. We should not try to make the other person hold the same views that we do. We should approach that person using his or her perceptions. The challenge is to build a bridge from your individual perceptions to a mutually acceptable solution.

Restraining yourself is one of the most important challenges in the midst of an argument. In the words of James 1:26, "If anyone considers himself religious and yet does not keep a tight rein on his tongue, he deceives himself and his religion is worthless."

—DAVID STIEBEL

MONDAY

SAD TO SAY, conflict is inevitable. Whether at the office, in the home, or at play, there will be times when disagreements occur. How do you handle them? Solomon says, "A wrathful man stirs up strife, but he who is slow to anger allays contention" (Prov. 15:18). That's the first line of defense. Outbursts of anger only make difficult situations impossible, so stay calm. Second, realize that there's more to solving a problem than talking about it.

Solomon says, "When a man's ways please the Lord, He makes even his enemies to be at peace with him" (Prov. 16:7). Now, we might think that a man who does things *decently* and in order creates an environment in which even his enemies will be conciliatory. But that would be wrong. The "He" in this passage is God, who directs our paths. The writer of Chronicles says, "For the eyes of the Lord run to and fro throughout the whole earth, to show Himself strong on behalf of those whose heart is loyal to Him" (2 Chron. 16:9).

Pray that as you walk daily with Him, God will steer you away from waters of strife. ▤

TUESDAY

DAVID STIEBEL, a mediator by profession, recites Paul's teaching that faith in Christ *compels* us to become peacemakers. We are not to insist on our own way, but to find ways in which the needs of others might be satisfied. In the same chapter cited by Stiebel, Paul makes the memorable statement: "If anyone is in Christ, he is a new creation; old things have passed away; behold, all things have become new" (2 Cor. 5:17).

Paul continues, "Now all things are of God, who has reconciled us to Himself through Jesus Christ, and has given us the ministry of reconciliation, that is, that God was in Christ reconciling the world to Himself, not imputing their trespasses to them, and has committed to us the word of reconciliation. Now then, we are ambassadors for Christ, as though God were pleading through us" (2 Cor. 5:18–20). What better motivation could we have to work for reconciliation in all our relationships.

Pray that as God draws you to Himself, He will give you the heart of a peacemaker. ▤

WEDNESDAY

HOW MANY TIMES have you heard someone trying to

settle a disagreement by saying, "Hey, you're not listening to me!"? In other words: "If you'd just stop long enough to hear what I'm saying you'd see how right I am!" Then that person is surprised when the other party refuses to change his mind or hear what the person has to say.

The peacemaker understands that two heads really are better than one, and coming to a mutually satisfactory agreement is better than just getting your own way. Jesus said, "Therefore if you bring your gift to the altar, and there remember that your brother has something against you, leave your gift there before the altar, and go your way. First be reconciled to your brother, and then come and offer your gift. Agree with your adversary quickly, while you are on the way with him" (Matt. 5:23–25).

Jesus taught that disagreement and division put us out of fellowship with either man or God. Pray today for the courage to be a man of peace. ▤

THURSDAY

TOO OFTEN, PEOPLE think that conflict resolution means twisting things around so that they can get their own way, by hook or by crook. But wisdom knows better. Manipulation only causes resentment and creates resistance. The apostle James asks, "Who is wise and understanding among you? Let him show by good conduct that his works are done in the meekness of wisdom.

But if you have bitter envy and self-seeking in your hearts," he warns, "do not boast and lie against the truth. This wisdom does not descend from above, but is earthly, sensual, demonic. For where envy and self-seeking exist, confusion and every evil thing are there. But the wisdom that is from above is first pure, then peaceable, gentle, willing to yield, full of mercy and good fruits, without partiality and without hypocrisy. Now the fruit of righteousness is sown in peace by those who make peace" (James 3:13–18).

Does James' description fit you? Pray that it will. ▤

Friday

"Therefore, having been justified by faith, we have peace with God through our Lord Jesus Christ, through whom also we have access by faith into this grace in which we stand, and rejoice in hope of the glory of God. And not only that, but we also glory in tribulations, knowing that tribulation produces perseverance; and perseverance, character; and character, hope. Now hope does not disappoint, because the love of God has been poured out in our hearts by the Holy Spirit who was given to us" (Rom. 5:1–5).

This famous passage from Romans offers both good news and bad. The good news is that God is in the business of building *character,* and that the fruit of His completed work in us is *hope.* The bad news is that, along the way, it will take various trials and tribulations—like the flame in a blacksmith's anvil—to prepare us to be pounded into shape so that we will be fit instruments in Christ's hands. If we really understand what justification by faith means, we will rejoice in the hope of glory. Pray for a sense of peace when the heat is on. ▤

Weekend

There may be no higher calling, and perhaps no harder, than that of peacemaker. After all, Jesus came to teach us the art of love, and to model for us the true meaning of brotherly love. It cost His life. In Philippians we read: "Let this mind be in you which was also in Christ Jesus, who, being in the form of God, did not consider it robbery to be equal with God, but made Himself of no reputation, taking the form of a bondservant, and coming in the likeness of men. And being found in appearance as a man, He humbled Himself and became obedient to the point of death, even the death of the cross" (Phil. 2:5–8).

Being a peacemaker means letting go of pride and practicing patience and humility, so that the greater good may be served. This kind of behavior calls for moral integrity and spiritual wisdom, but it's always worth the effort. Remember David's words? "But the meek shall inherit the earth, and shall delight themselves in the abundance of peace" (Ps. 37:11).

Consider how you can learn from Christ's example, and learn the ways of peace. ≡

Week 13

....

LONGSUFFERING

WHEN TRAGEDY STRUCK his family for a second time, Dave Biebel stunned his wife with a barrage of stark honesty: "If that's the way it's going to be, then God can go to hell! If that's the way it's going to be, I can't and I won't serve Him."

Dave had faced one of the worst nightmares a father could face—twice. After the death of one son, David was told that his other son had a rare disease that would leave him handicapped. One tragedy was enough—he didn't want to stomach another one.

When a godly man takes a punch of adversity, he can be shocked at his own fickle attitude toward God. One day he can lift his hands to praise Him, and the next day he shakes his fist at Him. Maybe you have been there. Something bad happens, and you curse God more than you have ever cursed a fellow human. Or you think about chucking the whole faith-in-a-good-God thing. In times like that, reading a nice little Bible story about Job's suffering doesn't always help much.

I have been there. One Saturday afternoon, my wife and I were talking over a family struggle. Once again, God had disappointed me because He hadn't done something my way. Finally I laid out our options: "We can do one of two things: We can toss God out of our lives and run away from Him; or we can remember all of His previous acts of goodness and mercy toward us, and trust Him to bring us through once again."

Our decision was clear: God had proven Himself faithful so many times, there was no way we could reject Him. That afternoon was important for us. We prayed, we released our disappointment, and we were at peace with God.

Later that day, we got a telephone call. My mother-in-law's car had been broadsided by a limo. She was killed instantly. I realized that God had prepared us in the afternoon for what was to come later that day. My wife and I still face the shock, and we are still grieving, but our faith in God is strong.

There was a happy outcome for Dave Biebel too. "I am here to say I know more about the love of God now than I ever could otherwise," he says. Out of his experience, Dave now has a heart to help other men make peace with God. "Too many people—lots of men—serve God with half a heart because they never admitted they don't like something they think He caused or allowed."

Such men stomach the bitterness they hold against God, sometimes without realizing it. But they need to get honest with God and make peace with Him. When men accept the fact that God has, and deserves, sovereign control, they will be in a place to love Him more. God often uses our suffering to change the hearts of men.

—BRIAN PETERSON

MONDAY

IT'S SO EASY to be faithful and pious and self-satisfied when we're comfortable, well-fed, and everything's going our way; but how suddenly we turn from God when things fall apart. Imagine being in David Biebel's shoes. Having lost one son already, suddenly news comes that your other child has a serious illness and handicap. How would you cope?

"For examples of patience in suffering," James writes, "look at the Lord's prophets. We know how happy they are now because they stayed true to him then, even though they suffered greatly for it. Job is an example of a man who continued to trust the Lord in sorrow; from his experiences we can see how the Lord's plan finally ended in good, for he is full of tenderness and mercy" (James 5:10–11, TLB). Yes, we have heard many times about the saints who suffered great loss before witnessing God's glory. But what we should learn from these models is not just patience but that God is faithful and just—He can be trusted.

Can you "count it all joy" as James advises? Pray for grace to trust Him more. ▤

TUESDAY

JESUS WAS LEERY of people who offered pious platitudes but failed to live out their example in a spirit of love and compassion. Do as they say, Jesus advised, but don't do as they do, because they don't practice what they preach! (Matt. 23:3). Jesus taught that we are to bear each other's burdens, and we ought to look to God for strength in tough times.

"Is anyone among you suffering?" James asked. "Let him pray. Is anyone cheerful? Let him sing psalms. Is anyone among you sick? Let him call for the elders of the church, and let them pray over him, anointing him with oil in the name of the Lord. And the prayer of faith will save the sick, and the Lord will raise him up." And then, to make sure than no other problems may be causing our problems, James continues, "If he has committed sins, he will be forgiven. Confess your trespasses to one another, and pray for one another, that you may be healed. The effective, fervent prayer of a righteous man avails much" (James 5:13–16).

Pray that God will prepare you to be a man of fervent and effective prayer. ▤

WEDNESDAY

WE LIVE IN a world that finds it easy to live by double standards, with no clear lines between right and wrong, cheating and honesty, loyalty and backstabbing. But God's Word pulls no punches. "Now the works of the flesh are evident, which are: adultery, fornication, uncleanness, lewdness, idolatry, sorcery, hatred, contentions, jealousies, outbursts of wrath, selfish ambitions, dissensions, heresies, envy, murders, drunkenness, revelries, and the like; of which I tell you beforehand," said Paul, "just as I also told you in time past, that those who practice such things will not inherit the kingdom of God.

"But the fruit of the Spirit," he hastens to add, "is love, joy, peace, longsuffering, kindness, goodness, faithfulness, gentleness, self-control. Against such there is no law. And those who are Christ's have crucified the flesh with its passions and desires. If we live in the Spirit, let us also walk in the Spirit" (Gal. 5:19–25). We really need to be men who have the fruit of the Spirit and live it out each day.

Pray that God will build you up in His Spirit. ▤

THURSDAY

WHEN LIFE IS unfair, we want to shake our fists at the heavens and demand that God give us *what* we deserve. Now, just saying those words should make us think twice. The Bible makes it pretty clear what we deserve! But even Job cried out, "Let me be weighed on honest scales, that God may know my integrity" (Job 31:6). Job had lived a good life and he was sure that something had gone terribly wrong with God's judgment. Then, when God finally answered Job's protests and let him know who was keeping score, the suffering saint hit the deck, face down, begging for mercy. "I have uttered what I did not understand," he cried, and added, "therefore I abhor myself, and repent in dust and ashes" (Job 42:3, 6).

God is never far away, even if it feels like He's out of town on business. Trust Him. In the meantime, stay in the Word daily, stay on your knees before God, and stay close to your brothers in Christ. Paul says, "Bear one another's burdens, and so fulfill the law of Christ" (Gal. 6:2).

Pray that, when needed, you may truly be a friend-in-need to someone. ▤

FRIDAY

WHEN WE FIND ourselves at a spiritual crossroads, wondering if we can trust God in our moments of crisis, Brian Peterson suggests we have two options: "We can toss God out of our lives and run away from Him, or we can remember all of His previous acts of goodness and mercy toward us, and trust Him to bring us through once again." As Brian says, our decision should be clear: God has proven Himself faithful so often, how could anyone consider rejecting Him? And who knows but what the afflictions you're enduring now may not be His way of building you up for other challenges in the future?

Solomon was no stranger to worry. Though he was the author of Proverbs and other Scriptures, and though he had tremendous wealth and power—like no other king in the history of Israel—he knew stress and doubt. Assessing his situation, he said, "Anxiety in the heart of man causes depression, but a good word makes it glad" (Prov. 12:25).

Pray that you may have a good word for those in stress—and receive one in turn. ▤

WEEKEND

FROM BEGINNING TO end, the Bible addresses the issues

of suffering and injustice, and in both Old and New Testaments, makes it clear that the best response to both situations is faithful endurance. At the end of his life, Joshua challenged the people of Israel to put up or shut up: either they would trust God, or they would trust the gods of the Amorites. So, he said, which will it be? "Choose for yourselves this day whom you will serve . . . But as for me and my house, we will serve the Lord" (Josh. 24:15). Even though they fell away later, they saw the wisdom of Joshua's words and chose the Lord. Jesus knew our tendency to waffle and said, "Because lawlessness will abound, the love of many will grow cold. But he who endures to the end shall be saved" (Matt. 24:12–13).

Whether or not we can "count it all joy when we suffer all manner of trials," as James suggested, we should know that, however bitter the pain and however long the trial, God is on our side, and He is good.

Pray that you will always trust Him, even in life's trials. ▤

Second

←·······················→

Quarter

Week 1
LOVE

AFTER TWENTY PLUS years of counseling, I am convinced that there are only five basic languages of love. Each of us speaks one of them, but seldom do the husband and wife speak the same language. By nature, we speak our own language and wonder why our spouse doesn't feel loved.

Let me show you the five love languages and how they work in a marriage.

1. *Using words of affirmation to build up the other person.* "Bob, I appreciate that you have a regular job. I really appreciate your hard work." Or, "Thanks for the meal, Mary. It was great." First Corinthians 8:1 says, "Love edifies." One of the ways to express love is to use words that *build up* the other person.

2. *Giving gifts to the one you love.* Giving gifts as an expression of love is universal. In my studies in anthropology, a culture has never been found where gift giving is not part of the love-marriage process. A gift says, "He was thinking about me." The gift need not be expensive—it really is the thought that counts.

3. *Acts of service.* Cooking a meal is an act of service. Washing dishes is an act of service, as is vacuuming floors or servicing the car or cleaning the commode. Try doing an act of service that your spouse has complained about doing for years, and see what happens.

4. *Quality time.* Giving someone your undivided attention is a strong expression of love. In order

to give your spouse your undivided attention, the television must be off, the computer must be down, the newspaper must be set aside. Your spouse must be the focus of your attention. To give her quality time is to give her a portion of your life. It is a powerful emotional communication.

5. *Physical touch.* Holding hands, kissing, embracing, sexual intercourse, touching on the shoulder, rubbing the back, placing your hand on her leg as you ride down the road—all of these are expressions of love. And to the person whose primary love language is physical touch, these physical expressions speak volumes of your affection.

Out of these five, each person has a primary love language. One means more to you than all the others. You may appreciate all of them, but one will speak to you more deeply. Seldom does a husband and wife have the same primary love language, so you may need to learn a new language. If you can keep each other's love tanks full, you are far more likely to accomplish the other objectives that God has in mind for each of your lives.

A love-starved wife will never reach her potential as a wife, mother, or Christian. Fill her love tank and watch her blossom. Discover her love language and speak it regularly. In turn, she will probably start speaking your love language, and your love tank will overflow again.

—GARY D. CHAPMAN

MONDAY

IN THE BEGINNING of time, God created the family and recognized the marriage bond of husband and wife as the essential building block of society. The relationship of husband and wife has been vital in every society. In some cultures men believed they could get love outside the home, but Christian culture specifically teaches that men are to love their wives and to live with them in harmony. Paul says, "So husbands ought to love their own wives as their own bodies; he who loves his wife loves himself. For no one ever hated his own flesh, but nourishes and cherishes it, just as the Lord does the church" (Eph. 5:28–29).

Now, that's a tall order—to love one another as Christ loves the church—but there are no options in the clause. Paul says, "For this reason a man shall leave his father and mother and be joined to his wife, and the two shall become one flesh" And then adds, "Let each one of you in particular so love his own wife as himself" (Eph. 5:31, 33).

Does that describe you? Pray that you will learn to speak your wife's love language. ▤

TUESDAY

MARRIAGE COUNSELOR Gary D. Chapman tells us there are five languages we speak with our mates. Some of these languages will mean more to you than others, and some will mean more to your wife. But Chapman suggests that you and your spouse will both be speaking in unknown tongues if you don't give some thought to speaking to each other.

The first love language is *words of affirmation.* It's not a complex language; it doesn't involve a lot of study or body-building exercises. Yet, when spoken with sincerity, Chapman says, it can build up our wives and help transform their attitudes and feelings toward us. Men aren't affirming by nature; we have been taught to hang in there, get the job done, and keep a stiff upper lip. We grit it out and keep on truckin'; but if we expect our wives to do the same, assuming they'll just know that we love them, they may not get the message. Paul says, "Husbands, love your wives. . . . " It doesn't get any simpler than that.

Pray that God will open your ears and help you to speak your mate's love language. ▤

WEDNESDAY

THE SECOND LANGUAGE is *giving gifts to your loved one.* Now this is a language the gift shops and card stores certainly understand. Gifts for every occasion; cards that do the talking for you. But do you think these places exist only to convince people that gift giving is a nice idea? Or are they so common and so successful because half the population—the female half—already understands the language of giving gifts and speaks it fluently?

Good guess. A gift says something special to your wife—it says you're thinking about her, and she needs to know that. The Bible says, "Therefore, as the elect of God, holy and beloved, put on tender mercies, kindness, humility, meekness, longsuffering; bearing with one another, and forgiving one another, if anyone has a complaint against another; even as Christ forgave you, so you also must do. But above all these things put on love, which is the bond of perfection" (Col. 3:12–14).

To make marriage the bond of perfection it can be, ask God to teach you how to show your love. ▤

THURSDAY

JESUS REBUKED THE Pharisees because of their desire to legalize divorce, reminding them that "from the beginning of the creation, God 'made them male and female. For this reason a man shall leave his father and mother and be joined to his wife, and the two shall become one flesh'; so then they are no longer two, but one flesh. Therefore," Jesus said, "what God has joined together, let not man separate" (Mark 10:6–9). Repeatedly, the Bible says, "God hates divorce," yet we fail to give our marriages the attention they deserve until one day we (or our spouses) feel so unloved, so unappreciated, we think we can just bolt.

Not so. Chapman's third language is *acts of service.* Perhaps no other area is so neglected by men today, and none speaks so clearly of your commitment to your spouse. Do you want to build your relationship and make it strong enough to withstand storms of adversity?

Pray that you will see how acts of service can speak your love louder than words. ▤

FRIDAY

LANGUAGE NUMBER FOUR calls for giving your wife a little *quality time.* That means, turn off the tube, ditch the remote, forget work for now, and get the kids busy somewhere else so you two can be together doing something you *both* enjoy. One husband said his idea of a good time was taking his wife to the driving range; another wanted seats at ringside for the Golden Gloves event. Chances are, that's not what either lady had in mind. Quality time means being together where the focus is on the two of you, not on some mindless sport or amusement. If the language you're speaking tells your wife she's just "one of the guys," don't be surprised if she takes a rain check next time you ask her out.

Paul says, "Let your gentleness be known to all men" (Phil. 4:5). Good advice. He might also have said, show some gentleness to your wife as well by learning to speak her language, and by making her the center of attention on a regular basis.

Pray that God will keep you sensitive, giving your mate the time she needs. ▤

WEEKEND

THE FIFTH AND last language Chapman describes is *physical touch.* Touch, even without words, is a powerful stimulant to which all living things respond. Children need it, pets thrive on it, and wives especially need to feel the sense of physical communication that comes from a gentle, loving touch.

An interesting study a few years ago reported that store clerks are so busy running people through the checkout line and making change that they hardly ever notice the faces of the customers who come through. In those conditions it's easy to be rude, and people can feel abused by their abrupt behavior. But the study said that if the hands of customer and checkout person should touch, even for a moment, the chemistry changes. Suddenly the customer and the clerk are humanized, they see each other, and the transaction is somehow less cold and perfunctory. If touch can do that in the checkout line, imagine what it can do for two people who are actually in love!

Pray for your mate. Pray for your language skills. ■

Week 2
VISION

WHEN YALE LAW professor Stephen Carter published his book, *The Culture of Disbelief* in 1993, a lot of people were talking about the need for virtue and morality in society. From the White House to the university campuses, people paid lip service to integrity and decency but made few visible changes in their own lives.

In the middle of this apparent hypocrisy in our nation, something unexpected is happening among Christian men. They're disturbed by the evils of society, but what seems to be convicting them even more is the upheaval in their own lives. Could it be that these "new" Christian men are finding the fulfillment that the secular men's movement had been trying to offer?

Paul Cole, of the Christian Men's Network, thinks so. The secular movements of the 1980s tried to help men find their inner strength and values, but their sources of authority were wildly different. "They were trying to figure out how men are supposed to deal with masculinity, and unfortunately," he says, "they weren't doing a very good job of it." The Wild Man groups that sprouted up may have seemed silly, but beneath all the ritual was a genuine search for meaning. "The secular movements told men to put themselves first," says Cole, "while the Christian movement said to put God first and to put others ahead of yourself."

Pastor Jack Hayford of The Church On The Way says, "I believe that what is taking place in the awakening among men across this nation is one of the three or four most significant things that the Holy Spirit is doing in the church right now. In God's order, it is historic that if men can be stirred to accept their responsibility, everything else begins to be rectified." Are these changes among men the stirrings of something for which so many have prayed for so long? "I believe that with all my heart," says Hayford. "I believe America can be turned around and restored. And I frankly believe that is what is already in motion to happen."

Such thoughts are on the hearts of many people today. The hope of revival touches all of us, and renewal and awakening are in the prayers of believers everywhere. Will the move of God among men help bring this to pass? Paul Cole says that what God is doing is "centered first on Jesus Christ and His model for living a meaningful and fulfilling life. And second, it is centered on the family. But the key for activating both of these is being centered on the Word of God."

"Things done in the Lord," he adds, "grow and have life. But things done in the world fade away, and the end of them is death. Our own movement may go through other stages, and things may continue to change, but we know that the things of God will prosper." This is the hope and the heart of many Christian men today.

—JIM NELSON BLACK

MONDAY

VIRTUE ISN'T A closet issue any more. Everybody's talking about the need for virtue and morality in society—even the White House. Unfortunately, not everybody has the same diagnosis. When Christians speak of integrity and decency, we're talking about a higher standard than most people recognize. But we all admit that some kind of change is needed.

The men's movements of the 1980s were primarily a

backlash against the radical feminism of the day. Women were getting tougher and more competitive, so bands of weekend wild men met in wigwams to vent their boyish frustrations. No wonder the world laughed! They recognized that men needed to get in touch with a higher power, but they couldn't see the forest for the trees. Today's awakening of Christian men has a far different goal. Instead of anger and revenge, it offers compassion, commitment, and true courage through a life-changing commitment to Jesus Christ. What a huge difference of vision!

If you want to be a man of God and a man of virtue, ask the Lord for guidance. ▤

TUESDAY

THERE MAY BE no finer statement of what Christ expects from Christian men than His words in the High Priestly Prayer. In it, He prays, "I have manifested Your name to the men whom You have given Me out of the world . . . I have given to them the words which You have given Me; and they have received them, and have known surely that I came forth from You; and they have believed that You sent Me . . . Now I am no longer in the world, but these are in the world, and I come to You.

"Holy Father," Jesus says, "keep through Your name those whom You have given Me, that they may be one as We are . . . I have given them Your word; and the world has hated them because they are not of the world, just as I am not of the world." Now, notice this: "I do not pray that You should take them out of the world, but that You should keep them from the evil one" (John 17:6, 8, 11, 14–15). If God leaves us in the world, He must have a reason!

Pray that you'll be all that Christ, by His endorsement, has commissioned you to be. ▤

WEDNESDAY

PASTOR JACK HAYFORD believes we're already in the midst of an awakening, and he says it's one of the most important things happening in the church today. "I believe America can be turned around and restored," he says, "and it's already happening." Do you agree? Are we experiencing a fresh new move of the Holy Spirit in our midst?

Throughout history, there's never been a great revival that wasn't preceded by fervent prayer. Are you praying? There has never been an awakening where there weren't great outpourings of the Spirit in massive gatherings of believers in churches, tents, arenas, or open fields. Seen any massive rallies lately? And no true revival has ever taken place without signs, wonders, and manifestations of God's divine power. Have you witnessed the hand of God in a miraculous way?

If there is to be revival, pray that it may start with you, and that God will manifest His glory in our midst, real soon. ▤

THURSDAY

PAUL'S LETTER TO the Galatians captures very well the spirit of reformation and revival that many find in movements like Promise Keepers. The letter offers important teachings on justification by faith and freedom in the Spirit, and calls the men of that Roman province to a higher standard. First, to support those who minister, and then to live godly lives. "Let him who is taught the word share in all good things with him who teaches," Paul said. Then, "Do not be deceived, God is not mocked; for whatever a man sows, that he will also reap. For he who sows to his flesh will of the flesh reap corruption, but he who sows to the Spirit will of the Spirit reap everlasting life. And let us not grow weary while doing good, for in due season we shall reap if we do not lose heart. Therefore, as we have opportunity, let us do good to all, especially to those who are of the household of faith" (Gal. 6:6–10).

As you think of your own vision of what it means to be a new man in Christ, reflect on Paul's words, and pray that you may gain a renewed passion for the household of faith. ▤

FRIDAY

WITHOUT WISDOM THAT comes through a change of heart and mind, and sound biblical instruction, we wander around like lost sheep. Solomon says, "There is a way that seems right to a man, but its end is the way of death" (Prov. 14:12). Isaiah describes the situation even better, saying, "All we like sheep have gone astray; we have turned, every one, to his own way; and the Lord has laid on Him the iniquity of us all" (Isa. 53:6). Man's ignorance and indifference to God results in sin, and sin demands a blood sacrifice that only the pure Son of God can offer. That's why we need a Savior; and that's why men of God need to be constantly in the Word. We need to experience genuine transformation.

Paul Cole, who shares in leadership of the Christian Men's Network with his father, Ed, recognizes that, "Things done in the world fade away; the end of them is death." If we want to grow in faith and wisdom as men of God, then let's get on His team.

Pray that God will give you a passion for the Word. ▤

WEEKEND

THE CITIZENS OF Macedonia were proud Greeks, descendants of Alexander the Great. Paul gave some of his greatest teaching there—but hear these powerful words to the men of God in the capitol: "Finally then, brethren, we urge and exhort in the Lord Jesus that you should abound more and more, just as you received from us how you ought to walk and to please God; for you know what commandments we gave you through the Lord Jesus.

"For this is the will of God, your sanctification: that you should abstain from sexual immorality; that each of you should know how to possess his own vessel in sanctification and honor, not in passion of lust . . . that no one should take advantage of and defraud his brother in this matter, because the Lord is the avenger of all such, as we also forewarned you and testified. For God did not call us to uncleanness, but in holiness. Therefore he who rejects this does not reject man, but God, who has also given us His Holy Spirit" (1 Thess. 4:1–8).

Let sanctification, or holiness, be your goal; and pray that your vision may expand. ▤

Week 3
....
AMBITION

▰ TODAY, AS NEVER BEFORE, men are being bombarded with an endless list of requirements supposedly necessary to be an effective husband, father, or disciple of Christ. Consider these unrealistic expectations:

1. *Time management.* I have attended numerous Christian seminars and read dozens of books on time management. To listen to some of these experts, you get the idea that every moment of your life should have profound significance. God is pictured as some divine efficiency expert, sitting on His throne with a giant day-timer, recording how well we use our time.

2. *Money management.* Christian men are saturated with advice about how to manage their money. We're told we should be saving thousands of dollars each year for our children's college and our own retirement. At the same time, we're encouraged to give an increasing percentage of money to support God's work. No wonder so many are suffering from floating anxiety about their finances.

3. *Marriage.* If you and your wife are not enjoying wedded bliss every moment, are you falling short of God's expectations for your marriage? I'm afraid that Christian books, radio programs, and seminars have so inflated our expectations that many couples are becoming needlessly discontent with their relationships.

4. *Prayer.* How many times have you heard stories

about great men of the past spending hours in daily prayer? Do those stories make you feel as guilty as they do me? Nowhere does the Bible teach that God hears us better when we're hungry and sleepy. Nor does the Bible place a premium on long prayers. Unfortunately, many men, unable to meet these unrealistic standards, give up praying altogether.

5. *Parenting.* One of the downsides of the flood of information about parenting is the myth of the "ideal Christian parent." Author Tim Hansel writes, "I'm so weary of all the images. At church I'm supposed to be some sort of bionic Christian. At work, I'm supposed to be some kind of robot. And now at home I'm expected to be some sort of Christian Super Dad. It's no wonder I feel like a failure most of the time . . . I thought Christianity was supposed to set us free."

I believe God wants to loosen the knots of unrealistic expectations enslaving us to guilt. Many men feel so weighed down by all the unrealistic expectations from other Christians that they give up trying to please God at all. If God were to sit beside us and place His loving arm around us, many of us would be shocked to hear Him say, "You're doing great. I'm proud of you. Quit being so hard on yourself."

Wishful thinking? Only for those who have become a slave to the unrealistic standards of others. Did Jesus heal every sick person, raise every dead person, or convert every sinner during His brief thirty-three years? No, but He knew He had completed the assignment God had given Him. Unshackle yourself from the expectations of others and begin to enjoy life in His grace!

—ROBERT JEFFRESS

MONDAY

WE LIVE IN a performance-oriented society. Sometime during our adolescent years we get the idea that life's rewards only come to high achievers, and from that moment on we begin pushing ourselves, striving for success and the respect of others. But Jesus has a different idea: "So don't be anxious about tomorrow," He says. "God will take care of your tomorrow too. Live one day at a time" (Matt. 6:34, TLB).

You can't work your way to heaven. Paul said, "But when the kindness and the love of God our Savior toward man appeared, not by works of righteousness which we have done, but according to His mercy He saved us, through the washing of regeneration and renewing of the Holy Spirit, whom He poured out on us abundantly through Jesus Christ our Savior, that having been justified by His grace we should become heirs according to the hope of eternal life" (Titus 3:4–7). Furthermore, the same grace that saves us covers us in all things.

Pray that you can find peace, knowing you are justified through God's grace. ▤

TUESDAY

FUNNY, ISN'T IT, how time management, which is supposed to make life easier and free up all sorts of wasted hours, actually drives people crazy? Instead of making it easier, suddenly we've got hundreds of off-the-wall rules and formulas and checkpoints that no sane person could remember! Who thought of this stuff anyway? All you really wanted was a little order and efficiency in your life, and what you got was a day crammed full of stuff—even your "free time" is regulated by some time chart.

Robert Jeffress reminds us that God is not a celestial efficiency expert clocking your every move. David says, "The Lord will give strength to His people; the Lord will bless His people with peace" (Ps. 29:11). And again, "As for me, I will call upon God, and the Lord shall save me. Evening and morning and at noon I will pray, and cry aloud, and He shall hear my voice. He has redeemed my soul in peace from the battle that was against me" (Ps. 55:16–18).

Pray that God will give you His peace in life's battles. ⬛

WEDNESDAY

SOME MEN HAVE the idea that the Bible's teaching on stewardship somehow requires every man to be a great money manager! Not only does such a view put undue pressure on us, but it actually distorts the Scriptures. When Jesus talked about being stewards, He used money as a metaphor for investing our talents in the kingdom of God.

If we do neglect the riches God has given us through Christ Jesus, we will surely inherit damnation; but Jesus had no interest in our accumulating wealth! Far from it. He said: "You cannot serve two masters: God and money. For you will hate one and love the other, or else the other way around. So my counsel is: Don't worry about things—food, drink, and clothes. For you already have life and a body—and they are far more important than what to eat and wear. Look at the birds! They don't worry about what to eat—they don't need to sow or reap or store up food—for your heavenly Father feeds them. And you are far more valuable to him than they are" (Matt. 6:24–26).

Pray that God will help you to focus on the real treasures. ⬛

THURSDAY

HOW MANY BOOKS have you seen lately that tell men how to be better husbands, lovers, leaders, and pals? A lot, no doubt, if you've been around a church or a Christian radio broadcast lately! There's no doubt most of us could use some help in all these areas, but the problem is the risk of letting the "self-improvement" mythology of secular culture infiltrate our lives to the point that the walk of faith looks more like an Olympic marathon.

Have you failed if you're not a red-hot lover? Do you feel guilty if you haven't mastered the latest formula for marital bliss? Give it a rest! The writer of Hebrews tells us, "Marriage is honorable among all, and the bed undefiled. . . . Let your conduct be without covetousness; be content with such things as you have. For He Himself has said, 'I will never leave you nor forsake you.' So we may boldly say: 'The Lord is my helper; I will not fear. What can man do to me?'" (Heb. 13:4–6).

Pray that you may be ambitious for the things of God and realistic about the rest. ▤

Friday

PRAYER WAS VERY important to our Lord—He majored in it. But He never taught that prayer is some kind of contact sport. He said, "And when you pray, you shall not be like the hypocrites. For they love to pray standing in the synagogues and on the corners of the streets, that they may be seen by men. Assuredly, I say to you, they have their reward. But you, when you pray, go into your room, and when you have shut your door, pray to your Father who is in the secret place; and your Father who sees in secret will reward you openly. And when you pray, do not use vain repetitions as the heathen do. For they think that they will be heard for their many words. Therefore do not be like them. For your Father knows the things you have need of before you ask Him" (Matt. 6:5–8).

Then, to show how really simple it is, Jesus gave us

His model prayer—just sixty-six words long including the Amen!

Pray now, and pray often. But next time you hear someone speak about the rigors of the prayer life, remember Christ's example of "simplicity of heart." ▤

WEEKEND

IT'S TRUE THAT we all could be better parents. There's no segment of the population so devastated by modern life as our kids, and most of the attention we give to making dads better dads and moms better moms is well placed. Unfortunately, as Robert Jeffress and Tim Hansel point out, we've set the hurdle of godly parenting so high even a pole vaulter would have trouble getting over it. Hansel says the prospect of being some sort of "bionic Christian" makes him feel like a failure most of the time! Whatever happened to the idea of "freedom in Christ"?

Our faith teaches us how to love. Paul says, "As you abound in everything—in faith, in speech, in knowledge, in all diligence, and in your love for us—see that you abound in this grace also" (2 Cor. 8:7). Christian love should not be under compulsion. Again, Paul says, "Stand fast therefore in the liberty by which Christ has made us free, and do not be entangled again with a yoke of bondage" (Gal. 5:1).

Pray for ambition tempered by grace. ▤

Week 4
FORGIVENESS

"TO ERR IS HUMAN, to forgive divine." It's easy to see how those words, penned by eighteenth-century poet Alexander Pope, are mistaken for Scripture. We all make mistakes, we all need forgiveness—and God makes this fact very clear. In the midst of daily failures—by our children, our spouses, and ourselves—forgiveness must be a central part of what we do as we seek to imitate our Father God.

One summer day several years ago I was called in to help resolve a small family dispute. I listened carefully, studied facial expressions, and assessed the situation. It seemed clear that my son, Joel, wasn't being honest but he wouldn't give himself away.

Finally, I made the call: "Joel, I don't believe you." As I doled out the appropriate punishment, Joel showed no sign of remorse. Only minutes later I found out through one of the other kids that Joel had in fact been telling the truth, and I had punished him unfairly. I was wrong. I don't think there's anything more gripping for a father than coming face-to-face with his own mistakes. What needs to be done is clear: confess that he was wrong, and ask for forgiveness. It is humbling, but it is also a father's ultimate moment of modeling.

Asking your children for forgiveness demonstrates that, as in all relationships, there is give and take. They learn that your rules are not arbitrary, and that it's a two-way street—you hold yourself accountable to those rules as well, and if you blow it, you owe them a repentant apology. You admit you're not perfect. You prove that restoring the integrity and trust of the relationship is more important than your own ego.

But it goes even further. Think of the relief your child must feel. He or she has been punished unfairly, but you haven't blown off their feelings. You don't just say, "Hey, life isn't fair, son," and expect him to understand. Seeking his forgiveness symbolizes that you are responsive to your child. He has suffered unjustly, and you want to make things right.

Have you blown it recently? We all sin against God and the people around us—including our children. And we all need forgiveness. Imagine what would happen if all fathers in the world today were willing to acknowledge their shortcomings to their children. What if they asked forgiveness for their constant criticism, or lack of affirmation, or lack of involvement in their lives?

We may never know what effect it would have, because that kind of widespread awakening is not likely. But as individuals, we must find out! The effects of forgiveness can be earthshaking. Children will flourish if they live with a gracious and repentant father. That power is ready to work for you today.

Let's allow the forgiveness of another Father to flow through us so we may accomplish the work of forgiveness in our families.

—KEN R. CANFIELD

MONDAY

AFTER HE HAD taught His disciples the model prayer, Jesus said, "If you forgive men their trespasses, your heavenly Father will also forgive you. But if you do not forgive men their trespasses, neither will your Father forgive your trespasses" (Matt. 6:14–15). Is that a frightening concept or what? We're so accustomed to holding grudges against everyone we think treated us badly, the idea of blanket forgiveness for everybody is a shocker! But Jesus didn't leave room for debate. We must forgive those who need forgiveness.

And have you thought about this?—The first person you need to forgive may be yourself. If that's so, why not say this prayer right now? "Dear God, before You, I forgive myself. You know what I've done, what I've said, and who I've hurt. I want to make those things right, but I know that, through Jesus Christ, You have forgiven me. So now I forgive myself." In that simple statement, you actually begin your journey to restoration.

As you consciously forgive yourself, you'll be better able to forgive those who've wronged you. ▣

TUESDAY

THE SECOND PERSON you need to forgive may surprise you. Many people who have felt wronged for a long period of time may be angry with God Himself, harboring resentment toward Him. They may have blamed Him for the death of a loved one, a child, or a friend. Some accuse God of breaking up their family or their marriage. Others are angry because God never showed His face when they were in desperate pain, poverty, need, loneliness, hunger, unemployment, or stress of one kind or another. Some are physically scarred and disfigured; some are hurting deep inside, and they are bitter toward God.

Take heart. God understands your anger, and He can deal with it. He does not hate you for it. But you can't experience His blessings while holding onto your bitterness. You have to get rid of those emotions by looking deep into your soul and bringing up all those feelings so you can confess them before God and seek His forgiveness. Would you release Him now?

Pray that God will free your heart from the past and truly make you a new man. ▣

WEDNESDAY

AS YOU CONTINUE down your list and forgive each person for whom you've held a grudge, you may not be able to remember, at one sitting, all the people you've resented; but pray over these things every day until God frees your heart from the clutches of bitterness and hatred. If you're driving down the freeway thinking about someone you've been angry with, take a moment right then to confess those feelings to the Lord, ask His forgiveness, and then forgive that person for whatever was done or said to wound you.

You may have every legal right to hold a grudge against the ones who've hurt you. You may have a case that would stand up in a court of law. But to be free of the weights holding you down in your relationship with Jesus Christ, you must cut loose the anchors. Toss out all the debris of those old emotions and hurts and wounded relationships, and start on a new course. That's what it means to be a new man; and this is the day to begin. If God has had the mercy to forgive you, surely you can do no less.

Pray for the power to forgive. ■

THURSDAY

CHILDREN ARE SO perceptive. They don't miss very much, and if they see a weakness in us, they may not say anything but they make a mental note. That's why Ken Canfield's suggestion to be open and honest with your kids, and even admit when you make a mistake, is so important. God has entrusted us with the privilege of raising the next generation.

Those young lives hold the future of the nations in their hands. What are they learning from you? What values will they soak up by seeing how you respond to life's trials and tribulations? When Moses brought the Ten Commandments to the Israelites, he told them God was to be honored at all times, and His Commandments were to be constantly on their minds: "You must teach them to your children and talk about them when you are at home or out for a walk; at bedtime and the first thing in the morning" (Deut. 6:7, TLB).

If your kids see that you're obedient to God's Word, they'll get the point that it's important.

Pray that you will always be open, honest, and a godly influence on your kids. ▓

FRIDAY

DAVID WENT THROUGH some ups and down in his walk with the Lord. He committed serious sins, got off on the wrong foot with his sons, and had to hide out in caves to avoid the wrath of King Saul. But David was honest and transparent in his faith, and God said, "I have found David the son of Jesse, a man after My own heart, who will do all My will" (Acts 13:22).

But perhaps most remarkable, David discovered the joy of God's forgiveness. He says, "There was a time when I wouldn't admit what a sinner I was. But my dishonesty made me miserable and filled my days with frustration. All day and all night your hand was heavy on me. My strength evaporated like water on a sunny day until I finally admitted all my sins to you and stopped trying to hide them. I said to myself, 'I will confess them to the Lord.' And you forgave me! All my guilt is gone. Now I say that each believer should confess his sins to God when he is aware of them, while there is time to be forgiven. Judgment will not touch him if he does" (Ps. 32:3–6, TLB).

Pray for a heart like David's. ▓

WEEKEND

"IMAGINE WHAT WOULD happen," says Ken Canfield, "if all fathers in the world today were to acknowledge their shortcomings to their children. What if they asked for-giveness for their constant criticism, or lack of affirmation, or lack of involvement in their lives?"

No doubt the world would be transformed before our eyes. But even if such a transformation is hardly likely in this fallen world, what's to stop each of us from taking the challenge right now? A forgiving spirit rec-ognizes that we're all capable of falling from time to time. It's a human thing. It doesn't say that sin's okay, or that bad behavior is no big deal. On the contrary, a forgiving spirit recognizes that you've done something both you and others find reproachful, and you admit you need forgiveness. But a forgiving heart says, when there is honest repentance (and sometimes when there isn't), I'm willing to forget it.

If you appreciate what Christ has done for you by forgiving your sins, would you pray that you will have a forgiving spirit, and that you'll be honest about your own failings? ▤

NURTURING

IN A WORLD OBSESSED with entertainment and sports heroes, how can a dad compete? My son Matthew occasionally comes to work with me. As offensive lineman for the Green Bay Packers, my job is football, and my "office" is Lambeau Field in Green Bay, Wisconsin. One day I found Matt standing near the locker of one of our team's superstars. There he was, mouth wide open, caught in the aura of the man he hoped would be his new hero.

Suddenly I saw another player, one of my football buddies, in a position of influence with my son. But he never even acknowledged the boy. Matthew was out in the cold, and so was I. I was at fault. My goal shouldn't be to hand off the role modeling to someone else. I realized there's one role model Matt could always count on, someone who had a home-field advantage: me. Our most important responsibility as role models is at home.

Fathering is a learning process. No dad starts out knowing it all. I played football for Coach John Robinson at USC where our objective was to wear our opponents down in the first three quarters so by the fourth quarter we could win the game. In some ways, we dads can apply this one-step-at-a-time approach to influence our children. But to do so, we have to be engaged with them. We have to participate in their victories and defeats. We can't just be observers; we need to make fathering a contact sport. I found three ways to do that.

1. *Dominate the clock.* A recent study reveals that

the average five-year-old spends only twenty-five minutes a week in close interaction with his father. Yet, the same child spends twenty-five hours a week watching TV. The average preschooler watches more TV in three years than the average college student spends in the classroom in four years. And the average teenager will listen to eleven thousand hours of rock music—more than twice the time he'll spend in class. Is it any wonder that people like Madonna and Snoop Doggy Dogg have a bigger impact on our children than we do?

2. *Make gains with patience.* Think of the first time you taught your child to throw a ball. You threw, the child missed. You wanted to say, "Here's how you do it." Your child would understand and that would be the end of it. But it doesn't happen that way. It's throw . . . pick up . . . throw . . . pick up. . . . We can't expect kids to immediately learn great moral concepts either; it takes time and patience.

3. *Guard your position.* Our kids are watching us intently. Sometimes we notice, sometimes we don't. But they're always watching, taking mental notes. Are you willing to risk being watched and imitated? If not, someone else may be the one they watch and imitate. But if you guard your position, your example can make an indelible impact on them. And they won't need to turn to another second-string role model again.

—KEN RUETTGERS

MONDAY

MOST OF THE TIME, the world's role models come with strings attached. Sports heroes hawking athletic gear, TV and film stars pushing their escapades (and lifelike action figures), or rock idols selling sex, drugs, violence, and a culture of death. Even the most wholesome celebrities frequently give all the wrong signals, and few offer the kind of example you'd want your kids to admire. Someone said, "Woe to the nation that needs heroes!" We only need heroes when we're in a jam— somebody to fight for us or save us when we can't save ourselves. Great generals and warriors? Those who bled and died on foreign soil maybe?

How about a real superhero! "But we see Jesus, who was made a little lower than the angels, for the suffering of death crowned with glory and honor, that He, by the grace of God, might taste death for everyone" (Heb. 2:9). The writer then calls Jesus "the captain of our salvation." Captain Jesus! It doesn't get any bigger than that!

As you nurture your kids, pray with them, and help them get to know the greatest role model of all. ▤

TUESDAY

REMEMBER WHEN YOU were a little guy? Remember your first images of your dad or of some other man you looked up to? Remember the sense of trust, hope, admiration, and even the fear you felt? Chances are that's what your kids feel for you, too. Kids naturally desire to look up to their dads, uncles, and adult males who are big and strong and know stuff. It's only when we no longer measure up, when we get too busy with our problems, or when others surpass our ability to inspire, that they start looking elsewhere for role models.

By all rights, Ken Ruettgers should have been a big-time role model to his five year old. He was not only a pro football player and a big powerful guy, he was Daddy. But Ken found out that if he wanted to be a role model, he had to be present and accounted for. The apostle Paul dared to say, "Imitate me, just as I also imitate Christ" (1 Cor. 11:1). Are you bold enough to model Jesus for your kids?

It's a tall order, but pray that you'll demonstrate the love and strength of character, and be the kind of man, that even your kids can admire. ▤

WEDNESDAY

UNDER COACH JOHN ROBINSON, Ken Ruettgers learned to play hard-nosed football and win big games. Ken's suggestions for dads help us to recognize the degree to which modern parenting really is a contact sport. His first principle, "Dominate the Clock," hits most of us right where we live. Associated Press reports that 31 percent of eight- to twelve-year-olds say that they don't spend enough time with their fathers. A University of Maryland study shows that parents today spend just seventeen hours a week with their children, a 40 percent drop since 1965. In fact, American parents spend less time with their children than parents in any other industrialized nation. What does that say about where we put our values?

Jesus said, "Where your treasure is, there your heart will be also" (Matt. 6:21). Apparently, we don't treasure our kids enough to give them what they want most—us. No wonder they look elsewhere for role models! If you really want to be a man of God, then you need to be a factor in some youngster's life.

Would you pray about how to do that? ▤

THURSDAY

RUETTGERS' SECOND PRINCIPLE is to "Make Gains With Patience." As a rule, we're a society that wants it all now. Deferred gratification is not something we're very fond of. But to make a lasting difference in the life of another person, and especially the life of a child, we need to take a steady, systematic approach. We need to show that we're there for the duration. And we need to be patient when it takes several times for the important lessons to sink in. The writer of Hebrews says, "Therefore do not cast away your confidence, which has great reward. For you have need of endurance, so that after you have done the will of God, you may receive the promise" (Heb. 10:35–36). Christ calls us to walk with patience and endurance if we expect to receive the promise of eternal life. We need some of that same spirit in our roles as parents and friends.

If you show patience, tenacity, courage, and respect in your behavior, you won't need a lot of words to gain your children's respect.

Pray you'll be that kind of role model. ▤

FRIDAY

DO YOU KNOW your position? Do you know the rules you're supposed to play by? Before you can lock onto Ruettgers third principle, "Guard Your Position," you need to be sure of your role as husband, father, friend, and child of God. And once you do, you need to "be strong in the Lord and in the power of His might" (Eph. 6:10).

Guarding your position means claiming your turf and holding it. It means sticking by the fundamentals of the game. It means not letting anybody push you out of position. Just listen to the passion in Paul's words: "O Timothy! Guard what was committed to your trust, avoiding the profane and idle babblings and contradictions of what is falsely called knowledge" (1 Tim. 6:20). And then, just verses later, these wonderful words: "For I know whom I have believed and am persuaded that He is able to keep what I have committed to Him until that Day" (2 Tim. 1:12–14).

As you pray for a loving, nurturing heart, pray for strength to guard your position. ▤

WEEKEND

WHATEVER YOU DO for a living—whether you're a football player, a traffic cop, or a sanitation engineer—it's important to remember who you work for, and give credit where credit's due. When Paul and Barnabas were preaching in Timothy's hometown of Lystra, Paul saw a man in the crowd who was born lame and couldn't walk. So he said, "Stand up straight on your feet." Suddenly the man leaped up and began to walk. Pandemonium broke out. They'd never seen miracles like this! "The gods have come down to us in the likeness of men!" they shouted. The priest of Zeus brought oxen and garlands to sacrifice to these new gods, but Paul was horrified and stopped them immediately. As he began to preach, the crowds grew angry and they stoned him and left him for dead. (See Acts 14.)

Later, Paul wrote: "Take up the whole armor of God, that you may be able to withstand in the evil day, and having done all, to stand" (Eph. 6:13).

That doesn't mean you won't take some hits, but pray that you can stand strong and remember who you work for. ▧

Week 6

STRENGTH

TEMPTATION KNOWS NO STRANGERS. Everyone is tempted, and always will be. Your mind, your body, your social nature—all will be avenues of temptation. Satan, our great enemy, is called the tempter. He prowls around like a roaring lion, poised to pounce. And he's had tremendous success with millions of members of the human race over thousands of years.

Temptation is not sin. Scripture says that Jesus was "in all points tempted as we are, *yet without sin*" (Heb. 4:15). In fact, temptation all by itself is powerless. To succeed, temptation needs a partner, someone to open the door and welcome it in. You can't stop temptations from coming, but you can decide what you're going to do with each one when it comes.

It is natural to look at a woman's physical appearance. But the downward slide to lust begins when we look in order to savor a tempting thought. This is the evil thought, the fantasy. The sin of lust is a process that begins in the mind. Therefore, guard your heart and mind. No wonder Paul talked about needing a "renewing of your mind" (Rom. 12:2).

If our conscience has been trained by the Bible and we are committed to its principles, we meet temptation with confidence instead of fear. God's warnings are the love words of a father telling his child not to run in the street, jump off the bridge, or trifle with drugs. They are loving protections, not capricious prohibitions. Here's a verse to remember: "I have strength for all things in Christ Who empowers me [I am ready for anything and equal to anything through Him Who infuses inner strength into me]" (Phil. 4:13, AMP).

Some would give anything if temptation could be eliminated. But every temptation is an opportunity to defeat the devil. Temptation gives us a chance to develop virtue and mastery—a stepping stone to building Christian character. The devil wants to use temptation for our destruction, but God can use it for our development. We were made to be victors, not escapists.

You cannot wait until you are nose to nose with temptation to decide your response. The decision must be made ahead of time and confirmed at the time you are tempted. Then you will be able to remove yourself from the situation.

Fix your thoughts on what is true and good and right. Think about things that are pure and lovely, and dwell on the fine good things in others. Think about all you can praise God for and be glad about. (See Philippians 4:8.) That doesn't mean shifting your mind out of gear and passively hoping some excellent thoughts will drop in. Research shows that 90 percent of the input we get is negative. This is why we must saturate our hearts and minds with the Bible and faith-building words.

Christ's response to temptation reveals three power sources: He was obedient to His Father, filled with the Holy Spirit, and wisely used the Scriptures. These same resources are available and necessary for us.

—J. ALLAN PETERSEN

MONDAY

IF YOU HAVE a weakness, you can be sure Satan will find it. He has a lot of experience at doing that, and he uses all the tricks in his bag to make us feel that our sins are so awful there's no hope of forgiveness. That's why Peter warns us, "Be sober, be vigilant; because your adversary the devil walks about like a roaring lion, seeking whom he may devour" (1 Pet. 5:8). But just in case the image of a wild beast stalking its prey seems too intimidating, Peter goes on to say, "Resist him, steadfast in the faith, knowing that the same sufferings are experienced by your brotherhood in the world" (v. 9).

Satan can be defeated. It happens every day whenever we resist his taunts. Paul assures us, "No temptation has overtaken you except such as is common to man; but God is faithful, who will not allow you to be tempted beyond what you are able, but with the temptation will also make the way of escape, that you may be able to bear it" (1 Cor. 10:13).

Pray for courage to resist, and God will give you the strength to defeat temptation. 〓

TUESDAY

ISN'T IT JUST like Satan to go after us when we're at our weakest point? After the Lord's grueling forty-day fast, Satan said, "If You are the Son of God, command that these stones become bread." Jesus was starved, but He said, "It is written, 'Man shall not live by bread alone, but by every word that proceeds from the mouth of God'" (Matt. 3:3–4).

What a relief to know that Jesus was tempted by Satan, even as we are, and yet He had the strength to resist and say no. The fact that the devil shot his hottest arrows at Him did not reflect badly on our Lord, because Jesus was able to resist Satan's attack by quoting the Scripture back at him. If we are steeped in the word of God, and if our hearts have turned away from the allure of the world, then we, too, can defeat Satan.

We can be grateful for the snapshot Matthew provides of that critical moment. In it, Jesus shows us how to resist temptation.

Pray that you'll have the strength to do the same. 〓

WEDNESDAY

IT MIGHT HAVE been nice if Satan had given up after his first attempt, but, wouldn't you know it, he came back again. We read, "Then the devil took Him up into the holy city, set Him on the pinnacle of the temple, and said to Him, 'If You are the Son of God, throw Yourself down. For it is written: "He shall give His angels charge over you," and, "In their hands they shall bear you up, lest you dash your foot against a stone"'" (Matt. 4:5–6). Notice that Satan knows the Scripture very well.

But so does the Lord—after all, He wrote it. So Jesus said to him, "It is written again, 'You shall not tempt the Lord your God'" (v. 7).

For his last trick, the devil took Jesus up on a high mountain, showed Him all the kingdoms of the world, and said, "All these things I will give You if You will fall down and worship me" (v. 9).

Jesus said, "Away with you, Satan! For it is written, 'You shall worship the Lord your God, and Him only you shall serve'" (v. 10). Then the devil left Him, and angels came and ministered to Jesus.

Pray for strength like that, so you can defeat Satan.▤

THURSDAY

TEMPTATION IS NOT a sin. Everybody has to face it sometime. The greatest risk of temptation is in allowing it to linger in our minds so the desire to do that which we know to be wrong begins to take possession of our thoughts. If we sense that Satan is creeping around trying to weaken us, our goal should be to cast out the evil thoughts and replace them with pure, holy thoughts. That's how we defeat the devil's plan. James shows us the two sides of that coin when he says: "Resist the devil and he will flee from you," then he adds, "Draw near to God and He will draw near to you" (James 4:7–8).

The words of Joshua come to mind, when he said, "Choose for yourselves this day whom you will serve. . . . But as for me and my house, we will serve the Lord" (Josh. 24:15). Power over temptation demands the same kind of resolve. Make up your mind right now that you will serve God and not the flesh, so that when a bad encounter comes you'll have the strength to say no.

Pray and build strength now, because you will need it later. ▤

FRIDAY

THE NIGHT HE was betrayed into the hands of His accusers, Jesus wanted to be alone with the Father, so He asked Peter, James, and John to come with Him to the garden to pray. But after a short time, He came back to see if the men were watching and found them fast asleep. "What! Could you not watch with Me one hour?" He asked. Then He said, "Watch and pray, lest you enter into temptation. The spirit indeed is willing, but the flesh is weak" (Matt. 26:41).

We know what happened next. Twice more Jesus went back, and twice more His most trusted disciples let Him down. Then Judas arrived with his pack of angry accusers to carry the Master off to be questioned by the Jewish leaders, beaten by the Roman guards, tried before Pilate, and finally condemned to death on the cross. There are many important lessons in this story—but we need to hear Christ's words that only vigilance and endurance, in the strength of the Lord can keep us from falling.

Let your prayer focus on this lesson today. ▤

WEEKEND

HOLLYWOOD AND MADISON Avenue play on our weaknesses. They tell us that we deserve the best; they encourage us to indulge in every exotic and erotic plea-sure and grab all the gusto we can get. But Jesus said we are not to indulge in the sins of the flesh or to fall for the allurements of this world. "When He had called the people to Himself, with His disciples also," Mark tells us, "He said to them, 'Whoever desires to come after Me, let him deny himself, and take up his cross, and follow Me. For whoever desires to save his life will lose it, but whoever loses his life for My sake and the gospel's will save it. For what will it profit a man if he gains the whole world, and loses his own soul?'" (Mark 8:34–36).

What an important statement! Allan Petersen says that God's warnings are the love words of a loving parent teaching us to avoid the mistakes we encounter in our lives. The best this world can offer is slavery and death to the soul. Why would anyone pick that when God offers life and joy forever?

Pray for the strength to choose Him, and do things God's way. ▤

DILIGENCE

THE PHILOSOPHER VOLTAIRE wrote, "God made man in His image, and man returned the favor." Ever since the Garden of Eden, mankind has been attempting to recreate God in man's own frail image. We want a God we can comprehend in human terms. We want a deity we can figure out. We want a deity we can control.

Slowly but surely, we have given God a "1990s makeover." At the expense of reverence for His sovereignty, we have made God over into a comfortable pal, a "user-friendly" God who makes allowances for sin; a non-judgmental God who will easily adapt to our lifestyles.

In his book *The Body,* Chuck Colson wrote, "The books selling in Christian bookstores today are the 'touchy-feely' ones that focus on self-esteem, self-fulfillment, and self-analysis, while devotionals and missionary biographies gather dust on the shelves. So do books encouraging self sacrifice."

A 1994 *U.S. News & World Report* cover story noted, "American religion has taken on the aura of pop psychology. Many congregations have multiplied their membership by going light on the theology and offering worshipers a steady diet of sermons and support groups that emphasize personal fulfillment."

The National Council of Churches felt the Bible was too "sexist," so it determined to make it more acceptable to Christians of the 1990s. The opening of their revised Lord's Prayer goes: "Our Father and Mother who art in heaven. . . ." One mainline denomination included references to our Creator such as "Grandfather," "Great Spirit," and "Our Grove of Shelter," as well as describing Him as "like a baker woman who brings the leaven that causes our hope to rise." *Give me a break!*

Recoiling from a negative distortion of an angry God, many have allowed the pendulum to swing too far in the opposite direction. When was the last time you heard a "hellfire and brimstone" message? For that matter, when was the last time you even heard a preacher politely mention hell?

While some still admire Jonathan Edwards' sermon, "Sinners in the Hands of an Angry God," I doubt Edwards would be welcomed in the pulpit today. Once he reworked it for the 1990s, he could call it, "People With Low Self-Esteem From Dysfunctional Families in the Hands of an All-Caring, Nonjudgmental Supreme Being."

As godly men, our job is to expose the incomplete gospel message as counterfeit. The apostle Paul warned, "I am astonished that you are so quickly deserting the one who called you by the grace of Christ and turning to a different gospel—which is really no gospel at all. Evidently some people are throwing you into confusion and are trying to pervert the gospel of Christ. But even if we or an angel from heaven should preach a gospel other than the one we preached to you, let him be eternally condemned" (Gal. 1:6–8, NIV).

Without repentance followed by forgiveness and respect for all of God's Word, Christianity isn't Christianity. It's *Christ* who changes us—not the other way around.

—GREG LAURIE

MONDAY

SOCIETY has done its best to craft a new, no-fault theology—a doctrine in which everything goes, there's no right or wrong, and no need for repentance or forgiveness. Greg Laurie writes that people are looking for a God in their own image; an easygoing, nonjudgmental God with a 1990s makeover. But the bad news for the makeover artists is that God will not sit still for their idolatrous plans.

Paul warned us, saying, "For the time will come when they will not endure sound doctrine, but according to their own desires, because they have itching ears, they will heap up for themselves teachers; and they will turn their ears away from the truth, and be turned aside to fables" (2 Tim. 4:3–4). So how should believers respond? Paul stated earlier, "Preach the word! Be ready in season and out of season. Convince, rebuke, exhort, with all longsuffering and teaching" (v. 2). Regardless of what images men may offer, we must do what's right. And never give up!

Pray that you will always be diligent, always ready to "contend for the faith." ▤

TUESDAY

IN HIS BOOK *The Body,* Chuck Colson writes about the search for a "touchy-feely" faith that satisfies the need for "therapy" without any sense of conviction for sin. It's what some have called the "McChurch" mentality. Colson says, "Thus the church becomes just another retail outlet, faith just another commodity. People change congregations and preachers and even denominations as readily as they change banks or grocery stores.

"What many are looking for," he adds, "is a spiritual social club, an institution that offers convivial relationships but certainly does not influence how people live or what they believe" (Colson, pp. 41–42). But God's truth can't be determined by majority opinion or surveys. The "special revelation" of the Bible—along with the witness of the Holy Spirit—teaches us the true nature of God. "Behold, I stand at the door and knock," Jesus says. "If anyone hears My voice and opens the door, I will come in to him and dine with him, and he with Me" (Rev. 3:20).

Pray for diligence in sharing the truth of the gospel with others. ▤

WEDNESDAY

EVEN *U.S. NEWS & World Report* recognized how far astray many Americans have wandered in their attempts to repackage God in their own image. We've made the Creator of the universe into a tribal chieftain, a "great spirit," a gentle guru, some unknowable force, a kindly old grandfather, and even a baker woman! Greg Laurie laughs, *"Give me a break!"*

The religious leaders of Jesus' day failed to comprehend who He was. They were looking for a different sort of God, too. Jesus confronted them, saying, "You know neither Me nor My Father. If you had known Me, you would have known My Father also" (John 8:19). Another time He said, "You do not know the Scriptures nor the power of God" (Mark 12:24). Ironically, when Jesus approached a man in the temple who had an evil spirit, the demon cried out, "I know who You are—the Holy One of God!" (Luke 4:34). The difference was that the demons had no false illusions about the identity of God. They knew and feared Christ's power.

Pray for diligence in knowing Christ and seeing Him as He is. ▤

THURSDAY

PUNDITS OF OUR day have tried to change our traditional teachings about *self-respect*—based on good behavior and a well-developed sense of personal responsibility—into a politically correct notion of *self-esteem.*

Instead of accountability for bad behavior, people are told that society is to blame for all their problems. There's no such thing as sin, they say, and no need to feel guilty for their bad choices. As a result, not only is God's truth ignored but society appears to be falling down around our ears. Over the centuries, many people have misunderstood the nature of God; but in our day men and women seem determined to "reinvent" God and to transform His Word into little more than a volume of helpful hints.

Paul says they have "exchanged the truth of God for the lie, and worshiped and served the creature rather than the Creator" (Rom. 1:25). But men of God should not accept such counterfeits.

Pray that you will have the discernment and diligence to stand on the Word of God and to stand up boldly in its defense. ▤

FRIDAY

WHAT ARE THE risks of serving man-made idols and ideologies? Paul says, "Professing to be wise, they became fools, and changed the glory of the incorruptible God into an image made like corruptible man. . . .Therefore God also gave them up to uncleanness, in the lusts of their hearts, to dishonor their bodies among themselves, who exchanged the truth of God for the lie, and worshiped and served the creature rather than the Creator, who is blessed forever" (Rom. 1:22–25).

Modern society may not like Jonathan Edwards' image of an angry God, but in their attempt to run away from it, they risk running headlong into absolute and final judgment. One day, on that great and dreadful day, God will rain down fire on the godless and unjust. But we shouldn't take comfort in that fact. Jesus said, "The Son of Man has come to seek and to save that which was lost" (Luke 19:10), and we can do no less.

Pray that God will give you a passion for the lost, to snatch some from destruction. ▤

WEEKEND

EVEN THOUGH THE hearts of men may change, the gospel has not changed. We know that "Jesus Christ is the same yesterday, today, and forever." And we are told, "Do not be carried about with various and strange doctrines" (Heb. 13:8–9). Paul reinforces this point when he says, "But even if we, or an angel from heaven, preach any other gospel to you than what we have preached to you, let him be accursed. As we have said before, so now I say again, if anyone preaches any other gospel to you than what you have received, let him be accursed. For do I now persuade men, or God?

"For if I still pleased men," the apostle says, "I would not be a bondservant of Christ. But I make known to you, brethren, that the gospel which was preached by me is not according to man. For I neither received it from man, nor was I taught it, but it came through the revelation of Jesus Christ" (Gal. 1:8–12). It is so important to be strong, and to stand diligently for the faith.

Pray that you may be an example of diligence to other men. ▤

Week 8
FAITHFULNESS

MY LAST HAPPY memory of my dad was at my college graduation. With my pastor escorting him, Dad traveled one hundred miles to attend my commencement ceremony. By then his cancer-ravaged body was weak and tired, but he came anyway. Seeing his only child graduate from college was one of my dad's great dreams, and he wasn't about to miss it.

Two weeks later, he was dead.

My dad's passing was a defining moment for me. My mother had died four years earlier, and that was tough. But with Dad's death, I was officially "on my own."

I had been adopted as a four-month-old. My mom and dad were older (both of them were in their fifties when they adopted me). At first glance, most people thought they were my grandparents rather than my parents. Growing up, I was sometimes ashamed because Mom and Dad were not as young as other kids' parents. Nor were they as educated. Both my parents grew up in the "Jim Crow" South, during an era that did not afford many African Americans the opportunity to receive a full education.

It wasn't until I was a teenager that I began to fully appreciate the uniqueness of my lot in life. Suddenly, the wisdom, history, and simplicity of my parents' lives began to take on new meaning. Their age and lack of credentials were no longer things to be embarrassed by, but something to be admired.

Above all, I began to see my parents' heart for me. If there is one thing I know my mom and dad possessed, it was a deep love for the little abandoned baby they had adopted. They were committed to their son.

Soon after my dad's death, I was struck with the realization that he had been my best friend. Regardless of my failures, my selfishness, or my shame of him— he was the one who was always there. Before I could remember my first sights and sounds, he had a love that had sought me out and taken me in. And Dad's love continued to be stubborn and strong until the day he died.

In a similar vein, those of us who have accepted Jesus Christ into our lives can also be assured of a strong, intentional love. From the foundations of the world, we have been chosen by the heavenly Father. Adopted into His family.

As associate editor of *New Man,* I have had the privilege of observing lots of dads—dads of all types— biological, adoptive, divorced, surrogate. All with one thing in common: They love their kids and have taken the job of fathering as an assignment from the Father above.

That love is the kind that doesn't quit. It puts others first and draws its strength from the fact that it gives without reservation. It's the kind of love that sent an only Son to die for the sins of many. And it is the kind of love men today need to emulate for their families.

—Edward Gilbreath

Monday

"But the fruit of the Spirit is love, joy, peace, longsuffering, kindness, goodness, faithfulness, gentleness, self-control. Against such there is no law. And those who are Christ's have crucified the flesh with its passions and desires. If we live in the Spirit, let us also walk in the Spirit" (Gal. 5:22–25). Sometimes, perhaps too often, we only grasp the real quality and character of those around us when they're gone. During his college years, Edward Gilbreath began to see just how unique his own experience had been, and he had the time to let his father know his love and appreciation for all he had been given. But some of us never have that chance—or, at least, we never take it.

When we think of those nine character traits Paul calls "fruit of the Spirit," we tend to focus on the words themselves and fail to hear Paul's comment: if we are truly Christ's, then we need to be men who have crucified the flesh and its passions, so that we might truly walk in the Spirit.

Pray for better understanding and application of these powerful words. ▤

TUESDAY

WAITING ON THE LORD, or anybody else, is simply not the American way. By nature, we're people of drive and ambition. We do things for ourselves. But David says there's a better way: "Trust in the Lord, and do good; dwell in the land, and feed on His faithfulness. Delight yourself also in the Lord, and He shall give you the desires of your heart. Commit your way to the Lord, trust also in Him, and He shall bring it to pass" (Ps. 37:3–5). Of course, David isn't saying that we can just sit back and do nothing, and then expect God to feed our families. We must still "do good" and "dwell in the land." But how often do we commit our way to the Lord, trusting Him fully, so that we can rely upon His faithfulness?

If we find it hard to appreciate the faithfulness of others, we'll have trouble even recognizing what God has done—or is doing—for us now.

Pray today that David's words will instruct your heart so that you might delight yourself in the faithfulness of the Lord. ▤

Wednesday

What God promises His children is not a wistful fantasy or fulfillment of some vague yearning in our lives. Rather, we can have the trusting expectation that God is faithful, and He will keep *all* His promises to us. That is the foundation of our hope in Him. The Bible's idea of hope involves the anticipation of a positive outcome through God's guidance. Paul tells us that hope gives us the confidence that God, who has been faithful in the past, will surely provide blessings and opportunities in the future as well.

In the joy of such thoughts, David says, "Oh, love the Lord, all you His saints! For the Lord preserves the faithful, and fully repays the proud person. Be of good courage, and He shall strengthen your heart, all you who hope in the Lord" (Ps. 31:23–24).

Do you live in that relationship with your Lord? Are you prompted to faithfulness to those around you by God's faithfulness to you?

Pray that you may always do so. ▤

Thursday

The Book of Lamentations is surely one of the saddest, most tragic books ever written. Composed by one of the Israelites taken into Babylonian captivity after the utter destruction of Jerusalem, the book is a darkly beautiful poem which expresses the deep sorrow and regret of a people who realized, too late and only too vividly, what they had truly lost. Yet, despite their sadness, the people also recognize that God is faithful and just, and that He had not utterly rejected them.

The writer says, "Through the Lord's mercies we are not consumed, because His compassions fail not. They are new every morning; great is Your faithfulness. 'The Lord is my portion,' says my soul, 'therefore I hope in Him!'" (Lam. 3:22–24). Many great hymns and songs of faith have been taken from those words! But must God's people always wait for some great loss before we recognize His goodness? Let's praise Him now.

Thank God for His faithfulness to you, and for His promises of deliverance. ▣

FRIDAY

WE ARE SO easily drawn to great men and women of faith who overpower us with their works of goodness, their worldwide outreach, and their swelling words of wisdom. We see their pictures on TV and in magazines and books; their voices flood the airwaves; and their names are on everyone's lips. Many of them have a dynamic revelation of God's power. But what about those who serve modestly, quietly, and in unseen ways? Are they also servants of the King? The Lord said to Samuel: "For the Lord does not see as man sees; for man looks at the outward appearance, but the Lord looks at the heart" (1 Sam. 16:7). Obviously, we don't have to be flashy or handsome or mighty to do God's work.

Paul says, "For he who sows to his flesh will of the flesh reap corruption, but he who sows to the Spirit will of the Spirit reap everlasting life. And let us not grow weary while doing good, for in due season we shall reap if we do not lose heart. Therefore, as we have opportunity, let us do good to all" (Gal. 6:8–10).

Ask God to teach you His way. ▣

WEEKEND

THE FOLLOWING PARABLE of Jesus has such a powerful message. He said, "Then the King will say to those on His right hand, 'Come, you blessed of My Father, inherit the kingdom prepared for you from the foundation of the world: for I was hungry and you gave Me food; I was thirsty and you gave Me drink; I was a stranger and you took Me in; I was naked and you clothed Me; I was sick and you visited Me; I was in prison and you came to Me.'

"Then the righteous will answer Him, saying, 'Lord, when did we see You hungry and feed You, or thirsty and give You drink? When did we see You a stranger and take You in, or naked and clothe You? Or when did we see You sick, or in prison, and come to You?' And the King will answer and say to them, 'Assuredly, I say to you, inasmuch as you did it to one of the least of these My brethren, you did it to Me'" (Matt. 25:34–40).

Do you grasp the triple impact of those words: Words for the people of that day, words for those in the final Judgment, but also words for us?

Pray that you may apply Christ's lesson to your heart. ▤

RECONCILIATION

TOM SKINNER AND I never really planned on becoming best friends—it just sort of happened. I have learned that reconciliation is not a group experience. Rather, it is a one-on-one personal kind of thing. It's one white man and one man of color sitting down over lunch or a cup of coffee and getting to know each other. As Tom always said, the problem is simple—we don't know each other. In any event, I did get to know Tom.

Then in 1991, I took an early retirement from business to give myself to ministry. After approaching some friends in Jackson, Mississippi, about doing a city-wide crusade, it became clear that a white middle-aged businessman wouldn't connect with black pastors. Since half the city is black, I asked Tom if he would "joint venture" with me. That's how we began Mission Mississippi, a ministry of racial reconciliation which continues to this day.

For several years I took a strong stand among whites that they must apologize to blacks for their sins of racism (active or passive) and the sins of their fathers. Oh, I have heard the arguments: "But, I'm not a racist. Why should I have to apologize?" But I have the Scriptures to back me up: Nehemiah 1:6, 9:2; Leviticus 26:40; and even the words of Jesus in Matthew 23:29–32, "Fill up, then, the measure of the sin of your forefathers!" (NIV).

Nevertheless, the white brothers were beating me up badly. Finally I prayed: "Lord, I'm getting killed here. I need some help. Can You give me a word for black people?" One day the thought came to mind, *Tell black people that it's time to move from 1 Corinthians to 2 Corinthians.* You may recall that Paul wrote 1 Corinthians because a man was involved in sinful behavior. Paul told the Corinthian believers to put him out of fellowship. But in 2 Corinthians he told them their punishment was sufficient and now they needed to forgive and comfort him.

"Therefore I urge you to reaffirm your love to him" (2 Cor. 2:6–8).

I have talked with hundreds of white men who have tried to reach out to African-American men. But because of years of distrust, most black men have been unwilling to reach back. Because of constant rebuffs, I fear that many, if not most, of these white Christians are on the brink of giving up. Blacks say, "They'll never change—you can't trust white people."

Then, rejected, whites turn around and say, "Oh, well, I tried."

So, my black brother, here is what I would ask you to do. Forgive me, and forgive us. You hold a powerful tool—the power to forgive. Yet, if you don't forgive, you bring trouble upon yourself because it is sin to withhold forgiveness. (See Luke 17:3–4.) Let's both take a step: When a white Christian reaches out with a repentant heart, reach back. Forgive. Comfort. Reaffirm your love.

It is time for us to move from 1 Corinthians to 2 Corinthians.

—PATRICK MORLEY

MONDAY

HOW MANY SERMONS have you heard telling Christians to love one another? Surely, the central challenge of faith is to learn to love one another even as Jesus loved us. During those last precious days before the crucifixion as recorded in the Book of John, Jesus tried to prepare the disciples for His death and Resurrection; He said, "A new commandment I give to you, that you love one another; as I have loved you, that you also love one another. By this all will know that you are My disciples, if you have love for one another" (John 13:34–35). This ministry of love was to be the hallmark—the sign and symbol—of those called to be sons of God. But how often we fail, choosing to dispense our love selectively, jealously, discriminating in how, when, and to whom we're willing to extend fellowship.

Black, white, brown, tan—we all have problems with prejudice until we've been transformed from within by Christ's love. Are you reconciled to Him? Then He commands that you be reconciled to your brothers.

Pray that you may be transformed by His love. ▤

TUESDAY

ARCHIE AND JACK argued on the job for thirty years about whether Jesus was black or white. Archie was certain Jesus was white, but Jack was just as sure He was black—and each had his reasons. As fate would have it, both men died on the same day, and they raced to the pearly gates to find out who was right. "St. Peter," they shouted, "is Jesus white or black?" Just at that moment Jesus walked up and greeted them: "Buenos dias!" He said.

When evangelist Luis Palau tells that story, he always gets a laugh, but for some people it's no joke. In life, Jesus was a brown-skinned, brown-eyed, Middle-Eastern Jew. Semitic by race, He looked like any other Jew or Arab of the day; but those who try to use His race for political or racial reasons make a big mistake. That's why Peter said: "In truth I perceive that God shows *no partiality*. But in every nation whoever fears Him and works righteousness is accepted by Him" (Acts 10:34–35). God's love is so great it surrounds all who come in repentance, regardless of race or color.

Thank Him today for his impartiality. ▤

WEDNESDAY

THE LESSON OF impartiality was a cornerstone of early church doctrine. Paul, who was ordained as an apostle to the Gentiles, proclaimed, "For though I am free from all men, I have made myself a servant to all, that I might win the more; and to the Jews I became as a Jew, that I might win Jews; to those who are under the law, as under the law, that I might win those who are under the law . . . to the weak I became as weak, that I might win the weak. I have become all things to all men, that I might by all means save some. Now this I do for the gospel's sake, that I may be partaker of it with you" (1 Cor. 9:19–23).

At a time when some men would like to exploit prejudice and intolerance for their own purposes, Paul's message is so important. Jesus said, "I have come as a light into the world, that whoever believes in Me should not abide in darkness" (John 12:46). We must shine the light of His love into the darkness of prejudice and hypocrisy so that we may all be one in Christ.

Would you pray that Christ will help you to see His outstretched arms? ▤

THURSDAY

PATRICK MORLEY observes that, despite our holy talk, there sometimes seems to be an insurmountable barrier of distrust between the races in this country. But the Bible condemns such behavior, saying that we are to demonstrate the love of God for all people, regardless of race or station in life—even kings and rulers. Paul says, "Therefore I exhort first of all that supplications, prayers, intercessions, and giving of thanks be made for all men, for kings and all who are in authority, that we may lead a quiet and peaceable life in all godliness and reverence. For this is good and acceptable in the sight of God our Savior, who desires all men to be saved and to come to the knowledge of the truth. For there is one God and one Mediator between God and men, the Man Christ Jesus, who gave Himself a ransom for all" (1 Tim. 2:1–6).

If the early Christians could bring themselves to pray for their wicked rulers, surely we can pray for our brothers in Christ of every race.

Pray today that this may be the generation to tear down those barriers of distrust. ▨

FRIDAY

WHEN PATRICK MORLEY asked for a word for black men, he felt God led him to teach the message of 2 Corinthians, which teaches us to set aside intolerance and distrust. In that letter, Paul makes the message of reconciliation pointedly clear, saying, "Therefore, if anyone is in Christ, he is a new creation; old things have passed away; behold, all things have become new. Now all things are of God, who has reconciled us to Himself through Jesus Christ, and has given us *the ministry of reconciliation,* that is, that God was in Christ reconciling the world to Himself, not imputing their trespasses to them, and has committed to us *the word of reconciliation*" (2 Cor. 5:17–19). Through the love of Christ, the apostle says, we have all been called to a new ministry: "Now then," he adds, "we are ambassadors for Christ" (v. 20).

If we are truly Christ's ambassadors, then we are commissioned to carry His message of love without prejudice of any kind.

Pray that you may be a willing ambassador. ■

WEEKEND

JESUS LIVED AMONG the broken-hearted, the weary, the poor, the despised, and lonely. His mission was to share the love of God with all people. For us to do any less is the most ungrateful response imaginable. Listen to His words: "This is My commandment, that you *love one another as I have loved you.* Greater love has no one than this, than to lay down one's life for his friends. You are My friends if you do whatever I command you. No longer do I call you servants, for a servant does not know what his master is doing; but I have called you friends, for all things that I heard from My Father I have made known to you. You did not choose Me, but I chose you and appointed you that you should go and bear fruit, and that your fruit should remain, that whatever you ask the Father in My name He may give you. These things I command you, that you *love one another*" (John 15:12–17).

Jesus, who has given us all things freely, asks one thing of us—that we keep His commandment, which is that we love one another.

Pray for wisdom that you may obey Him. ■

Week 10
....
SUBMISSION

▤ SOONER OR LATER, every man comes face-to-face
with a very important principle: God is sovereign. As our supreme Monarch, He has a title deed on
everything we own, every relationship we count dear,
and every dream we possess.

It's easy for preachers to tell us to yield control of
our lives to a sovereign God, but what that really means
is not always clear. Do we throw out the other principles we have heard, such as "Pull yourself up by your
bootstraps," or, "Where there's a will, there's a way"?
The concept of yielding control sounds a lot like quit-
ting, giving up, or becoming passive. And that goes
against our nature of overcoming and competing.

The thought of yielding control of your life to God
conjures up images of people who gave total control to
cult leaders and were led like sheep to the slaughter.
Those who come to Christ are asked to do exactly the
opposite. You are asked to be "transformed by the
renewing of your mind" (Rom. 12:2). Yielding control
does not mean being passive. It means finding out what
God has to say about every aspect of life.

As Christians, we can make plans, set goals, fight
with all our strength, and as Churchill said, "Never,
never, never give up." We do so with bent knees and a
bowed heart, knowing that we can rejoice at the victories accomplished and that our failures have a purpose
larger than our understanding.

Most non-Christians and many believers have trouble
conceiving of a God who is kind. They view life's
tragedies as proof that nothing or no one intervenes or

protects—and that is understandable. But Jesus makes an appealing offer to those who will trust Him with their lives: "Seek first his kingdom and his righteousness, and all these things [life's necessities] will be given to you as well" (Matt. 6:33, NIV).

Once people are committed to be "kingdom followers," they realize God controls the script of their lives. That doesn't mean life will be trouble free or exempt from heartache, but it will be purposeful. Throughout Scripture God reveals that He works by a plan. In the Book of Genesis, God called a people to be His own, planned for their redemption, planned their present and future livelihood, and then planned for their growth and success as a nation.

In Psalm 40:5, David declares: "Many, O Lord my God, are the wonders you have done. The things you planned for us no one can recount to you; were I to speak and tell of them, they would be too many to declare" (NIV). He didn't say that everything we experience would be delightful. But David assumes God is good, and all of life's experiences weave a tapestry that is good beyond our understanding.

Although the backside of each tapestry reveals a tangle of gnarled knots and twisted threads, the front side ultimately reveals how meaningful each life experience can be for those who are yielded to Him.

—LARRY KREIDER

MONDAY

SOME OF US make a religion of our own self-sufficiency. We've got ways to handle every difficulty, and the idea of trusting God to pull us through is the last thing on our mind. But consider the story of the Exodus. When Moses led the children of Israel out of Egypt, they were saved miraculously from Pharaoh's armies, saved from the elements and starvation; and when the rebels led by

Dathan threatened violence, the earth swallowed them up. Humbled time after time by God's awesome power, Moses sang, "Who is like You, O Lord, among the gods? Who is like You, glorious in holiness, Fearful in praises, doing wonders? You stretched out Your right hand; the earth swallowed them. You in Your mercy have led forth the people whom You have redeemed; You have guided them in Your strength to Your holy habitation" (Exod. 15:11–13).

The Israelites only had one recourse: complete submission, but God always pulled them through. Why can't we learn from their example?

Pray for strength to trust Him more. ▤

TUESDAY

LARRY KREIDER SAYS the idea of submission causes some people to think of cult leaders and their zombie-like followers. But those who follow Christ not only resist that kind of mind control, they find that they need real strength of character to bring their minds and bodies into submission to the Word of God. Remember Paul's wise instruction?

"I beseech you therefore, brethren, by the mercies of God, that you present your bodies a living sacrifice, holy, acceptable to God, which is your reasonable service. And do not be conformed to this world, but be transformed by the renewing of your mind, that you may prove what is that good and acceptable and perfect will of God." That part you know, but Paul goes on to say, "For I say, through the grace given to me, to everyone who is among you, not to think of himself more highly than he ought to think, but to think soberly, as God has dealt to each one a measure of faith" (Rom. 12:1–3).

True submission means putting aside our pride so that Christ may reign in our lives. Ask Him to show you how. ▤

Wednesday

Perhaps no writer has captured the spirit of faithful submission better than James, who reminds us that "God resists the proud, but gives grace to the humble." The apostle challenges men to have an active faith. We're not sheep; we're not to be passive. God wants to see our love demonstrated in the types of fruit we bear. But notice the paradox in James' teaching. He tells us that we serve fully only through genuine submission. He says, "Submit to God," but then offers these words of counsel: "Resist the devil and he will flee from you. Draw near to God and He will draw near to you" (James 4:7–8). What a remarkable promise! God is not looking for human dynamos who can do it all by themselves, and he is certainly not looking for mindless zombies.

Again, James says it best: "Humble yourselves in the sight of the Lord, and He will lift you up" (v. 10). It is Christ who strengthens us as He prepares us for service.

Are you willing to give yourself completely so that Christ can lift you up? Would you pray about it? ▤

Thursday

At times Jesus seemed dismayed by the lack of faith among His followers. He told them, "If God cares so wonderfully for flowers that are here today and gone tomorrow, won't he more surely care for you, O men of little faith?" They nodded, no doubt, and said they understood, then they continued living in fear and panic. Jesus said repeatedly, "Don't worry at all about having enough food and clothing. Why be like the heathen? For they take pride in all these things and are deeply concerned about them. But your heavenly Father already knows perfectly well that you need them, and he will give them to you if you give him first place in your life and live as he wants you to."

"Don't be anxious about tomorrow," He said. "God will take care of your tomorrow too" (Matt 6:31–34, TLB). Or as the King James Version puts it, "Sufficient unto the day is the *evil* thereof." If we really trusted God in that manner, we would gladly submit to Him. But do we?

Pray that you may discover the fulfillment that come through total submission. ▤

FRIDAY

IF WE NEED a model of submission, we could do worse that reflect on the lives of the apostles. Completely sold out for Christ, each one gave his life for the kingdom. But clearly our best model is Christ Himself, who was obedient to the Father, even unto death.

Paul says: "Let this mind be in you which was also in Christ Jesus, who, being in the form of God, did not consider it robbery to be equal with God, but made Himself of no reputation, taking the form of a bondservant, and coming in the likeness of men. And being found in appearance as a man, He humbled Himself and became obedient to the point of death, even the death of the cross. Therefore God also has highly exalted Him and given Him the name which is above every name, that at the name of Jesus every knee should bow, of those in heaven, and of those on earth, and of those under the earth" (Phil. 2:5–10).

Once again, notice the paradox: through total submission to the Father, Jesus gained ultimate authority.

Let your prayer be that the mind that was in Christ might also be in you. ▤

WEEKEND

THE PROBLEM WITH submission is that it often means we're obliged to wait upon the Lord. We don't like waiting. We want our prayers answered right now! But, as Larry Kreider says, at some point we have to give our plans to God and trust Him to manage the details. David's words give us a sense of this: "I waited patiently for the Lord," he says, "and He inclined to me, and heard my cry. He also brought me up out of a horrible pit, out of the miry clay, and set my feet upon a rock, and established my steps. He has put a new song in my mouth; praise to our God; many will see it and fear, and will trust in the Lord."

If you know the context of David's life, it means a lot when he says, "Blessed is that man who makes the Lord his trust, and does not respect the proud, nor such as turn aside to lies. Many, O Lord my God, are Your wonderful works which You have done" (Ps. 40:1–5).

But we can trust Him too! Would you pray for a fully submitted heart? ▤

Week 11
SELF-CONTROL

My FRIEND GASPED when I told him what my wife and I were giving our children for Christmas. "I can't believe you bought one of those video entertainment systems," he chided. "It'll ruin your family." But despite his comments, we gave them a video game machine as planned. We had considered the decision for a long time and laid down the ground rules for having a video game system in the house.

The system has rested on top of the TV for several months now. It hasn't destroyed our family life, but it did bring some unexpected challenges. When you sit down to play a quick video game, forty-five minutes can fly by before you know it. Most games take five to six minutes, but the attraction of doing a little better each time can trap you in a game for hours.

Our solution to the problem of wasted time was to set a time limit. Our children earn time on the machine. Getting all their chores done early gives them a bonus of thirty minutes. We encourage them to play outside while it's daylight and leave game time for after dark, but we still limit video games to an hour or less per day.

We have chosen not to allow violent games in our house. We have found that if we're uncertain about a particular game, we can often rent the game in question and try it before buying it. Many Christian bookstores carry games based on biblical characters—there are games based on Exodus, Noah's ark, and even spiritual warfare. We have found that, if used properly, the machine can bring other positive results besides building eye-hand coordination.

The video machine gives me another activity to share with my kids. We sometimes play as father/son or father/daughter teams. When we save games, we can work toward a shared purpose for longer periods. This is helpful in teaching my kids to work with others in achieving their goals. I have also found that they appreciate having their parents taking an interest in their activities.

When parents don't care, their children may wind up playing an arcade machine in the dark corner of the local convenience store or at the home of a friend with no controls. We have only had our machine a short time, but we have learned a lot. We must not allow it to become our master, but rather we must master it. This emphasizes the value of self-control to me and my kids.

When time is up, it's hard to turn off the game. It's also tempting to click on the machine and play a quick game despite work needing to be done. Teaching my kids to be responsible begins with self-control. As a father, I, too, must remember that the video machine has an on-off switch.

I believe the game machine can be more than mindless entertainment. It can be a tool to help parents relate with their children—and teach them in the way they should go.

—James Sandell

Monday

When he walked with Jesus, Peter was usually out of control. Enthusiastic, eager, excitable, he frequently had his foot in his mouth. But, later, as "the apostle Peter," he was able to teach the believers: "Add to your faith virtue, to virtue knowledge, to knowledge *self-control,* to self-control perseverance, to perseverance godliness, to godliness brotherly kindness, and to brotherly kindness love." Peter didn't have to make it up; he had learned his lessons the hard way, and could say with certainty: "For if these things are yours and abound, you will be neither barren nor unfruitful in the knowledge of our Lord Jesus Christ. For he who lacks these things is shortsighted, even to blindness, and has forgotten that he was cleansed from his old sins. Therefore, brethren, be even more diligent to make your call and election sure, for if you do these things you will never stumble" (2 Pet. 1:5–10).

Who better to teach about the benefits of self-control and the dangers of stumbling?

As you reflect on Peter's words, pray that your heart may be renewed through self-control. ▤

TUESDAY

ON A WILDERNESS adventure to Pike's Peak, in Colorado, during the 1920s, Katherine Lee Bates, an English professor at Wellesley College, was so stunned by the beauty of the mountains, and so moved by the hand of God upon this nation, she composed a poem of just four stanzas that, when set to the music of Samuel Ward, would become an unofficial national anthem. Since that time, the words of "America the Beautiful" have stirred the hearts of millions and encouraged America's fighting men from Iwo Jima to Kuwait City.

"O beautiful for spacious skies," we sing, "for amber waves of grain." And we pray, "God shed His grace on thee; and crown thy good with brotherhood, from sea to shining sea." Then, in the second verse, we sing, "God mend thine ev'ry flaw; Confirm thy soul in *self-control,* Thy liberty in law." More than a hymn to the creation, the anthem recognizes that America's goodness comes from God, and our national character from faith and self-control.

As men of God, let us celebrate our Creator and dedicate our lives anew to Him. ▤

WEDNESDAY

THE PROVERBS OF Solomon were written as a source-book on wisdom, from a father to his son. In many ways, this book offers a practical seminar on self-control. Solomon says, "Take firm hold of instruction, do not let go; keep her, for she is your life." David's son knew what temptations could do, but strong conviction and self-discipline can lift us above our impulses. "Do not enter the path of the wicked," he said, "and do not walk in the way of evil. Avoid it, do not travel on it; turn away from it and pass on."

The wicked lurk about looking for trouble, Solomon warned. "For they do not sleep unless they have done evil; and their sleep is taken away unless they make someone fall. For they eat the bread of wickedness, and drink the wine of violence. But the path of the just is like the shining sun, that shines ever brighter unto the perfect day" (Prov. 4:13–18). Today we have Christ's words: "I am the light of the world. He who follows Me shall not walk in darkness, but have the light of life" (John 8:12).

Pray that you may always walk in His light. ≡

THURSDAY

WHEN DAVID SINNED by taking Bathsheba, the wife of Uriah, he fell from favor with God and man and had to be confronted by the prophet Nathan. From that moment on, David expressed profound regret and repentance for his sin. In the Psalms he pledged to mend his ways and follow the Lord with all his heart. In Psalm 101 he says, "I will behave wisely in a perfect way . . . I will walk within my house with a perfect heart. I will set nothing wicked before my eyes" (Ps. 101:2–3).

The best way to control behavior is to begin by controlling what we allow into our minds. If we look upon evil, we will entertain wicked thoughts. If we allow pornography or lust or violence to enter our lives, then we give control of our hearts and minds to the forces of darkness. David said, "Your word I have hidden in my heart, that I might not sin against You!" (Ps. 119:11). He knew there could be no room for sin in a life overflowing with God's Word.

Pray that you will be fed on the Word so you can walk with a perfect heart. ▓

FRIDAY

A FRIEND NOTICED a daddy looking after his small son while his wife was shopping at the neighborhood grocery store. The kid was kicking and screaming and throwing a fit the whole time, but the father just spoke softly, "Okay, Robert, stay calm. Keep your temper. It's gonna be okay."

As my friend passed the place where the young man was waiting, he felt he should say a word of encouragement, so he said, "I really admire your self-control, speaking so calmly to Robert when he's acting up like that."

"Are you kidding?" the man shouted. "I'm not talking to him. *My* name's Robert!"

It takes real strength to keep your cool when things aren't going right, but that's why self-control is one of the fruits of the Spirit. Solomon says, "If you faint in the day of adversity, your strength is small" (Prov. 24:10). Ultimately, it is God who gives us strength when our resources are low, but we need to practice patience.

Pray that God will help you to be calm, and give you strength to maintain self-control when the going gets tough. ▓

Weekend

When we fill our minds with trash, vulgar sitcoms, steamy movies, dirty music, and the casual disrespect for the things of God that we find in today's culture, and especially in the media, we spit in the face of a holy God. How can we claim to be *new men* and live like the devil all day long? How can we claim to love the Lord then fill our minds with junk?

Solomon's instructions to his own son begins by saying, "The fear of the Lord is the beginning of knowledge, but fools despise wisdom and instruction" (Prov. 1:7). Maybe a healthy dose of fear is appropriate as we think about the importance of self-control for the Christian. But it's also helpful to hear Paul's advice to young Timothy when he says, "Flee also youthful lusts; but pursue righteousness, faith, love, peace with those who call on the Lord out of a pure heart. But avoid foolish and ignorant disputes, knowing that they generate strife" (2 Tim. 2:22–23).

If you long to see this world transformed and renewed through faith, then why not start now, by praying that God will give you real self-control? ▤

Week 12
RESPECT

My RESEARCH AND the time I have spent speaking to groups of pastors have made it powerfully clear to me that pastors and ministerial leaders are father figures to many. They may not realize it, but other people look to them as reference points. People watch the way they treat their wives and children, the way they relate to others, the way they carry themselves in public day in and day out.

I suggest we need to approach our pastors with the same attitude with which we should think about our fathers—focus on their strengths. For the most part, pastors are healthy examples of manhood. Every year we at the National Center for Fathering gather data among the men at Promise Keepers' conferences. After running the numbers, I have found that pastors are blazing the trail in two important areas.

1. *They are walking their talk when it comes to sexual fidelity and integrity.* I know you have seen the past media splashes about Christian leaders, but those are the exceptions. In comparison with other Christian men, pastors score significantly higher in talking with their wives about sexual temptations they are facing and seeking to maintain purity in the eyes of the world.

2. *Pastors are providing a good model when it comes to integrating the emotional side of life.* It isn't easy for men to expose themselves honestly and with integrity. But our research shows that many pastoral leaders are understanding

> the purpose and power of emotions, and are
> learning to express them in a healthy way.

I always encourage men to seek to understand the challenges their fathers faced. In the same way, I encourage you to consider the unique challenges your pastor faces. I hope you have come to appreciate what your pastors are dealing with, not only as spiritual leaders but also as men, husbands, and fathers. Pastors must deal with isolation, with what I call "glass house scrutiny," and with flock/family conflict, which places undue stress on them. Few lines of work provide such a test of a man's ability to balance his work and family responsibilities.

Let me suggest three principles that can help ease their burden. First, we can honor them by forgiving and seeking to restore our pastors when they have personal struggles. Realize that they are juggling a lot of heavy responsibilities and you can help lighten the load. Second, honor them in special ways: Give your pastor and his wife a week off to go on a marriage retreat. Excuse him from a meeting or two so he can be with his family. Third, support him in casual, personal ways. Take him to lunch, and don't mention the church—ask about his kids; take him to a football game; and, in general, let him know he has worth to you as a person and a friend.

When we do these things, we give them the strength and praise that may just bring about the type of spiritual and social reformation that America needs.

—KEN R. CANFIELD

MONDAY

IT'S NATURAL TO expect our leaders to provide a good example of the Christian life. For pastors, however, life in the spotlight can be pretty demanding. Surely that's one reason why the apostles warned about entering the ministry. James says, "Not many of you should presume to be teachers, my brothers, because you know that we who teach will be judged more strictly. We all stumble in many ways." Then, as if he anticipated the scandals of our day, he says: "When we put bits into the mouths of horses to make them obey us, we can turn the whole animal. Or take ships as an example. Although they are so large and are driven by strong winds, they are steered by a very small rudder wherever the pilot wants to go. Likewise the tongue is a small part of the body, but it makes great boasts. Consider what a great forest is set on fire by a small spark" (James 3:1–5, NIV).

It's important to treat pastors with respect, giving them encouragement and support; and it's equally important that they live respectably.

Pray for your Christian leaders today. ▣

TUESDAY

TITUS WAS THE pastor of the church at Crete, and he faced withering opposition from the pagans and various sects on the island. Paul's letter was designed to offer encouragement, instruction, and credibility to the young pastor so that he could withstand these pressures. The main lesson Paul offers deals with the importance of character and integrity in Christian leadership. He says, "Encourage the young men to be self-controlled. In everything set them an example by doing what is good. In your teaching show integrity, seriousness and soundness of speech that cannot be condemned, so that those who oppose you may be ashamed because they have nothing bad to say about us" (Titus 2:6–8).

Paul was aware of the risks—he had just finished one jail term, and he was hated and tormented relentlessly by the Jews. As we focus on what it means to be men of integrity and leaders in our homes and churches, let's take Paul's words to heart.

Pray that you may demonstrate the kind of character in your own life that will draw others to Jesus Christ. ■

WEDNESDAY

"GOD HAS GIVEN each of us the ability to do certain things well," writes Paul. "So if God has given you the ability to prophesy, then prophesy. . . . If your gift is that of serving others, serve them well. If you are a teacher, do a good job of teaching. If you are a preacher, see to it that your sermons are strong and helpful. If God has given you money, be generous in helping others with it. If God has given you administrative ability and put you in charge of the work of others, take the responsibility seriously. Those who offer comfort to the sorrowing should do so with Christian cheer. Don't just pretend that you love others: really love them. Hate what is wrong. Stand on the side of the good" (Rom. 12:6–9, TLB).

In his research at Promise Keepers' events, Ken Canfield finds that pastors are doing an above-average job, maintaining accountability and integrity, and using their gifts. But that doesn't mean they don't need a little help along the way. Why not pause now to think of some ways you can help your pastor?

Pray for your pastor, and find ways to show your respect. ■

THURSDAY

ALONG WITH HIS advice to pastors, Paul's instructions for deacons give us a good idea of how a temperate and responsible leader should behave. "Likewise," he says, "deacons must be reverent, not double-tongued, not given to much wine, not greedy for money, holding the mystery of the faith with a pure conscience. But let these also first be tested; then let them serve as deacons, being found blameless. Likewise their wives must be reverent, not slanderers, temperate, faithful in all things. Let deacons be the husbands of one wife, ruling their children and their own houses well. For those who have served well as deacons obtain for themselves a good standing and great boldness in the faith which is in Christ Jesus" (1 Tim. 3:8–13).

Obviously the high requirements for leadership of this type will limit the field of candidates, but that's a good thing. Not everyone can claim to live such orderly lives, but not everyone can expect to lead.

Those who do deserve our respect and our prayers.▤

FRIDAY

ELDERS AND BISHOPS, mentioned at least five times in the New Testament, were to be the watchmen and over-seers of the church. At one point Peter used the term in reference to Jesus, calling Him "the Shepherd and Overseer of our souls." In the book of Acts, Paul says that, through the Holy Spirit, Christ gives all leaders the responsibility of overseer and bishop, "to shepherd the church of God which He purchased with His own blood" (Acts 20:28). Such men demand respect by virtue of their exemplary lives and selfless conduct.

"A bishop then must be blameless," says Paul, "the husband of one wife, temperate, sober-minded, of good behavior, hospitable, able to teach; not given to wine, not violent, not greedy for money, but gentle, not quarrel-some, not covetous; one who rules his own house well, having his children in submission with all reverence (for if a man does not know how to rule his own house, how will he take care of the church of God?)" (1 Tim. 3:2–5). Does this describe leaders in your church?

Pray that God will enable them to feed the flock. ▤

WEEKEND

THE BIBLICAL DEMANDS on pastors, along with all the

expectations heaped on them by church members, can become a back-breaking burden. Every year thousands of pastors go through burnout, and many leave the profession because of stress. If we want our leaders to stay strong and vital, we need to take Ken Canfield's three suggestions very seriously.

First, he says, honor them through forgiveness and restoration when they're tested by struggles of various kinds. Second, honor them in special ways, particularly if it helps them grow closer to their wives and families. A little time off can make a big difference. This doesn't mean you should treat them like celebrities, but when you encourage them in a few special ways, they'll know you respect what they're doing. Third, honor them in casual but practical ways, remembering birthdays and anniversaries, taking them out for a meal, or offering tickets to a ballgame.

Then, one more thing: Don't forget to hold them up in your prayers.

Pray for each of them, often. In fact, why not do it now? ■

COURAGE

IF YOU HAVE HEARD Matthew Ward sing, you know the guy has skills. His crisp tenor voice weaves its way around melodies—part classical, part Stevie Wonder, part wailing maniac. As the male member of the vocal trio, the Second Chapter of Acts, Ward and his sisters garnered respect not only for their trademark harmonies but also for their desire to minister to audiences. Ward, now a solo artist, has made several albums and sang at nearly half the Promise Keepers' conferences in 1996.

His dangling blond locks and spontaneous wit are the first features you note about the man. Seeing the spirited, thirty-eight-year-old singer today, it's hard to believe that just three years ago he nearly lost his life to cancer. He was diagnosed with a rare form of testicular cancer. After removing the cancerous organ, doctors did a CAT scan to see if the cancer had spread.

"Those were five of the longest days of my life," Ward says. "Of course, I was afraid. But it wasn't necessarily dying I was afraid of." Death had lost its sting many years before. At age twelve, Matthew lost his mother to a brain tumor and his father to leukemia. "I can remember seeing my dad suffer for a long time before he died," he says. "My worst fear was a slow, painful death from cancer like Dad's. I didn't want my wife and daughters to have to go through what I did when I was a kid."

The good news was that the CAT scan revealed that the cancer had not spread. The bad news, however, was that there was a 50/50 chance of the cancer returning unless he underwent chemotherapy. He was well-versed on the horrors of chemotherapy: dramatic weight loss, hair loss, nausea and fatigue, and shrunken lung capacity (not good for a singer). He investigated alternative treatments but after much prayer decided that chemo was the way to go.

His weight dropped more than seventy pounds, but there were unexpected bright spots. "I didn't lose that much hair," he smiles. And his lung capacity actually increased. "The doctors were amazed," he says. "They asked me what my secret was. I said, 'I believe in the power of God.'"

He even sang for the hospital staff. "I tore up this soulful version of *Amazing Grace* for three technicians," he remembers. Halfway through the song, the doorway was clogged with curious people. "When I was done, one technician said to me, 'Man, if I could sing like that, I'd never stop singing.' They saw a little bit of the Source of my hope. It was great!"

Today, Ward has even more to sing about. He is fully cancer-free and at work on his next album. "It helps to have faith in God," he says. "You can either draw closer to God or . . . grow bitter and angry. But cancer is not the end of the world if you know Christ. Even if it kills you, it's not the end."

—EDWARD GILBREATH

MONDAY

FOR CENTURIES, some who have felt the hand of God have composed hymns of praise to glorify our great King and exalt His name. David sang, "Make a joyful shout to God, all the earth! Sing out the honor of His name; make His praise glorious. Say to God, 'How awesome are Your works! Through the greatness of Your power Your enemies shall submit themselves to You. All the earth shall worship You and sing praises to

You; they shall sing praises to Your name.' Come," David cries out, "and see the works of God. He is awesome in His doing toward the sons of men" (Ps. 30:1–5). Surely the songs of praise that pour freely from the hearts of the redeemed must delight the heart of God.

When Matthew Ward began ministering to the saints as a child, he had no way of knowing the tribulations he would endure one day. Now, having crossed through the valley of the shadow, he knows his hope is certain—and his clear tenor voice rings out in praises to the King.

With David, and with all those who trust in the Lord, let your praises ring. ▰

TUESDAY

GENERAL DOUGLAS MacArthur was a bold and courageous military leader with visions of a just and lasting peace in the Pacific. He tried to stabilize the governments of Japan, the Philippines, and Korea, but ran headlong into resistance from the leadership in Washington. When he was dismissed in 1951, he gave a dramatic speech to Congress that reminded the nation that true victory demands true courage. At the end of his list of the qualifications for leaders, he offered: "Last, but by no means least, courage—moral courage, the courage of one's convictions, the courage to see things through. The world is in a constant conspiracy against the brave. It's the age-old struggle—the roar of the crowd on one side and the voice of your conscience on the other." MacArthur sided with conscience and never looked back.

Do we have that kind of courage? Paul says, "Let us not grow weary while doing good, for in due season we shall reap if we do not lose heart" (Gal. 6:9). Whether or not we know victory in this life, we can be sure of the prize.

Ask God to fortify and encourage you. ■

WEDNESDAY

HOW DO YOU deal with bad news? What do you say to yourself, your loved ones, and your friends when life suddenly makes a hard left turn? Andrew Jackson, seventh president of the United States and a veteran of many fiery trials, said, "One man with courage makes a majority." But sometimes in the midst of adversity, even wise counsel seems meaningless. David had won many gallant victories for Israel. He defeated Goliath, led the armies of Judah against the Philistines, delighted the king with his music and his songs, and yet he was a hunted and haunted man, forced to hide out in caves to escape the wrath of Saul.

"Hear, O Lord, when I cry with my voice!" he said. "Have mercy also upon me, and answer me." David was faithful, and he eventually found victory. Then he sang: "I would have lost heart, unless I had believed that I would see the goodness of the Lord in the land of the living. Wait on the Lord; be of good courage, and He shall strengthen your heart; Wait, I say, on the Lord!" (Ps. 27:7, 13–14).

Thank Him for the hope of second chances. ■

THURSDAY

IT'S A GOOD THING to make up your mind and accomplish your goals; but it's just as important to make sure that you understand the objective and the realistic limits of your actions. It was minister and speaker Oliver J. Hart who first said, "Give us the fortitude to endure the things which cannot be changed, and the courage to change the things which should be changed, and the wisdom to know one from the other." That prayer, often a part of twelve-step rehabilitation programs, expresses the idea that courage is a combination of wisdom and resolve. We need to be willing to do whatever it takes to accomplish our goals, but it's just as important to know when to struggle and when to let go.

The writer of Ecclesiastes says, "Enjoy prosperity whenever you can, and when hard times strike, realize that God gives one as well as the other—so that everyone will realize that nothing is certain in this life." But he adds, "If you fear God, you can expect his blessing" (Eccl. 7:14, 18, TLB).

Pray that you'll have courage to see His hand in all things. ▤

FRIDAY

MATTHEW WARD KNEW Peter's advice, "Always be ready to give a defense to everyone who asks you a reason for the hope that is in you" (1 Pet. 3:15). So when the doctors asked about his remarkable recovery and his trusting spirit, he was more than ready to share, as he says, "the Source of my hope." And you can be certain that when he unleashed his unique vocal talents for that group of technicians, their spirits and their hopes were raised, along with the hair on the back of their necks!

Too often, we let the pressures of the world convince us that our faith in Jesus is not welcome. Matthew could have mumbled something meaningless or explained his hope in other ways; but who knows but what God had given him that precise moment to touch someone's life, or perhaps to save a soul? James says, "Therefore, to him who knows to do good and does not do it, to him it is sin" (James 4:17).

Let's pray always that we can avoid those sins of omission. Time is much too short to let those precious moments slip away. ▤

WEEKEND

HE HAD BEEN beaten, stoned, imprisoned, shipwrecked,

spat upon, and held up to ridicule by religious and political leaders alike. His body was falling apart, his sight was bad, he stuttered, and had trouble speaking before crowds. When he wrote down his thoughts, people said he was obscure and hard to understand. No wonder Paul thought of death as a friend. "For to me, to live is Christ," he said, "and to die is gain." There must have been times when he longed for release from this life so he could be with his Lord.

"But," he said he had a mission to fulfill, and "if I live on in the flesh, this will mean fruit from my labor; yet what I shall choose I cannot tell. For I am hard pressed between the two, having a desire to depart and be with Christ, which is far better. Nevertheless to remain in the flesh is more needful for you" (Phil. 1:21–24). It may be a bit much to expect people to have joy in adversity, but surely we can have courage.

Matthew Ward said that physical death isn't the end; but let us also *live with courage,* to fulfill God's plan for us. ■

THIRD

◄········►

QUARTER

Week 1
WISDOM

"SUCCESS PANIC" passed the threshold of my door when I was forty-four. It hit me with a blunt object: my slavish devotion to the art of the deal and the thrill of the kill. Like most thrills, the excitement of making money was beginning to wear off. I had begun to ask myself, "How much is enough?"

At some point in every man's life we wonder, *Is this all there is?* What disturbed me was that I didn't have the answer. I had the big house, the Jaguar; I really did have it all, including my faith. I was active in church. Unlike many of my successful peers, I also had a great marriage and no skeletons locked away in a closet. So why was I in such turmoil?

In my hour of need, grace led me to an atheist. Mike Kami is a strategic planning consultant. He is brilliant, intuitive, demanding. He does not believe in God, but I can testify that God worked unmistakably through him. I went to Mike because I wanted him to draw up a strategic plan for my life. I had tons of questions: What should I do with my life? Where should I invest my time, talents, and treasures? In this blizzard of wonderment, Mike asked a simple question: "What's in the box?"

I didn't have a clue as to what he was getting at and asked him to fill me in. "I have been listening to you for a couple of hours," he said, "trying to figure out what's in your box. It's either money or Jesus Christ, but I can't tell you the strategic planning implications unless you can tell me which one it is."

After a few minutes, I answered, "Well, if it has to be

one or the other, I'll put Jesus Christ in the box." It was an act of faith, it was my answer to the question. Like many men, my belief in God was in the background while I pursued my career. I'm convinced many men are afraid to put Jesus in the box because they fear where it will lead. Ironically, once God got me to surrender, He set me on a path very similar to the one I already was on.

Jesus said He came so we might have abundant life, life to the fullest. Most of us miss out on that because we think religion is restricting. But giving God total freedom to use me in any way He wishes is leading me to a larger life, not a small and narrow one.

There is nothing magical about Mike's exercise. But it was a tool God used to get my attention. I can't tell you what to put in your box, but sooner or later you *will* choose. Your life will race toward the thing that is most important to you. Don't wait for disaster; listen to that still small voice and do some honest soul-searching. What is in your box?

—BOB BUFORD

MONDAY

SOMETIME TOWARD the middle of our lives, each man runs headlong into a brick wall called "reality." For some, it's a simple matter of getting up, dusting ourselves off, and moving on to the next thing. For others, however, this mid-life adjustment can be a life-threatening emergency that throws everything we once took for granted up for grabs. Those in the first group seem to be able to go on with only minor repairs, either because they're generally satisfied with the changes taking place in their lives, or because they're able to find—quickly and naturally—a reliable source of security and answers to their questions.

Bub Buford's brick wall, which he calls "success

panic," brought him straight to the bottom line: "What's in the box?" Suddenly money, power, and privilege had to take a back seat to the real priority in his life—his faith in Jesus Christ. The psalmist says, "The fear of the Lord is the beginning of wisdom" (Ps. 111:10). That truth made all the difference for Buford, and it can be our greatest source of strength.

Pray that you may rest in His strength. ▤

TUESDAY

"BUT GOD HAS chosen the foolish things of the world to put to shame the wise, and God has chosen the weak things of the world to put to shame the things which are mighty; and the base things of the world and the things which are despised God has chosen, and the things which are not, to bring to nothing the things that are, that no flesh should glory in His presence" (1 Cor. 1:27–29).

The modern world, with all its high-tech wizardry, high-dollar values, and high-pressure demands, scoffs at the simplicity and self-sacrifice of the Christian life. But when we try to live by the world's theology—to grab all the gusto we can get—we soon find that sensual pleasures, self-indulgence, and even wealth and professional success do not fill the void in our souls. We cry out, "Is that all there is?" and find that, truly, the weak things, the simple things, and the gentle things of God put all our sophistication and glamor to shame. It's no accident—God designed it that way.

Thank Him today for His marvelous design. ▤

WEDNESDAY

SOMETIMES WE SEEM to have split personalities: We go to church on Sunday and pray and say all the right things; then we rush from one success seminar to another, reading all the latest advice on striking it rich, and chancing the almighty dollar with the unwashed masses.

But David offers another model. He says: "Blessed is the man who fears the Lord, who delights greatly in His commandments. His descendants will be mighty on earth; the generation of the upright will be blessed. Wealth and riches will be in his house, and his righteousness endures forever. Unto the upright there arises light in the darkness; he is gracious, and full of compassion, and righteous. A good man deals graciously and lends; he will guide his affairs with discretion. Surely he will never be shaken; the righteous will be in everlasting remembrance. He will not be afraid of evil tidings; his heart is steadfast, trusting in the Lord" (Ps. 112:1–7).

Pray that God will help you focus your priorities and rely upon His wise counsel. ▤

THURSDAY

IN HIS MARVELOUS little book *Your God Is Too Small,* English theologian and author J. B. Phillips says that many Christians seem to want a "God in a box." We want a generous Benefactor in the sky who can be easily described, quickly understood, and put to practical use whenever we need Him, and then, just as quickly, shoved back in the box when He begins to meddle in our plans. But, says Phillips, such a shallow conception of the Author of life will never do. "We can never have too big a conception of God, and the more scientific knowledge (in whatever field) advances, the greater becomes our idea of His vast and complicated wisdom." He is so vast, so powerful, so wise: the only way to conceive of such a God is to accept His own focusing of Himself in the person of Jesus Christ.

"Oh, the depth of the riches both of the wisdom and knowledge of God! How unsearchable are His judgments and His ways past finding out! (Rom. 11:33). To tame the panic in our hearts, let us pray for rest in the reality of God's love for us, through His Son. ▤

FRIDAY

IN THE FOURTH chapter of Proverbs, Solomon praises the power and excellence of wisdom, which delights the heart and teaches lessons that lead to a long and prosperous life. But, for all his learning, Solomon failed to grasp that true wisdom comes through a life devoted to God and through obedience to the commands of our Lord. Despite tremendous wealth, power, and wisdom, Solomon went through his own "success panic," a "mid-life crisis" of sorts, and the last years of his life were deeply troubled, in part because he trusted more in human knowledge and learning than in the "unsearchable riches" of God's wisdom.

"For this reason," says Paul, "we also, since the day we heard it, do not cease to pray for you, and to ask that you may be filled with the knowledge of His will in all wisdom and spiritual understanding; that you may walk worthy of the Lord, fully pleasing Him, being fruitful in every good work and increasing in the knowledge of God" (Col. 1:9–10).

Pray for spiritual understanding, that you may walk worthy of the Lord, fully pleasing Him. ▤

WEEKEND

IS THERE A SECRET for successful living? Is there any way to guarantee that things will go smoothly and trouble free in this life? The problem with such questions is that our sight is so limited by our human condition, and we cannot see as God sees. David assures us that God does, sometimes, at least, grant success and prosperity to those He loves. Yet, we also know that even abject failure in this life may be the doorway to success in the kingdom of heaven. Paul says, "Has not God made foolish the wisdom of this world?" (1 Cor. 1:20).

If we desire to be wise and to live godly lives, then we have to learn to trust God for His guidance when our finite, earthbound wisdom fails. Through Jeremiah, God says, "Let not the wise man glory in his wisdom, let not the mighty man glory in his might, nor let the rich man glory in his riches; but let him who glories glory in this, that he understands and knows Me, that I am the Lord, exercising lovingkindness, judgment, and righteousness in the earth. For in these I delight" (Jer. 9:23–24).

Pray that you may know Him in that way. ▤

Week 2
PURITY

WHEN I WAS a young Christian, I decided to clean up my mind. When I made that decision, the battle of temptation got harder. After spending four years in the Navy, I had seen enough pornography to where it was a serious problem. I hated it. I struggled every time I went to a place where pornography was available. I finally got the victory. Let me share how.

Think of your mind as a coffee pot. You desire the water inside to be pure, but unfortunately you have put in some coffee grounds. There is no way to take out the coffee once it has been put it. So the water inside is dark and polluted. Sitting beside the coffee pot is a huge bowl of crystal clear ice that represents the truth of God and the reality of your identity in Christ.

You are only able to put in one or two cubes a day so it may seem a little futile at first. But over time the water begins to look less polluted. Finally, you can hardly taste or smell the presence of coffee. The process works provided you stop putting in more coffee grounds.

For many people this will be a two-steps-forward-and-one-step-back process in winning the battle for their minds. Slowly it becomes three steps forward and one back, then four and five steps forward as every thought is taken captive in obedience to Christ. You may despair with all the steps back, but God isn't going to give up on you.

It is essential to remember this: Christ died only once for all your sins. The issue is no longer forgiveness. This has been done. You only need to fight for your personal victory over the destructive acts of sin. This is a winnable war since you are alive in Christ and dead to sin. The battle over sin has already been won by Christ.

As you learn more about who you are as a child of God, and the nature of the battle that is going on for your mind, the process can get easier. Eventually it is twenty steps forward and one back, and finally the steps are all forward with only an occasional slip in the battle for the mind.

Paul writes, "Let the peace of Christ rule in your hearts, since as members of one body you were called to peace. And be thankful" (Col. 3:15, NIV). How to do that is in the next verse: "Let the word of Christ dwell in you richly" (Col. 3:16, NIV). We fill our minds with the crystal clear Word of God. God has no alternative plan. Just trying to stop thinking bad thoughts won't work, we have to choose to think upon what is true, lovely, and pure (Phil. 4:8–9).

If we know who we are in Christ, we will not carry out the desires of the flesh. Jesus is more than our bondage breaker. He is our life.

—NEIL T. ANDERSON

MONDAY

"CREATE IN ME a clean heart, O God, and renew a steadfast spirit within me. Do not cast me away from Your presence, and do not take Your Holy Spirit from me. Restore to me the joy of Your salvation, and uphold me by Your generous Spirit. Then I will teach transgressors Your ways, and sinners shall be converted to You" (Ps. 51:10–13).

When David, who offered that prayer, let the lust of the eyes get the better of him, he fell hard and had to be challenged by Nathan in order to be restored in his walk with the Lord. In today's world of constant and abundant temptations, men of God must walk with caution, avoiding the lure of evil and shunning the casual flirtations with sin that have destroyed so many lives. John says, "For all that is in the world—the lust of the flesh, the lust of the eyes, and the pride of life—is not of the Father but is of the world. And the world is passing away, and the lust of it; but he who does the will of God abides forever" (1 John 2:16–17).

Pray that God will give you strength to reject the impure and to abide in His grace. ■

TUESDAY

WHAT CAUSES A man of God to fall? Jesus said, "You have heard that it was said to those of old, 'You shall not commit adultery.' But I say to you that whoever looks at a woman to lust for her has already committed adultery with her in his heart. If your right eye causes you to sin, pluck it out and cast it from you; for it is more profitable for you that one of your members perish, than for your whole body to be cast into hell" (Matt. 5:27–29). The graphic nature of Christ's teaching makes it clear that lust in the heart is a gateway to sin. And since God judges the heart, if we allow impure thoughts to linger, to grow, or especially if we let them fester into impure behaviors, then we are guilty of sin.

But there are many excellent resources to help men overcome the allure of sin—the Word of God, the counsel of brothers who hold us accountable, the counsel of pastors and other professionals, as well as many good books. All these can help us avoid danger, and we shouldn't hesitate to use them.

Pray that God will empower you to live a life of purity. ■

WEDNESDAY

AUTHOR NEIL T. ANDERSON says that the secret of overpowering an addiction to pornography is to channel such a constant flow of Christian counsel pouring into our hearts that there can be so room for anything that is off-color or impure. Like crystal clear, clean ice cubes deposited regularly into a coffee pot, the refreshing truth of God's word will soon flush out grime and sin and lewdness until we may be fully "transformed," as Paul says, by the renewing of our minds.

In Romans, Paul says, "Let us walk properly, as in the day, not in revelry and drunkenness, not in lewdness and lust, not in strife and envy. But put on the Lord Jesus Christ, and make no provision for the flesh, to fulfill its lusts" (Rom. 13:13–14). If we seek only and always the things of God, the things of Satan will soon disappear.

Pray that you may be filled to overflowing with godly influences, godly friends, and with the Word of God, so that fleshly lusts will have no place to linger in your life. ▰

THURSDAY

THE IMAGES FAVORED by Hollywood and the mass media are saturated with sex and sin. Much of what passes for "adult" entertainment is designed entirely around pornography and sensuality, to the point that even the most secular among us has to admit that films and TV in this country are not always *suitable* as entertainment. The simple fact that popular entertainment must be rated by censors according to sexual content, violence, and language, is an admission that parents, educators, government leaders, and even producers and directors themselves recognize the damaging effects of these materials. Yet it continues.

But is "adult entertainment" adult? Is it wise? Is it wholesome? Or isn't it, in fact, the most juvenile behavior imaginable? Paul says, "Let no one despise your youth, but be an example to the believers in word, in conduct, in love, in spirit, in faith, in purity" (1 Tim. 4:12). Good judgment and decent behavior isn't just for kids—it's for everybody.

Pray today for strength to possess your own vessel, and courage to resist the corruptions of society. ■

FRIDAY

NEIL ANDERSON REMINDS us of these words of the apostle: "And let the peace of God rule in your hearts, to which also you were called in one body; and be thankful. Let the word of Christ dwell in you richly in all wisdom, teaching and admonishing one another in psalms and hymns and spiritual songs, singing with grace in your hearts to the Lord" (Col. 3:15–16). Again, this is the idea that the more we fill our hearts with God's Word and with His purity, the less room there will be for evil thoughts to enter our lives.

In his letter to the Galatians, Paul warns about allowing our "freedom in Christ" to develop into license, which leads to sin. He says, "Walk in the Spirit, and you shall not fulfill the lust of the flesh" (Gal. 5:16). If we expect to be faithful to Christ and to be men of God, then we need to saturate ourselves with the Word and live in single-minded devotion to Him, so that we will not be tempted to stray. Pray that God will fill you with His Spirit, so the Word of Christ may dwell in you richly. ■

WEEKEND

SOMEONE HAS SAID that whatever you think about most of the time is what you worship. What do you think about? Is it money? Your job? Your possessions? Or maybe it's that someone special in your life? Whatever fills your thoughts, waking and sleeping, must be something you're devoted to in a very special way.

Paul says, "Finally, brethren, whatever things are true, whatever things are noble, whatever things are just, whatever things are pure, whatever things are lovely, whatever things are of good report, if there is any virtue and if there is anything praiseworthy—meditate on these things" (Phil. 4:8). Why do you think he challenges men to think pure thoughts? Is the apostle asking us to be philosophers or poets? Or isn't he really saying that whatever we think about most of the time is what will control our lives and behavior? God is a jealous God. He wants to be first in our thoughts; and He deserves to be, because "He has loved us with an everlasting love."

Pray that you will love Him with all your heart. ▤

Week 3

PATIENCE

MY FRIEND JIM Grassi and I came to the Sea of Galilee to organize a fishing festival for Christian fishermen. But in my search for fish, the Sea of Galilee caught *me*—with truth as deep as its waters. I believe I now know what Jesus sought when He came here. He sought the makings of a man.

Capernaum's many fishermen, including the apostle Peter, wintered here, spending their days and nights catching schools of tasty fish called musht, mending their nets, and spinning fish stories. When Jesus arrived, He observed the men on the water. Perhaps He noted the tight rhythm with which they worked, looking for the men who worked best together.

Christ called one twosome as they cast their nets, "Come, follow me . . . and I will make you fishers of men!" (Mark 1:17, NIV). What sort of men were they who attracted the eye of the Lord of the universe? The men Jesus sought were team players. Net fishing requires cooperation. They couldn't man a boat, cast, and retrieve nets alone. Surely the Lord knew such self-less teamwork was basic to good ministry.

The Gospels mention Christ's use of a boat more than forty-five times. He preached from them, traveled in them, and slept in them. As the crowds pressed in on Jesus, He asked the disciples to have a boat ready for Him, and they responded. Am I as eager as they were to answer Christ's call? Christ desires the company of team players, and of men eager to place their most prized possessions at His service.

I think of that evening when Christ slept in the boat

as the disciples watched the gathering storm. "Don't disturb the Master," they said. "We're the professional boatmen. We'll navigate this storm." But as the winds grew fiercer, they screamed, "Teacher, don't You care if we drown?"

Of course He did. With three words, He handled the matter: "Quiet, be still!"

"Where is your faith?" He asked. "Why linger in fear? Why try to handle your problems alone?" How often we foolishly try to handle business, family, or ministry situations on our own. "Let's not bring God into this one," we say.

Christ replies, "Where is your faith? Accept My peace."

I watched as two local fisherman let out their nets, moving in concentric circles. After thirty painstaking minutes, they began to haul them in, remove the fish, then repeat the process maybe eight times that day. American fishermen claim patience—they should see these guys!

Returning to shore, I hear Jesus asking me, "Man, do you truly love Me more than these?" Jesus seeks men who love Him with real passion, who will dive out of the boat and swim or walk to His side. I went out on the Galilee seeking fish; but in the end, it was I who was caught, by the vision of a Man standing on the bank calling out to us to follow Him. How can we say no?

—JOE MAXWELL

MONDAY

JESUS COULD HAVE chosen disciples who were shepherds or carpenters or weavers or bakers. Surely any of those professions would have offered more than enough experiences and metaphors for understanding the Christian life—so why do you suppose He chose fishermen instead? Joe Maxwell believes it was because the fishermen of Galilee, and the men He chose in particular, had unique patience and character for becoming "fishers of men."

Many years after Jesus had completed His earthly mission and ascended to the right hand of the Father, the apostle James wrote: "My brethren, count it all joy when you fall into various trials, knowing that the testing of your faith produces patience. But let patience have its perfect work, that you may be perfect and complete, lacking nothing. If any of you lacks wisdom, let him ask of God, who gives to all liberally and without reproach, and it will be given to him" (James 1:2–5). James, a fisherman, understood what Jesus had said, that perfect faith only comes with patience.

Pray that you, too, may claim this lesson. ▤

TUESDAY

PETER WAS CLEARLY the loudest, most visible, most demonstrative of all the disciples. He was a big man with a big heart, and when he spotted Jesus walking on the water, he rashly cried out, "Lord, if it is You, command me to come to You on the water." Jesus told him to come ahead, but halfway across the lake Peter lost his nerve and started to sink.

So what happened? Even though the burly fisherman was bold enough to jump in the water, he didn't have the confidence or the faith to stay on top of it. Jesus took his hand and helped Peter back into the boat, then said, "O you of little faith, why did you doubt?"

The men in the boat said, "Truly you are the Son of God." But it was a learning process for them. They had to take it a step at a time. That's why the writer of Hebrews advises, "Therefore do not cast away your confidence, which has great reward. For you have need of endurance, so that after you have done the will of God, you may receive the promise" (Heb. 10:35–36).

Pray for patience, so you may continue to grow in grace and confidence. ▤

WEDNESDAY

WE KNOW BETTER. We know we need to focus on higher things, yet we let the desires of the moment distract us. Paul says, "But those who desire to be rich fall into temptation and a snare, and into many foolish and harmful lusts which drown men in destruction and perdition. For the love of money is a root of all kinds of evil, for which some have strayed from the faith in their greediness, and pierced themselves through with many sorrows" (1 Tim. 6:9–10). We know that God provides for those who trust in Him, yet in our impatience we go rushing after this world's goods thinking we can save ourselves.

Paul adds, "But you, O man of God, flee these things and pursue righteousness, godliness, faith, love, patience, gentleness. Fight the good fight of faith, lay hold on eternal life, to which you were also called and have confessed the good confession in the presence of many witnesses" (vv. 11–12).

If we truly understood the riches that God has laid up for us, we would pray for patience to trust Him, and place our possessions at His service. ▪

THURSDAY

JOE MAXWELL PAINTS a colorful picture of the fishermen of Galilee struggling in their small boat against the rising wind and waves. Intellectually, they know that Jesus is their Lord and Master, their Messiah and Redeemer; emotionally, however, they fear the reality of the approaching storm. But are we any different? We go to church on Sunday. We read the Bible. We've been to conferences and rallies, and we say all the right words. But can we really trust Jesus to save us when life's storms come crashing down upon us?

This is the lesson of godly patience. In Hebrews we read, "For God is not unjust to forget your work and labor of love which you have shown toward His name, in that you have ministered to the saints, and do minister. And we desire that each one of you show the same diligence to the full assurance of hope until the end, that you do not become sluggish, but imitate those who through faith and patience inherit the promises" (Heb. 6:10–12).

Pray that God will hold you up through the storms, so you may inherit the promises. ■

FRIDAY

WE NEED TO understand that patience is never to be confused with disinterest or boredom or laziness. Patience is a virtue that must be practiced. It is the willingness to defer the gratification of action now in the belief that, by waiting patiently, we will gain a greater reward in the future. If you're one of those who believes in the modern notions that teach, "Lift yourself up by your own bootstraps" or, "God helps those who help themselves," then you'll probably miss out on this important lesson. Neither of these maxims is biblical; and neither has much to do with the life of faith.

In Romans we read, "But if we hope for what we do not see, we eagerly wait for it with perseverance. Likewise the Spirit also helps in our weaknesses. For we do not know what we should pray for as we ought, but the Spirit Himself makes intercession for us with groanings which cannot be uttered" (Rom. 8:25–26).

We wait eagerly for the fulfillment of God's purpose in our lives, but true patience trusts in His provision for our needs. ■

WEEKEND

NOW AND THEN a man will give his life to Christ, go through the motions of living the Christian life, and then slowly drift back into his old ways. He wants to do the right thing, and he wants to be sure he has eternal life, but the gratification of the senses still has a hold on his soul. At root, we admit at those times that we don't have the patience to wait upon the Lord and trust Him to provide for us.

Peter, who learned his lessons in patience the hard way, warns about turning our backs on the truth: "For if, after they have escaped the pollutions of the world through the knowledge of the Lord and Savior Jesus Christ, they are again entangled in them and overcome, the latter end is worse for them than the beginning. For it would have been better for them not to have known the way of righteousness, than having known it, to turn from the holy commandment delivered to them" (2 Pet. 2:20–21).

Pray that you may run the race with endurance, not quibbling, not being entangled in sin, so that you may win the prize. ▦

THE EXPLOSIVE GROWTH of Promise Keepers is evidence of renewal in the church. But outside the church, the battle is just warming up. Of the ninety-four million American men over age eighteen, twenty-six million, or roughly a fourth of them, attend church; twenty-seven million read the Bible, leaving sixty-seven million who don't; and thirty-one million are "born-again" Christians, while sixty million trust some other means of salvation.

Why have so many men chosen to reject Jesus? A majority have concluded that participation in church life cannot be justified because the return on investment of time, attention, and energy is too slim. You may reject their view, but our survey shows that 85 percent of all unchurched men were previously churched. We found that they are least enthusiastic about the education, youth programs, and management of churches. They're not impressed with the music, preaching, or family programs. But they do respond to the friendliness, facilities, and leadership. So what are they looking for? Five things:

1. *Understanding.* They want a church that helps them truly understand the Bible. Men desire a more systematic, cohesive, and relevant understanding of Christianity.

2. *Relationships.* Though they hate to admit it, they feel lonely, isolated, and disconnected. They want a church that brings them into contact with peers in a non-threatening setting.

3. *Instruction for kids.* Many want their children to have a Christian learning experience. They struggle as fathers and want the church to help them.

4. *Solutions.* Nearly thirty million described themselves as "stressed out." These men are less anxious to learn spiritual principles than to discover how to "make life work." They see no connection between spiritual wisdom and marketplace success.

5. *Knowing God.* Unchurched men have given up on churches but not God. They want to know Him, but don't know how.

If you invite men to church, remember they need "space." They want their visit to be low-key, non-threatening. They ask: *Is this the kind of place I would like to spend time?* They tend to believe all religions are about the same; there are no absolutes; the Bible is a good book but not reliable; Jesus didn't actually rise from the dead; and God is not actually involved in our lives. Many believe "God helps those who help themselves"—the opposite of what Christians believe.

So how do you reach such people? Like it or not, you need to speak to their felt needs. Create a friendly church that is sensitive to male needs. Challenge your own assumptions instead of just rattling off "church speak" such as "washed in the blood," "Christian walk," or "convicted," and "redeemed by the Lamb." Don't abandon your theology, but make it accessible to the uninformed. And pray that God will help you fill the spiritual void in these men's lives.

We are ripe for a moral and spiritual revolution, but it will require the passion of Christ, not dead religion. It requires God's grace, compassion, and wisdom. So choose your side.

—GEORGE BARNA

MONDAY

JUST A QUARTER of adult men attend church regularly; only slightly more read their Bibles; a third claim to be "born again," but most are chasing after the gods of this world. What's wrong with this picture? Jesus told the multitudes, "You are the salt of the earth; but if the salt loses its flavor, how shall it be seasoned? It is then good for nothing but to be thrown out and trampled underfoot by men. You are the light of the world. A city that is set on a hill cannot be hidden. Nor do they light a lamp and put it under a basket, but on a lampstand, and it gives light to all who are in the house" (Matt. 5:13–15). Once they heard the truth Jesus gave them, they were to take the good news to the ends of the earth. That's the substance of the Great Commission. So how is it that so many men today are so far from God?

Could it be that the light they see in us is not compelling? Jesus continued, "Let your light so shine before men, that they may see your good works and glorify your Father in heaven" (v. 16).

Pray that your light may glow brightly and compel men to come to Christ. ▤

TUESDAY

ACCORDING TO GEORGE Barna's research, unchurched men say they'd be attracted to a church that offers a clear understanding of God and the Bible. David says there is one basic understanding that every man must recognize: "The fool has said in his heart, 'There is no God.' They are corrupt, they have done abominable works, there is none who does good. The Lord looks down from heaven upon the children of men, to see if there are any who understand, who seek God. They have all turned aside, they have together become corrupt; there is none who does good—no, not one" (Ps. 14:1–3).

If we want others to understand the reality of faith, we need to help them understand that all men are sinners, that without a Redeemer to reconcile us to God, we are out of fellowship with Him and have no hope of salvation. It's a hard truth, but an essential fact of faith that men must hear.

Will you pray that God will help you to share your understanding of His Word so that others may be attracted to Him? ▤

WEDNESDAY

RELATIONSHIPS ARE important to men. We're social beings, and no matter how tough we appear to be, we all need others to complete us and give us a sense of personal worth. But God knows our hearts, and He takes pleasure in arranging the days of our lives, putting us in touch with other people, and teaching us how to live together in peace.

That's why the psalmist says, "Delight yourself also in the Lord, and He shall give you the desires of your heart. Commit your way to the Lord, trust also in Him, and He shall bring it to pass. He shall bring forth your righteousness as the light, and your justice as the noonday" (Ps. 37:4–6).

As you endeavor as a new man to stand on the promises of God, to be faithful to Him and to those around you, pray that you may be a friend to other men who need to know the Savior.

Ask God to give you insight and a sense of commitment to help build bridges for those in need of Christ's message of hope and salvation. ▤

THURSDAY

THE IRONY IS that even when men want the freedom to continue leading lives of sin and self-indulgence, something tells them it's still a good idea for their kids to grow up in Sunday school or to have some sort of religious instruction. Why? Because without some kind of moral training, and some idea of right and wrong as taught by the Bible, kids can easily turn out to be wild beasts with no respect for others and no sense of discipline. Surely our own culture teaches that truth.

Proverbs says, "Train up a child in the way he should go, and when he is old he will not depart from it" (Prov. 22:6). But in His instructions to Moses, God says that teaching the kids isn't enough: "Only take heed to yourself," God says, "and diligently keep yourself, lest you forget the things your eyes have seen, and lest they depart from your heart all the days of your life. And [then] teach them to your children and your grandchildren" (Deut. 4:9).

Ask for wisdom and conviction to share this double-edged truth with others. ■

FRIDAY

MEN WHO HAVE run into the brick walls out there realize the need for real-world solutions that make life make sense. They've been programmed to think that religious answers are for the weak and simpleminded; but sometimes people in desperate need will pause to hear the truth. Let them hear the prophet who says: "Who is wise? Let him understand these things. Who is prudent? Let him know them. For the ways of the Lord are right; the righteous walk in them, but transgressors stumble in them" (Hos. 14:9).

Those who trust in the Lord grow strong, while sinners fall prey to their own weaknesses. David says, "Those who trust in the Lord are like Mount Zion, which cannot be moved, but abides forever. As the mountains surround Jerusalem, so the Lord surrounds His people from this time forth and forever" (Ps. 125:1–2).

If you have a commitment to reach the lost, pray that the Lord will help you to grow in knowledge so that you can be a source of strength to the perishing. ▤

WEEKEND

MODERN MEN HAVE learned to trust in the quick fix. They want to know God, but they don't want to pay anything for it. They want their life made whole, but they don't want to make any long-term commitments. More than four thousand years ago, God offered the Israelites this assurance, "You will seek the Lord your God, and you will find Him if you seek Him with all your heart and with all your soul. When you are in distress, and all these things come upon you in the latter days, when you turn to the Lord your God and obey His voice (for the Lord your God is a merciful God), He will not forsake you nor destroy you, nor forget the covenant of your fathers which He swore to them" (Deut. 4:29–31).

What a wonderful promise! But there's a catch. Paul says, "But without faith it is impossible to please Him, for he who comes to God must believe that He is, and that He is a rewarder of those who diligently seek Him" (Heb. 11:6).

As men of God we are committed to reach others; so pray that your witness may demonstrate the redemptive power of faith. ▤

Week 5
MERCY

WHAT IS MERCY? Ask David McAllister, a blind, seventy-seven-year-old ex-convict. Twenty years ago, he kidnapped a ten-year-old child, shot him, and left him for dead in the Florida everglades. Although blinded in his left eye by the bullet, the boy survived. McAllister escaped, and for two decades the case went unsolved. Then in the fall of 1996, a distraught McAllister, his frail body bedridden in a nursing home, confessed to the crime.

Learning of the confession, the victim, Chris Carrier, now thirty-two, visited him in the nursing home. He didn't go in anger. He went to pray with him and share the Good News of Jesus that had transformed his own life. You see, Chris lives on the side of mercy.

For most of us, mercy is a good thing in theory. But place it in the messy context of real life and it's a different story. After all, who wouldn't be upset if someone offended you, cheated you, stole from you, or, as in Chris's case, kidnapped you and left you for dead? Those actions deserve judgment, right?

Only if you're living on the side of judgment. Mercy is an application of unconditional love toward those who deserve it least. God still has to judge sin. However, in the person of Christ He found a way to do it and still maintain His master quality of love.

The foundation of Christ's whole ministry is on the side of mercy. If God decided to act only in judgment, He would have to destroy the world. Instead, He bestows mercy. With such profound love and grace shown to us, how can we resist living as God's instruments of mercy?

As I reflect on my life as a Christian leader and the people to whom I have ministered, I know how prone we can be to judging the spiritual progress of others. But God has been saying to me, "Wellington, get off the side of judgment and get on the side of mercy."

God could deal with us according to our sins, but He doesn't. Why not? A primary attribute of His nature is love (1 John 4:16). Through His love, God sent His Son to die in our stead (John 3:16). And He sent Him not only to save "righteous" people, but to save sinners as well. He didn't wait for us to get ourselves together—He sent Jesus to get us together.

God wants us to move to the *next step,* to rise to the level of His matchless promises and draw on the deposits of His mercy. Mercy is selfless and acts without pretense. Mercy is unconditional love. Mercy triumphs over judgment (James 2:13).

"Nobody could imagine that I would shake the hand that had tried to kill me," Chris Carrier said of his meeting with his abductor and would-be slayer. What a powerful picture of the mercy of God flowing through man. It's awesome to realize that this same God-given mercy is ours for the taking (Heb. 4:16).

—WELLINGTON BOONE

MONDAY

BY ALL APPEARANCES, those who are strong and powerful, flushed with success, have no need for mercy. According to the dictionary, mercy is the compassionate treatment of someone else, especially someone under our power. Mercy is the disposition to be kind and forgiving toward someone; it is something for which the recipient of mercy should be thankful. Mercy is a blessing extended by one person to another, often when the receiver of that blessing may have done nothing worthy of it.

Could there any better description of the kind of mercy that God has shown to us in offering up His own Son as payment for our sins? Jesus, our Redeemer, says, "Therefore be merciful, just as your Father also is merciful. Judge not, and you shall not be judged. Condemn not, and you shall not be condemned. Forgive, and you will be forgiven" (Luke 6:36–37). Christian mercy doesn't keep score; it is not blind; but it gives freely despite the weakness of the recipient.

Pray that you may take this important lesson to heart. ■

TUESDAY

IF THE CHRISTIAN faith were a man-made religion, the good would get heaven, and the bad, weak, and careless would get hell. But that's not the way it works. For a holy and perfect God who knew our weaknesses only too well, sent a holy and perfect Son, who lived a perfect and righteous life, to die on the cross, to be humiliated and spit upon, to be buried in a borrowed tomb, so that God Himself might pay the price of our sin. What an incredible act of mercy! But that's not all. For Jesus turned the tables on love and hate as well.

"There is a saying," He said, "'Love your friends and hate your enemies.' But I say: Love your enemies! Pray for those who persecute you! In that way you will be acting as true sons of your Father in heaven. For He gives His sunlight to both the evil and the good, and sends rain on the just and on the unjust too. If you love only those who love you, what good is that? Even scoundrels do that much" (Matt. 5:43–46).

Can you thank God for His act of mercy and love? And would you ask Him to teach you how to love like that? ■

WEDNESDAY

WHO CAN PUT a price on mercy? Who can describe the value of forgiveness? Surely David McAllister, who left ten-year-old Chris Carrier for dead more than twenty years ago, must have some idea of these things, since the young man made such a point of seeking David out to share the love of God and to offer him mercy and forgiveness despite his crimes.

When we give mercy, we give up the right to restitution and revenge. The man who gives mercy acknowledges that he will never get back what he has lost, just as Chris Carrier recognized that he would never regain sight in his blinded eye. Daniel prayed: "O Lord, to us belongs shame of face, to our kings, our princes, and our fathers, because we have sinned against You. To the Lord our God belong mercy and forgiveness, though we have rebelled against Him" (Dan. 9:8–9). Like Daniel, we need to recognize our debt to a merciful God we can never hope to repay; but if we have received mercy, shouldn't we also be merciful to others?

Pray for compassion, so that you may demonstrate mercy in your own life. ▤

THURSDAY

JUST IN CASE you'd like to argue that you don't have to be so merciful because your situation is so much worse than those described here, maybe you'd better think it over. The writer of Hebrews says, "For we do not have a High Priest who cannot sympathize with our weaknesses, but was in all points tempted as we are, yet without sin. Let us therefore come boldly to the throne of grace, that we may obtain mercy and find grace to help in time of need" (Heb. 4:15–16). Jesus Christ lived as we live, suffered as most will never suffer, and died a cruel and humiliating death, yet lives at this very hour to make intercession for us, demonstrating the mercy of

God upon all those who bear His name.

It should be comforting to know that there is no sorrow, grief, disappointment, or pain we can experience that Christ has not already endured; yet "God demonstrates His own love toward us, in that while we were still sinners, Christ died for us" (Rom. 5:8). Talk about mercy!

Pray today that God will make you grateful for His acts of mercy and love. ■

FRIDAY

WELLINGTON BOONE SAYS God expects us to move beyond selfishness, nursing our wounded pride over some slight, and go on to the next level—which is to love one another even as Christ loved the church, demonstrating mercy in all our personal relations. The idea is as ancient as the Bible. In the Old Testament, the prophet Zechariah said, "Thus says the Lord of hosts: 'Execute true justice, show mercy and compassion, everyone to his brother'" (Zech. 7:9). In the New Testament, the apostle James says, "For judgment is without mercy to the one who has shown no mercy. Mercy triumphs over judgment" (James 2:13).

But what we need to understand is that God is building in each of us a miniature version of His Son: each of us is meant to exhibit the love and mercy and compassion of Jesus, and, through our example, to teach others what God is like. Sound like a tall order? It is, and unless we come humbly before Him, asking for mercy and grace, we're bound to fail.

Pause now to seek His face, and ask God for wisdom to model Christ in your life. ■

WEEKEND

THE TWENTY-THIRD Psalm is everybody's favorite. For thousands of years, men have recited those reassuring words, which attest that God guides us through the dangers of this life as a gentle Shepherd guides His sheep. And at the end of that short and powerful verse, we say, "Surely goodness and mercy shall follow me all the days of my life, and I will dwell in the house of the Lord forever" (Ps. 23:6). But isn't it interesting that the very culmination and hope of the whole passage is that we may rest forever in the goodness and mercy of God?

What Chris Carrier offered David McAllister was just a little taste of God's mercy. What God asks each of us to give to others is to be an object lesson in love. Mercy, as the meditation tells us, is the gift of unconditional love, and nothing better describes God's gift to us, the redeemed. We have a right to be angry when we've been wronged, but so did God when callous, hard-hearted men took the life of His Son. But rather than exact punishment, God gave His love. Can you do the same?

Pray for a heart of mercy. ▤

FREEDOM

ON A COLD DAY in 1994, fifty Englishmen took the day off to pray. Desperate for a touch from God, they hardly noticed the rock band tuning up for an outdoor performance on the college campus nearby. "As the fifty men began to sing," says Pastor David Carr, "we sensed the presence of God in such a way that the men's worship drowned out the band and students just five hundred yards away . . . the sound of our meeting was heard all across the campus."

What people heard that day was the sound of a fire starting in the hearts of those fifty men whose lives have been radically changed, and they're not alone. All over Britain, a move of God's Spirit is igniting churches and the men in them.

Why Britain, and why now? Carr believes it's because British men have begun to put down their legendary pride and started to admit that they are spiritually destitute. "The men of our nation are realizing that unless we're touched by God we have got nothing to give anybody." True to His Word, God is pouring out His grace upon the humble.

On every continent, God has put out a call for men. But the ways He's drawing them into the fold are as diverse as the cultures themselves. Alex Mitala plants churches in the jungles of his native Uganda. So far he and his team have started 132 churches. "In our men's groups, we don't talk about heaven," says Mitala. "We talk about work, family, hygiene. When you're the man, it's not just a matter of praying. You must be clean, you must be working. God is teaching men how to be the priests and prophets of their homes."

Across the Indian Ocean from Africa, God has given a small but growing army of Australian men a different strategy for seeing homes come into order. Conditioned by the media to view Christianity as an irrelevant sub-culture, the average Aussie won't listen to any message that's labeled Christian, so Michael Murphy, head of the Australian Men's Network, is helping to organize groups of men with a united voice speaking a common-sense Christian message, but without the Christian label.

In country after country, God is rallying men to His cause and tailoring His approach precisely to their needs. Ukrainian men are learning principles of stew-ardship and personal responsibility. The Nicaraguan secretary of education, unwilling to see another generation of men substitute a false "macho" for real fatherhood, has invited a missionary to bring Bible-based teaching into every school in the country.

Where men say yes to God, He is responding in ways that leave the world scratching its head in wonder. Pick any spot on the globe. God is looking for men there, and He's not letting traditions, expectations, bor-ders, or prison walls stop Him. "If people emphasize a particular method, they're worshiping the package, not the gift," says David Carr.

The gift is Jesus Christ, and men need Him more than anything else.

—DAVID CULP

MONDAY

AS AT NO other time in living memory, men and women all over the world are seeking for something to believe in. The emptiness and disappointment of their lives has left them adrift. The world offers no permanent values, and no convincing beliefs to hang onto. As a result, people everywhere are looking for something real, something true. It was to people like these that Jesus proclaimed, "You shall know the truth, and the truth shall make you free" (John 8:32). That's the first step of faith: looking for the Source of freedom.

For the fifty men gathered on that English university campus, however, God had an even bolder message: a demonstration designed to give them a sense of God's presence, to teach them to look to Him for empowerment. It is in this sense that Paul says, "If then you were raised with Christ, seek those things which are above, where Christ is, sitting at the right hand of God. Set your mind on things above, not on things on the earth" (Col. 3:1–2).

Let that be your prayer today—that God will focus your mind on the things above. ▦

TUESDAY

IN THE AGE of modern democracy, some people have confused freedom with absolute liberty. They've fallen for an idea as old as Eden, that freedom gives them unlimited license. As missionaries reach out to the lost in Asia, Africa, Europe, the Americas, and other places today, they are trying to set men free from bondage to sin, so they can experience new life and freedom in Christ. But along with freedom from sin, they must also learn that God has given us a standard of righteousness, as demonstrated by the life of His Son.

Peter was speaking of this standard when he said, "For this is the will of God, that by doing good you may put to silence the ignorance of foolish men; as free, yet not using liberty as a cloak for vice, but as bondservants of God" (1 Pet. 2:15–16). When we experience true redemption, we rejoice in the freedom it brings, but we are to use our freedom to do good, to serve others, to teach the Word.

Pray that God will show you how a life of faith can

free you up to serve and do good. 🔳

WEDNESDAY

DESPITE CHRIST'S PROMISE of freedom, many people have fallen for the deceptive allurements of this life. As Paul warned, they have "exchanged the truth of God for the lie, and worshiped and served the creature rather than the Creator" (Rom 1:25). The result is a dangerous form of bondage to this world and its carnal desires. In Great Britain, Australia, and parts of North America, some men are so hardened against God's Word they cannot accept the idea that the Christian faith can be good for their health.

As we reach out to these men, let us pray that they might understand the truth of David's words, when he says: "Happy is he who has the God of Jacob for his help, whose hope is in the Lord his God, who made heaven and earth, the sea, and all that is in them; who keeps truth forever, who executes justice for the oppressed, who gives food to the hungry. The Lord gives freedom to the prisoners. The Lord opens the eyes of the blind; the Lord raises those who are bowed down; the Lord loves the righteous" (Ps. 146:5–8). 🔳

THURSDAY

THE ENTICEMENT SATAN used so effectively on Eve in the Garden of Eden was the notion that self-indulgence and disobedience could lead to liberty. But, no sooner had she bitten into the apple and shared her sin with Adam than both of them realized what they had done; and suddenly, for the first time in their lives, they were ashamed of their nakedness and their sin. Pride, the sin that cost Lucifer his place in heaven, that cost Adam and Eve their life of ease in the Garden, is the sin that haunts millions of men today, and prevents them from worshiping the one true God. It is the sin that destroys freedom, and it is the shame that prevents millions from experiencing the joy of peace with God.

David says, "When pride comes, then comes shame; but with the humble is wisdom" (Ps. 11:2). Solomon adds, "A man's pride will bring him low, but the humble in spirit will retain honor" (Prov. 29:23). To know the experience of real freedom in Christ, we must defeat Satan's power by resisting the sin of pride.

Pray for strength to resist, and to overcome. ≣

FRIDAY

WHEN WE EXALT the name of God and praise Him for His love toward the redeemed, we draw down the very power of heaven upon our endeavors. In Psalm 22:3, David tells us that God inhabits the praises of His people. When we rejoice in His love, we come into the very throne room of God.

Surely this is the sense of joy the apostle John must have felt when he exclaimed: "Behold what manner of love the Father has bestowed on us, that we should be called children of God!" How can we help but rejoice! But we also recognize that peace with God creates enmity with this world. John says, further, "Therefore the world does not know us, because it did not know Him. Beloved, now we are children of God; and it has not yet been revealed what we shall be, but we know that when He is revealed, we shall be like Him, for we shall see Him as He is. And everyone who has this hope in Him purifies himself, just as He is pure" (1 John 3:1–3).

Let us live in this truth and rejoice in the freedom of His love. ≣

WEEKEND

"THERE IS ONE body and one Spirit, just as you were called in one hope of your calling; one Lord, one faith, one baptism; one God and Father of all, who is above all, and through all, and in you all. But to each one of us grace was given according to the measure of Christ's gift. Therefore He says: 'When He ascended on high, He led captivity captive, and gave gifts to men'" (Eph. 4:4–8).

This is the hope that is awakening men in every nation to the redeeming truth of God's Word. In Nicaragua, a secretary of education sees that faith can help men to become better fathers; in the Ukraine, men are finding out how to shepherd their resources from the Bible's teaching on stewardship; in Uganda, thousands are learning purity, decency, and chastity from God's Word. The Savior of mankind, who defeated death and hell by His death on the cross, has taken captivity captive so that we can be free.

Will you pray that millions on every continent will discover the freedom that comes through faith in Jesus Christ? ▤

Week 7
HONESTY

DAVE BEGS OFF when his boys want him to throw the football around with them—he says his old knee injury is kicking up again. Actually, his easy chair and TV remote are calling. Andy tells his wife they can't afford that winter vacation they have been planning. But he's really afraid he'll look like a fat old fool when he tries to learn to ski.

Mike's daughter is thirteen, and her computer knowledge surpassed his a couple of years ago. Rather than switch roles and learn from her, he loudly denies any interest in new software, saying he's too busy. Maybe such home-brew hypocrisy isn't on the scale of the Pharisees of old, but it is a problem.

"Hypocrisy is always an attempt to escape pain, embarrassment, or discomfort," says author Bill Beausay in his book, *Boys!* We seem to become blind to our own efforts to maintain our image for our family. It's a subtle, infectious trap that grows in size and complexity. Ultimately it makes integrity impossible and builds a wall between ourselves and our family, and worst of all, between ourselves and God.

Wives have a remarkable ability to see through our facades. What's more, they're always willing to give us plenty of rope to hang ourselves. But any compromise in integrity must lead either to repentance or to hypocrisy. Pastor John Maxwell says integrity is the factor that determines which choice we make. "Integrity will not allow our lips to violate our hearts," he says. "When integrity is the referee, we will be consistent; our beliefs will be mirrored by our conduct. There will be no discrepancy between what we appear to be and what our family knows we are."

To get to the bottom of the hypocrisy problem, we have to remember that hypocrisy itself is not the problem—deceit in the heart is the problem. "Jesus wasn't bluffing when He said a house divided against itself will fall," says Beausay. "And every time you knowingly allow a bit of hypocrisy to flourish in your heart, pride wins and creeps forward in your life." But there is hope. "Jesus wants to 'flush us out of the pocket' of comfort," He adds, "and make us scramble in the open field of risky honesty."

The experts agree that making a clean break with ongoing hypocrisies is the toughest part. But getting real with our families can be a real relief. Beausay says, "I think most guys can relate to the exhaustion we feel when we have to work so hard to maintain our image. It's pathetic—we ruin our health, sacrifice our homes, risk major embarrassments just to keep our image squeaky clean."

One reformed hypocrite put it this way: "I thought I had the world faked out, but the only person I really faked out was me. But God is much bigger and more able than I ever thought. He even loved the deceitful phantom I'd become. He 'out-clevered' me. Imagine that."

—KIP BURKE

MONDAY

THE PROPHET JEREMIAH was a man of uncanny vision. He saw man as he is, blessed by God, but often unworthy of His love. He says, "Blessed is the man who trusts in the Lord, and whose hope is the Lord. For he shall be like a tree planted by the waters, which spreads out its roots by the river, and will not fear when heat comes; but its leaf will be green, and will not be anxious in the year of drought, nor will cease from yielding fruit" (Jer. 17:7–8). The prophet saw that God is holy, and a rewarder of those who live honest and godly lives.

But, through Jeremiah, God also describes human nature as it is, and says in the very next verses: "The heart is deceitful above all things, and desperately wicked; who can know it? I, the Lord, search the heart, I test the mind, even to give every man according to his ways, according to the fruit of his doings" (v. 9–10). Despite man's weakness, God seeks men who practice honesty and integrity. Can we live that way?

Pray that God will help you to be forthright and honest with those around you. ■

TUESDAY

SOLOMON WAS A keen observer of human behavior, and in Proverbs he speaks of seven sins that provoke the heart of God. "These six things the Lord hates," he says, "Yes, seven are an abomination to Him: a proud look, a lying tongue, hands that shed innocent blood, a heart that devises wicked plans, feet that are swift in running to evil, a false witness who speaks lies, and one who sows discord among brethren" (Prov. 6:16–19).

In this week's reading, Kip Burke says our families can generally see through our tendency to mislead, to lie, to put on a false face, or to deceive in any of these ways. Wives, in particular, have a knack for seeing through their husbands' deceptions. But how do we let ourselves slip into such bad habits? Shouldn't we strive to defeat those seven sins? And if we are truly *new men,* shouldn't we live like it?

Pray that you may be able to say, with David, "But as for me, I will walk in my integrity" (Ps. 26:11). ■

WEDNESDAY

BURKE USES A modern football metaphor to make the point that Christ will not allow us to continue living in dishonesty. Jesus wants to flush us out of the pocket of deceitful lifestyles, he says, and make us scramble in the open field. In a similar vein, Solomon uses the image of a merchant's scales, saying, "Dishonest scales are an abomination to the Lord, but a just weight is His delight" (Prov. 11:1). In both cases, the message is that God cannot tolerate deception and dishonesty in those who claim to be men of faith.

Sooner or later, the truth always comes out. Solomon tells us that those who live honorably will have nothing to fear, while those who practice deceit will be found out. "He who walks with integrity walks securely," he writes, "but he who perverts his ways will become known" (Prov. 10:9). Do you want to be known as a man who tricks and cheats and scams because he can't face the truth?

As you think about areas of your life where you need to be accountable, pray that God will help you to walk always in integrity. ▨

THURSDAY

THE PROPHET MICAH cut through the fog of rhetoric with this lucid observation. "And what does the Lord require of you but to do justly, to love mercy, and to walk humbly with your God?" (Mic. 6:8). It's as simple as that: Men of God are to live honest, godly lives.

Later, the apostle James offered an equally simple witness, saying, "Who is wise and understanding among you? Let him show by good conduct that his works are done in the meekness of wisdom. But if you have bitter envy and self-seeking in your hearts, do not boast and lie against the truth. This wisdom does not descend from above, but is earthly, sensual, demonic. For where envy and self-seeking exist, confusion and every evil thing are there. But the wisdom that is from above is first pure, then peaceable, gentle, willing to yield, full of mercy and good fruits, without partiality and without hypocrisy" (James 3:13–17). With such clear advice from Old Testament and New, no one can pretend he doesn't know how to behave.

Pray that God will help you to be a man of honor and integrity. ▤

FRIDAY

SO MANY OF life's annoying problems would go away if we lived as the prophets and the saints of the Bible have described. David says, "Blessed is that man who makes the Lord his trust, and does not respect the proud, nor such as turn aside to lies." Honesty, the old axiom says, is the best policy. But even more, honesty and integrity are the essence of the godly life. David goes on to say, "Many, O Lord my God, are Your wonderful works which You have done; and Your thoughts toward us cannot be recounted to You in order; if I would declare and speak of them, they are more than can be numbered" (Ps. 40:4–5).

The traits of the man of God are not a mystery; there are no secret rules or hidden agendas to be discovered. The principles that lead to health, wisdom, and prosperity are spelled out clearly—and the wonderful works of God are so numerous they can't even be counted. Let us, like David, rejoice in the blessings and the wonders of our Lord.

Thank Him today for His Word, which speaks so eloquently of the habits of the man of God. ▤

WEEKEND

IT'S EASY TO slide into a life of hypocrisy, this week's meditation suggests, and to convince ourselves we've faked everybody out. But Paul tells us, "Do not be deceived, God is not mocked; for whatever a man sows, that he will also reap" (Gal. 6:7).

Many men who find themselves going through periods of loss and despair may not make the connection between their deceitful lives and their hardships. But that's one of the most important lessons we can learn. In the midst of his sorrows and anguish, Job reflected on this truth, saying, "God is wise in heart and mighty in strength. Who has hardened himself against Him and prospered?" (Job 9:4). We may be able to hide dishonesty from others; we may even fool ourselves some of the time; but we can't hide our sin from God.

Job adds that God is always greater than we imagine. "He does great things past finding out," he says, "Yes, wonders without number" (v. 10).

Knowing that we serve so great and wonderful a Savior, let us praise Him today, and ask for discretion in our lives. ▓

CREATIVITY

IN THE SUMMER of 1983, Steve Green was an up-and-coming singer. He and wife Marijean were part of the backup group for Bill and Gloria Gaither, but Steve's classically trained voice was attracting notice. Sparrow Records offered him a recording contract. Raised in Argentina by missionary parents, Steve could sing in English or Spanish; but his spiritual life was stuck on the launch pad where it had been since his college days.

"Although I grew up in a spiritual home," he says, "I turned my back on the level of commitment to Christ that I had seen in my parents. My desire to be free was really a license to sin. I rebelled and grieved the heart of God." Growing up, Steve wasn't allowed to go to the cinema. When he was on his own, he was attracted to raunchy movies on TV.

In August 1983, Steve went to his sister's wedding, and it didn't take him long to notice that older brother Randy had been through some sort of "revival" experience. Randy cornered each family member and asked where they stood with the Lord. Steve kept his distance, but one afternoon, the family jumped into a car to visit a hospitalized friend, and Randy had a captive audience.

Steve resisted his questions but after several minutes Randy began crying. He said God wanted to use Steve, but He couldn't because there was something bottled up inside him. That night, sleep did not come easily. His older brother had peeled away a layer of his heart and exposed the hypocrisy that his life had become.

Something powerful was tugging at Steve's conscience, and after an hour of internal debate, he fell out of bed and dropped to his knees.

When he got home after the wedding, Steve started from the beginning, confessing things to his wife Marijean that she did not know about her husband of five years. Driven by a newfound passion for God, Steve spent the next two weeks making restitution with those he had wronged. He was saying goodbye to an old life.

Several weeks later, he gave his first solo concert at Liberty University in Virginia. Normally he didn't say much in public, but that night he told the audience how his brother lovingly confronted him at a time when he needed it. As he looked down at the front row, he saw men and women dabbing their eyes with handkerchiefs. That had never happened before.

These days, Steve Green is into accountability. "These are some of the reasons I have made myself accountable to Christian artists Michael Card, Wes King, and Phil Keaggy," he says. "If I have stumbled, I contact them about it and ask them to pray for me . . . I know I'm one of the most unlikely candidates to be used by God because of my eight-year period of running away from Him as a prodigal. I see my own frailties even now," he says, "since God rescued me and turned my life around."

—MIKE YORKEY

MONDAY

THE STRUGGLE OF living a double life can put tremendous strain on a man's heart—not just physically, but spiritually and emotionally as well. Those who have tried it can testify to the pain it causes. That's one reason David declared in the thirty-second Psalm, "Blessed is he whose transgression is forgiven, whose sin is covered. Blessed is the man to whom the Lord does not impute iniquity, and in whose spirit there is no deceit" (Ps. 32:1–2).

Dumping the sin and hypocrisy that accumulates in our lives can be a liberating experience. It allows us to face up to the truth, to put away the guile and guilt, and come back to basics with God. Letting go of those stupid sins so that we can take hold of Christ is the most creative and the most intelligent thing any man can do. When singer Steve Green looked into his own heart and decided—because of the relentless probing of his brother, Randy—to work it out with God and with those around him, he was finally free to be the man God designed him to be.

Pray that you, too, will be everything God wants you to be. ■

TUESDAY

THIS REMARKABLE PSALM gives us a record of David's transformation from a man of selfishness and sin to a man who rejoices in the freedom of forgiveness. In complete honesty and openness, David admits that, "When I kept silent, my bones grew old through my groaning all the day long. For day and night Your hand was heavy upon me; my vitality was turned into the drought of summer."

David could not live under the weight of his sin, so he fell on his face before God, confessing everything. He says, "I acknowledged my sin to You, and my iniquity I have not hidden. I said, 'I will confess my transgressions to the Lord,' And You forgave the iniquity of my sin. For this cause everyone who is godly shall pray to You in a time when You may be found; surely in a flood of great waters they shall not come near him" (Ps. 32:3–6).

Truly the key to finding new life in Christ is

throwing off the shackles of sin so God's creative power can renew us from within. Praise Him today for His liberating love. ▤

WEDNESDAY

SET FREE FROM the despair that comes with sneaking around, hiding his thoughts and behaviors, and his secret life, David broke into songs of praise. How else could he feel when such a great weight had been lifted from his shoulders? That may also be what Steve Green experienced when he first unburdened his heart to God, and then began making things right with his wife and loved ones. Hear David when he sings: "You are my hiding place; You shall preserve me from trouble; You shall surround me with songs of deliverance." And then the psalmist hears the loving response of the Lord whose voice echoes, "I will instruct you and teach you in the way you should go; I will guide you with My eye" (Ps. 32:7–8).

What a joy to know that God leads us to repentance, that He teaches our lips the very words to say, that He renews and restores our hearts, and then gives us sanctuary from the taunts of Satan and a world of sin. Surely we must praise Him from whom all blessings flow!

How do you respond today to the God who loves you with such a tender love? ▤

THURSDAY

NO SOONER HAD David learned his lesson and experienced repentance and redemption than he became a teacher, instructing others to flee from the follies of sin. "Do not be like the horse or like the mule, which have no understanding, which must be harnessed with bit and bridle, else they will not come near you. Many sorrows shall be to the wicked; but he who trusts in the

Lord, mercy shall surround him" (Ps. 32:9–10).

In the same way, when Steve Green sings today he touches the hearts of millions. Whether singing in English or Spanish, whether in hymns of praise or in upbeat songs of celebration, his music speaks of the freedom that comes through surrender to the One who loves us. All over this country and around the world, men who have come to faith in Christ can sing those words; they can know the same joy and salvation. The creative Spirit of love that we find in our heavenly Father frees us up to discover the creativity within us.

Pray today that God will express His creative and redeeming power in you. ■

FRIDAY

IN THE FINAL verse of the psalm, David calls all men to sing out for joy in the knowledge that we have been saved from sin and wickedness, and made righteous through faith in our loving Savior. "Be glad in the Lord and rejoice, you righteous; and shout for joy, all you upright in heart!" (Ps. 32:11). David had been on the mountaintops, a hero, a leader of men, companion to kings, and a child of God; but he had also been in the valleys of sin and despair, corrupted by lust, passion, and anger. He could have died in his sin and lost the blessing that God had planned for him. But, instead, he fell on his face and begged for forgiveness.

Paul assures us, "There is none righteous, no not one" (Rom. 3:10). We all sin and "fall short of the glory of God" (v. 23). But God loves us so much that He made a way to turn us around: He gave us His Son. What an incredible act of mercy! What an act of love!

Let us each claim that marvelous free gift, and praise our Lord for His creative, redeeming power! ■

WEEKEND

WHEN WE FALL into sin, human nature tells us it's no big
deal. Everybody does it. And besides, we can hide it!
But that is Satan's big lie. Steve Green tells his own
story with such candor and painful honesty because he
knows that secret sins can prevent God's love from
working in us. Sin and guilt are like caustic chemicals
that eat away at our hearts, our relationships, and our
nerves, weakening and endangering all our hopes for a
better life. We can't buy God off with good works; the
only remedy is genuine repentance.

"Now to him who works," Paul says, "the wages are
not counted as grace but as debt. But to him who does
not work but believes on Him who justifies the ungodly,
his faith is accounted for righteousness, just as David
also describes the blessedness of the man to whom God
imputes righteousness apart from works: 'Blessed are
those whose lawless deeds are forgiven, and whose sins
are covered; blessed is the man to whom the Lord shall
not impute sin'" (Rom. 4:4–8).

Share your heart with God, and thank Him for His
love. ▤

Week 9
GRATEFULNESS

■■■ Bob and Sandy Varney and fifteen-year-old
■■■ daughter, Karly, had just completed an exotic
two-week Egyptian cruise and were on their way to
visit friends in Kuwait. They would soon return to
Reston, Virginia, where Bob is CEO of an Internet
provider and Sandy has a thriving dental practice. But
that day—March 17, 1996—would be one they'd never
forget. Their flight to Cairo had been delayed, and they
caught this one at the last minute; but just as they were
about to land, the plane shot back up. Bob knew something was wrong: "I think we're being hijacked," he
said.

In the cockpit, Mohammed Hamid Salim held a
revolver to the pilot's head. His son, armed with petrol
bombs, stood nearby. Salim claimed he had a divine
message for Libyan leader Moammar Gadhafi, Egypt's
Hosni Mubarak, and Bill Clinton. The 145 passengers
on board would be his hostages until he was flown to
Libya. Embassy officials in Kuwait said there were no
Americans on Flight 320, but when news of the kidnap-
ping was announced, Jack and Deborah Niblock
somehow knew their friends were on board. They
called Reston. News spread like wildfire, and within
hours hundreds of people were praying.

Low on fuel, the pilot told the hijacker they had to
land immediately. He swooped through the clouds and,
miraculously, there was an empty airstrip smack in the
middle of the desert. "Not knowing what was happening was the worst," Bob recalls. "You didn't know
whether the plane was going to blow up or if they were

going to shoot you." As the Varneys prayed silently, Bob remembered the passage in Daniel about Shadrach, Meshach, and Abednego. They said, "The God we serve is able to save us . . . but even if He does not, that's okay." (See Daniel 3:17–18.) At that point Bob was filled with peace.

When the terrorists departed the plane, passengers broke into cheers and applause. But Bob had another gut feeling: "We're being hijacked again!" he said. The passengers were told to deplane and board several buses lined up on the tarmac. Finally, around 4 A.M., they arrived in the coastal town of Benghazi. Half asleep, the hostages were herded into a hotel and thrust into the middle of a press conference. No settlement had been reached, but at 11 A.M. Colonel Gadhafi arrived. In a white suit, he barely resembled the brutal military dictator from the cover of *Time* magazine.

One enterprising photographer prodded Karly to stand next to Gadhafi. That picture appeared on the front page of Arab newspapers the next day. Negotiations were concluded at 4 P.M. and the hostages were driven to the airport. Two hours later, they arrived in Cairo.

Bob Varney looks at life differently now. "God reminded me that life is like a vapor which vanishes quickly," he says, "and I must seek first His kingdom. The hijacking has helped me to be thankful right now for each and every blessing that He showers upon me. God is in control!"

—JENNIFER FERRANTI

MONDAY

OF ALL THE things that could happen to you on any given day, a hijacking is about the least likely thing anyone would expect. Yet, on that spring day in 1996, that's exactly what did happen to the Varneys. But what do you say in such a situation? How do you respond?

We've all seen the made-for-TV movies and read the headlines about the cruelty and twisted sense of justice of hijackers and Middle-Eastern terrorists.

Watching as their aircraft approached the Cairo airport and then shot back skyward, Bob Varney knew one thing: He needed to pray. At just such a time, David prayed: "O my God, I trust in You; let me not be ashamed; let not my enemies triumph over me. Indeed, let no one who waits on You be ashamed; let those be ashamed who deal treacherously without cause" (Ps. 25:2–3).

If you found yourself in a crisis situation, would you have the confidence to trust God and pray without ceasing?

Pray that you will, and thank Him for the power of prayer. ■

TUESDAY

SITTING ON THE airplane with the Varneys were some three hundred men and women who may or may not have had the peace of mind Bob, Sandy, and Karly experienced that day. Most, no doubt, had tried to live a pretty good life; they had paid their taxes and kept their noses clean. They had friends and connections and enough money to take care of the basics, and they probably felt they could take care of themselves pretty well, without anybody's help. It's the way most people want to feel.

But as the shock of their situation began to sink in, many were suddenly troubled and sick to their stomachs. All the possibilities raced through their minds: gunshots, torture, maybe a plane crash, or worse! Yet, despite the apprehension, the Varneys rested in the knowledge that God would see them through. David prayed, "So teach us to number our days, that we may gain a heart of wisdom" (Ps. 90:12).

This is the confidence we may have in Christ: that

our days are safe in his loving hands, whatever happens. Thank Him for that. ▤

WEDNESDAY

SCRIPTURE TEACHES US that the way to be at peace with God is to live as if each day were the last, so that, whatever happens, there can be no devastating surprises. If we know that we are secure in the Father's hands, other men cannot hurt us. And when we encounter great difficulties, as the Varneys did, we know that the Holy Spirit is already interceding on our behalf.

Paul says, "Likewise the Spirit also helps in our weaknesses. For we do not know what we should pray for as we ought, but the Spirit Himself makes intercession for us with groanings which cannot be uttered. Now He who searches the hearts knows what the mind of the Spirit is, because He makes intercession for the saints according to the will of God." And then he offers those tremendous words of comfort: "And we know that all things work together for good to those who love God, to those who are the called according to His purpose" (Rom. 8:26–28).

Pray that God will keep your heart and mind in perfect peace. ▤

THURSDAY

BEFORE THE FOUNDATIONS of the world were laid, God had a plan to redeem mankind from the ravages of sin and death. God is Spirit. He is eternal and all-powerful. But we are flesh and blood: We suffer, we bleed, we die. Knowing that we would need a Redeemer who could intercede for us, who could bridge the unfathomable gulf that separates us and our mortal bodies from the immortal and awesome holiness of God, He sent a missionary in human flesh to share our sorrows and bear our sins.

To His anointed Son, God declares through the prophet Isaiah: "Fear not, for I am with you; be not dismayed, for I am your God. I will strengthen you, yes, I will help you, I will uphold you with My righteous right hand" (Is. 41:10). Christ endured our weaknesses and experienced all our pains. Now, having died for us and paid our debt, He lives today to give us continual access to God. Shouldn't we celebrate the promise and the provision of God's love?

If you realize what Christ has done for you, thank Him with a grateful heart. ■

FRIDAY

WHEN HE LIVED and traveled on the shores of Galilee, Jesus was constantly teaching the disciples to look to their heavenly Father for all their needs. Over and over again, He told them that if they had faith no bigger than a mustard seed they could tap into the very power of heaven. But just think of all the times recorded in the Gospels when those men failed to understand or to claim the lessons their Master taught them face-to-face.

Today as we face so many perplexing problems, dangers, threats, and concerns, we have a lot in common with those guys—we forget the most important part. Jesus said, "But seek first the kingdom of God and His righteousness, and all these things shall be added to you. Therefore do not worry about tomorrow, for tomorrow will worry about its own things. Sufficient for the day is its own trouble" (Matt. 6:33–34).

How can we be so blind to the power that Christ has offered us? How can we be so ungrateful when the bounty of heaven is already ours? Ask God to help you to trust Him. ■

WEEKEND

THE PICTURE OF GOD that many men carry around inside

their emotional wallets is of an angry, scowling Father just looking for an excuse to slap them around. Sometimes we feel that way because our own fathers were stern and humorless; but sometimes it's because a Sunday school image that God is a tyrant bent on revenge was seared into our minds.

How very, very false that image is! Are you carrying that snapshot around today? Take it out now, and rip it up. Please see the heart of a God who is yearning to love you and hold you in His arms. "I, the Lord, have spoken," He says through Ezekiel. "I will make a covenant of peace with them, and cause wild beasts to cease from the land; and they will dwell safely in the wilderness and sleep in the woods. I will make them and the places all around My hill a blessing; and I will cause showers to come down in their season; there shall be showers of blessing" (Ezek. 34:24–26).

God will hold accountable all those who prey on His flock, and He promises to bless the sheep. Thank Him now for His infinite love. ▤

Week 10

DEPENDABILITY

▰▰▰ IF A MAN IS worth his salt, he'll deliver on his
▰▰▰ promises. Let me illustrate what I mean. For as
long as anyone could remember, the Oklahoma Sooners
had intimidated our Colorado Buffaloes, not only with
their talent, but also with their downright offensive
demeanor. Colorado had become a cakewalk for them
as they won thirteen of fourteen games with an average
of more than forty points per game.

Clearly, we needed to try a new approach, so I
decided to issue a challenge based on my players' word
as young men. The morning before our trip to Oklahoma,
I summoned each player into my office and said, "Now,
son, I want to know what I can expect from you when
we play the Sooners." One by one, they looked me in
the eye and told me they'd play their heart out for us
and be the best player they'd ever been. Then I'd say,
"I'm going to hold you to your word."

Having set the tone with those meetings, the team
that boarded the plane was on a mission. The game was
played at night, nationally televised on ESPN, so I realized a lot of the high-school players we wanted to
recruit would be watching. What they saw before the
night was over, was that Colorado would no longer lay
down for O.U.! We eventually lost the game, but the
good news was that each of us knew he had given himself for the team. Each player kept his promise, and we
had taken a significant step forward as a team.

If that kind of dynamic exists in a football game,
how much more when men gather in Jesus' name, look
each other in the eyes, and say what can be expected of

them? Just as my football teams didn't become national contenders overnight, so we won't instantly become perfectly godly men. But just as Colorado began its transformation with that one game, so we start by committing our lives to Jesus Christ and becoming a new creation. (See 2 Corinthians 5:17.)

When you make a promise to a brother, you declare your intentions. You actually look into the future and determine that part of it related to your promise.

We're in a war, men. The enemy is real, and he doesn't like to see men of God take a stand for Jesus Christ and contest his lies. But almighty God is for us, and we know that if we walk the narrow road that leads to life, we have an extremely capable leader in the King of kings. And He is faithful to provide the grace and strength we need along the way.

You and I serve royalty, and we have a costly responsibility. But listen to this promise in John 12:26: "My Father will honor the one who serves me" (NIV). Accordingly, there's nothing I want more in life than to serve Jesus Christ, because I want almighty God's favor on me. How about you?

—BILL MCCARTNEY

MONDAY

WE MAKE A lot of promises in our lives. We promise our parents to be obedient children when we're young. We promise our teachers and coaches we'll do our best in school or on the practice field. We promise employers, church, and government leaders, and even God that we'll be faithful and do our best. But some men fail so often and break so many promises so routinely that it's amazing anybody even believes them anymore.

When Bill McCartney's team hit a major roadblock, he knew he'd need their best efforts, so he made each man promise to do his best. Was it enough? In the end, they still lost the game; but the coach knew it was their personal commitment that really counted.

Jesus said, "For everyone will be seasoned with fire, and every sacrifice will be seasoned with salt. Salt is good, but if the salt loses its flavor, how will you season it? Have salt in yourselves, and have peace with one another" (Mark 9:49–50). Dependability is such an important trait of a godly man.

Pray that your sacrifices will always be seasoned with it. ■

TUESDAY

MOST OF US have a reverence for Jesus that comes from years of Sunday school and church, and it's hard for us to imagine the mockery that He suffered from the men of His day. Contrary to the paintings and icons we've seen, Jesus didn't have a halo. There were no angels hovering overhead or choirs singing His praises. For the people of that day, Jesus was just a humble carpenter's son from Nazareth. He even had a strange accent and acted funny, telling people He was going to destroy the temple and rebuild it in three days.

But when Jesus taught the people, they sensed that this wasn't just another country bumpkin. Luke says, "And they were astonished at His teaching, for His word was with authority" (Luke 4:32). Furthermore, when He made a promise or gave His word, He never let them down. He was absolutely dependable. What an important lesson for us: If Christ was completely trustworthy, shouldn't we strive to be the same? That *is* what He expects.

Pray today that as a follower of Christ, you may be reliable in every word and deed. ■

WEDNESDAY

EVERY CHRISTIAN MAN discovers sooner or later that he

has two enemies—the world that is using every trick to break his will and resolve, and his own sinful nature. That's why Bill McCartney reminds us that we're in a war. The enemy is, indeed, real. Secular society would like us to believe that Satan is a silly myth or an ancient superstition; but those who have confronted him on the battleground of the soul know what a fierce competitor he is.

When Paul was teaching young Timothy a lesson about dependability, he told him to stand firm against the taunts of the devil, and to persevere with workman-like determination. "Be diligent to present yourself approved to God," he says, "a worker who does not need to be ashamed, rightly dividing the word of truth" (2 Tim. 2:15). If we try to conquer our ancient foe in our own might, we will be destroyed. But Paul says that diligent preparation, prayer, and spending quality time in the Word of God will give us the ability to overcome.

Are you doing those things? Pray that God will build you up daily through His Word. ▤

THURSDAY

IT'S NOT EASY to change old habits. Some men who try to quit smoking find that they have to change every-thing—drive to work a different way; make new friends; eat at different places; even wear different clothes. The reason, they believe, is that a whole new approach to life will make it easier to change the old habits. In other words, they're trying to trick their emotions into conforming to a new way of life.

Freedom in Christ doesn't depend on mental gym-nastics. We don't have to wrestle with old behaviors if God does the work in our hearts. Paul says, "Therefore, if anyone is in Christ, he is a new creation; old things have passed away; behold, all things have become new"

(2 Cor. 5:17). Through the Holy Spirit, we have authority over sin. We can defeat old habits, attitudes, and emotions that have troubled us for years; but we have to ask for it, believing that Christ can and will renew our minds completely.

Since our Lord is dependable, will you trust Him to renew your heart and mind? ▤

FRIDAY

IN MATTHEW 21, Jesus poses a tough question for his critics. Two sons were told to go to work in their father's vineyard. One said he'd go but didn't, the other said he would not go but ended up going anyway. So, which one, Jesus asked, pleased his father?

The answer is important not only for the Lord's critics but for us, because the way to please our Father is to *keep His commandments.* This is the lesson the apostle John had in mind when he said, "Now by this we know that we know Him, if we keep His commandments. He who says, 'I know Him,' and does not keep His commandments, is a liar, and the truth is not in him. But whoever keeps His word, truly the love of God is perfected in him. By this we know that we are in Him. He who says he abides in Him ought himself also to walk just as He walked" (1 John 2:3–6).

The man of God who wants to walk honorably with God must, first of all, be a man of his word. Do as you're asked, and pray that you may always walk as Jesus walked. ▤

WEEKEND

MAYBE IT WOULD be easier if the Christian life were a football game. You could suit up, put on your pads and helmet, then go out on the field and fight it out with the opposing team. Fans in the crowd would be yelling for one side or the other, and you'd always know whether you were winning or losing by the scoreboard and the yard markers.

That might be easier. But, unfortunately, Paul tells us our warfare isn't against flesh and blood. We're up against powers and principalities of the invisible world. That's a much tougher battle, and there's a lot more at risk. Jesus made it clear that a man must give up everything if he wants to win the prize. "The man who loves his life will lose it," he said, "while the man who hates his life in this world will keep it for eternal life. Whoever serves me must follow me . . ." But then He gives this wonderful promise. "Where I am, my servant also will be. My Father will honor the one who serves me" (John 12:25–26, NIV).

What a tremendous promise! Pray that God will teach you real dependability. ▤

Week 11

SERVANTHOOD

EVERY WEEK, RAIN OR shine, groups of men gather in Cincinnati to work. They never get paid for it. One recent Wednesday I went out with one of these groups. We split into teams of two and, after a prayer, hit the streets. Our mission: cleaning toilets.

One man explained what happened when he walked into a beauty salon and offered to clean toilets as a practical expression of God's love. "Conversations stopped. Dead silence. Our offer was so stunning to the manager, she asked us to repeat what we had just said. After we finished cleaning and were on our way out the door, the whole place was abuzz.

"I heard one lady say, 'I wonder what kind of Christians will wash your toilet to show God's love.' At that moment I knew we had made a lasting impression on each heart with the active love of God." Tears formed in Bob's eyes as he shared the story and I knew God had done something remarkable in both the served and the servant.

For the past eight years, Vineyard Community Church in Cincinnati has been experimenting with "servant evangelism." Using simple acts of kindness, we have been able to build a bridge into the lives of the unchurched. After trying all the usual approaches with little results, I concluded two things: I don't like being pushy; and the watching world is often left cold by traditional evangelism because they observe little or no love in the process.

Picture the difference: a fever-pitched evangelist on a soapbox, or small groups of men with squeegees, brushes, and snow shovels saying, "Hi, we'd like to serve you today to show you God's love." Last year alone, we shared the love of God with more than one hundred thousand people. People ask us: "Who are you guys? Why are you doing this? What do you believe?"

Over the years I have discovered three myths that keep us from touching people with God's love.

1. *I don't have enough free time to share God's love.* Servant evangelism is simply finding out where people are in pain, touching that point by bringing some relief, then pointing to the love of Jesus as your reason for serving.

2. *I don't have the gift for evangelism.* Only about 10 percent of us are naturally gifted at traditional evangelism, but 100 percent of us can serve. If we touch people with a kind act, they tend to ask the right questions and it's easier to evangelize.

3. *I don't have the courage to do this.* How much courage does it take to clean a toilet? After cleaning a lot of bathrooms, washing cars, and handing out soft drinks, I have noticed a new freedom in serving God through servant evangelism.

If you make yourself available to God, He will use you to bring His life to your city. Through your acts of kindness, your city will understand what real men are all about: simple servants with a profound message.

—STEVE SJOGREN

MONDAY

WHAT'S THE POINT of scrubbing toilets or washing windows? No doubt a lot of people in Cincinnati were surprised, and probably asked themselves that question when the men from Vineyard Community Church showed up. But one thing's for sure. When the fellows left, those people knew they'd been served in a most remarkable way. What makes servant evangelism so unique is that, for most of us, the idea of serving freely is inconceivable.

Jesus had little use for the self-serving materialism of His day. He told the Pharisees, "No servant can serve two masters; for either he will hate the one and love the other, or else he will be loyal to the one and despise the other. You cannot serve God and mammon." The Pharisees, who loved money, laughed at Him. But Jesus said, "You . . . justify yourselves before men, but God knows your hearts. For what is highly esteemed among men is an abomination in the sight of God" (Luke 16:13–15). Jesus said He came, not to be served, but to serve.

Pray for understanding of this teaching so you can bless those around you. ▤

TUESDAY

FROM THE EARLIEST birth pangs of the nation of Israel, God desired to teach men to be faithful, loving, obedient servants—men who loved the Lord and served one another. The Ten Commandments were given to them, not to penalize them or make their lives difficult, but as a standard by which they (and we) could live just and honorable lives. Those ten rules—think about it, He could have given them hundreds!—outline a way of life that will allow all of us to live in peace and harmony with one another.

When Moses came down from Mount Sinai carrying the tablets of the Law, God spoke to him, saying, "And now, Israel, what does the Lord your God require of you, but to fear the Lord your God, to walk in all His ways and to love Him, to serve the Lord your God with all your heart and with all your soul" (Deut. 10:12). The

Commandments spell out our debt of service to God; yet, in serving Him, we serve and bless others as well.

Pray for a spirit of obedience, so that you may honor the Lord with faithful service. ▦

WEDNESDAY

THE LORD'S DISCIPLES argued about who was the greatest, and they must have been humiliated when Jesus gave them the answer. "You know that the rulers of the Gentiles lord it over them, and those who are great exercise authority over them," He said. "Yet it shall not be so among you; but whoever desires to become great among you, let him be your servant. And whoever desires to be first among you, let him be your slave—just as the Son of Man did not come to be served, but to serve, and to give His life a ransom for many" (Matt. 20:25–28). From the world's perspective, the Christian life is upside down!

Those who would be greatest must be servant of all? And He who became our King had to die on a cross to pay our debt of sin? Yes, that's the way it works. Paul says, "God has chosen the foolish things of the world to put to shame the wise, and God has chosen the weak things of the world to put to shame the things which are mighty" (1 Cor. 1:27).

As you pray today, consider how God can develop a servant's heart in you. ▦

THURSDAY

HOW FORTUNATE WE are to serve a God who sees the heart and not simply the outer person! What if God determined our eternal destiny based on what anybody can see with their eyes? Unfortunately, that's what we seem to do much of the time. We're so conscious of outer appearances that we make snap judgments based on how attractive someone is, or how well they speak.

But God sees us by another dimension altogether: Samuel says, "For the Lord does not see as man sees; for man looks at the outward appearance, but the Lord looks at the heart" (1 Sam. 16:7).

But that raises another question. What does God see when He looks on your heart? Is it a giving heart, a heart of compassion, a servant's heart? Pray that it may be; and then strive to become the sort of man God wants you to be. Jesus says, "Blessed is that servant whom his master will find so doing when he comes. Truly, I say to you that he will make him ruler over all that he has" (Luke 12:43–44). Obedient service brings us nearer to Him. ▓

FRIDAY

THE IMAGE OF Christianity popularized by the secular media is one of a religion that is repressive, judgmental, and melancholy, with little fun and few liberties. But how far that is from the truth. Yes, we do give up the shallowness of self-indulgence, sensuality, and sin, but what we gain is so much greater. For Christ has taught us how to live at peace with our brothers here in this life, and peace with God forevermore. And the key to that kind of life is the work of transformation that Christ has accomplished in our hearts.

One of the most delightful things we see in new Christians is a desire to serve others. The message of redemption and forgiveness is so powerful that followers of Christ want to bless other people. And that is precisely what Jesus wants. Paul says, "For you, brethren, have been called to liberty; only do not use liberty as an opportunity for the flesh, but through love serve one another. For all the law is fulfilled in one word, even in this: 'You shall love your neighbor as yourself'" (Gal. 5:13–14).

Thank Him for the liberty He gives. ▓

WEEKEND

HEAR THESE WORDS of God to Moses: "For this commandment which I command you today is not too mysterious for you, nor is it far off. It is not in heaven, that you should say, 'Who will ascend into heaven for us and bring it to us, that we may hear it and do it?' Nor is it beyond the sea, that you should say, 'Who will go over the sea for us and bring it to us, that we may hear it and do it?' But the word is very near you, in your mouth and in your heart, that you may do it. See, I have set before you today life and good, death and evil, in that I command you today to love the Lord your God, to walk in His ways, and to keep His commandments, His statutes, and His judgments, that you may live and multiply . . . "

As you reflect on His Word today, hear His challenge: "And the Lord your God will bless you in the land which you go to possess. But if your heart turns away so that you do not hear, and are drawn away, and worship other gods and serve them, I announce to you today that you shall surely perish" (Deut. 30:11–18).

Would you pray for a servant's heart? ▤

Week 12
FLEXIBILITY

How come some fathers start out close to their children but, somehow, something happens, and their relationships with their children do not survive the journey to adulthood? During our research on fathering, we got the answer, but it was surprising: If we want to build relationships that will stand the test of time, we need to become *adaptable dads*.

How do we become adaptable dads? While doing the research for our books on fathering, we spoke with three dads who exemplified adaptability. Daniel's dad wasn't prepared for a baby with Down's Syndrome. With two grown children, the pregnancy itself had been a complete surprise. David consulted every expert he knew to find out what his new son's needs would be, and he decided to change whatever had to be changed to meet those needs. Today David works part-time, lives in a smaller house, and spends hours with his youngest son. They have a special bond. But it only happened because David put his son's needs first.

And that is the first key to being an adaptable dad: *Put your children's needs first.* That flies in the face of our culture's "me-first, take-care-of-yourself" value system. But it is the foundation for becoming an adaptable dad.

Fred talks about his own father with a sense of awe. He loved and respected his dad, but Fred isn't the same kind of dad his own father was. "My dad was from the old school where perfection was expected and . . . failure was punished. I decided I didn't want to be that kind of dad. I learned from his mistakes and from my own as a

WEDNESDAY

EVEN THOUGH WE try to maintain our composure and give the impression we're always on top of things, most dads have to admit they don't always know all the answers. We all make mistakes, but the biggest mistake of all may be pretending we don't make mistakes! Jack and Jerry Schreur offer this practical advice: Learn from your own mistakes, and those of others, and use them as practical examples in raising your kids.

In the Book of the Law, we discover that God was concerned that parents should teach children to know the truth. He said to Moses, "Gather the people together, men and women and little ones, and the stranger who is within your gates, that they may hear and that they may learn to fear the Lord your God and carefully observe all the words of this law, and that their children, who have not known it, may hear and learn to fear the Lord your God . . . " (Deut. 31:12–13).

God wants the best for us; pray that you'll know how to teach the best to your kids. ▤

THURSDAY

WE LIVE IN modern times, and things change so rapidly these days it's easy to get the idea we're old-fashioned and out of date. And if you don't feel that way on our own, your kids will certainly give you the idea! Flexibility, as the Schreurs say in their article, is a valuable asset for today's parents. But don't get the idea that means truth is flexible or that essential core values of Christian families have to change. Far from it! The point in being adaptable today is not to change your values, but to change your methods and models.

If your kids see that you care enough to come to them on their level, they're more likely to listen when you say, as Solomon said: "Hear, my son, and receive my sayings, and the years of your life will be many. I have taught you in the way of wisdom; I have led you in right paths. When you walk, your steps will not be hindered, and when you run, you will not stumble. Take firm hold of instruction, do not let go; keep her, for she is your life" (Prov. 4:10–13).

Pray for the wisdom to be a man of strong values and a flexible heart. ▤

FRIDAY

WE'RE ALL LOOKING for ways to build lifetime friendships with our children. Parents who are stern and unforgiving when their children are young will have a hard time staying in touch with them when they're grown. And parents who are irresponsible or careless with their kids will have even less hope of maintaining good relationships. The most important lessons we teach our children are the ones they take to heart; truth and wisdom shape the heart, and love helps them build those life-long habits that bring happiness, health, and joy.

The aging apostle John spoke to the early church as his children when he wrote to them: "My little children, let us not love in word or in tongue, but in deed and in truth. And by this we know that we are of the truth, and shall assure our hearts before Him. For if our heart condemns us, God is greater than our heart, and knows all things" (1 John 3:18–20). John's relationship with his flock can be a model for dads, too.

Pray that you will be able to teach your children the important things—the lessons of love—for this is what God approves. ▤

WEEKEND

COMPROMISE IS A dirty word in some circumstances; but for dads learning to get in touch with their kids, compromise doesn't mean giving up what you believe in.

Rather, it says that you're trying to see things through the eyes of your family in order to accomplish some important goals and objectives in the most compatible and agreeable way.

Think of the compromises that God has made for us—not in establishing the rules or in identifying essential truths, but in reaching out to us in ways we can understand. Again, John recognized the dynamic power of God's love when he said: "Behold what manner of love the Father has bestowed on us, that we should be called *children* of God! Therefore the world does not know us, because it did not know Him. Beloved, now we are children of God; and it has not yet been revealed what we shall be, but we know that when He is revealed, we shall be like Him, for we shall see Him as He is" (1 John 3:1–2).

Pray that you'll have the strength to bend without breaking, to be an adaptable dad. ▤

PERSISTENCE

IF THINGS GOT bad enough, would you leave your wife? What if a car accident left her with brain damage that wiped out her memory? I was in the back seat trying to rest a bad cold, and my wife, Krickitt, was driving near Gallup, New Mexico. A truck ahead of us was throwing smoke like crazy. By the time Krickitt realized he was going twenty-five miles per hour, she was on top of it. She swerved into the passing lane, clipping the truck's bumper, and was rammed from behind by a pickup following too close.

Our car flipped and rolled, and when we came to a stop Krickitt was silent. I was in major pain myself, cracked ribs, damaged lungs, a broken hand and nose, but nothing compared to Krickitt. It took twenty minutes to get help and forty minutes to pry her out of the car. When I saw her later in the emergency room I didn't recognize her. It was the ugliest sight I'd ever seen. Her head was as big as a basketball; her ears and lips were black and purple. I grabbed her limp hands and said, "We're gonna get through this. Don't you die on me." I began praying as they raced her to a waiting helicopter for the emergency airlift to Albuquerque.

After five days in intensive care, Krickitt stablized and was taken off life support. The nurses would say, "The pressure inside her brain is too high; it's going to kill her." I'd go with my in-laws and a couple of friends and start praying. Twenty minutes later the pressure would be lower. More than once, the staff was amazed at her improvements.

Her physical signs improved, but mentally, this was

not Krickitt. She had no memory of me or our life together. I learned that head trauma cases result in divorce more than 80 percent of the time. But I wasn't going to give up. My wife had always motivated me; now it was my turn to give 200 percent. The trouble was, I could make her move her muscles, but I couldn't do anything to repair her brain.

Those were the hardest months of my life. Krickitt didn't feel comfortable with me. Slowly, she began to accept what everyone told her—that she was indeed married to this guy in New Mexico—and five months after the crash she moved back to our apartment. She had no memories of me, so, on Valentines's Day 1996, I proposed again. She said yes, and on May 25, 1996, we repeated our vows. Krickitt's brother, a minister, said, "We're not here to perform a wedding. We're here rather to create a memory for Krickitt."

Inside Edition and *People* magazine told our story. Disney is making a movie about us, and they act as if I'm some kind of hero. I'm not. I'm a sinner saved like anyone can be. But I have learned, firsthand, the grace and courage that Christ extends to help us keep our vows. Only He can take a disaster like ours and redeem it for good.

—KIM J. CARPENTER WITH DEAN MERRILL

MONDAY

FOR ANYONE WHO has not been through a similar tragedy, Kim Carpenter's nightmare must seem like the worst experience imaginable. How does anyone cope with the kind of accident the Carpenters experienced? How does anyone hold on to their faith in God when the worst that could ever happen actually happens?

For Kim, waiting patiently for his wife's recovery was a long, painful, heartbreaking ordeal. In the Psalms, David describes a similar loss, saying, "I would have lost heart, unless I had believed that I would see the goodness of the Lord in the land of the living." His only hope after suffering tragedy was his belief that God is good, and sooner or later there would be relief. David says, "Wait on the Lord; be of good courage, and He shall strengthen your heart; wait, I say, on the Lord!" (Ps. 27:13–14).

Sometimes, we all have those dark nights, and we all need persistence to pull us through. Trust in the Lord with all your heart, and pray for the strength to endure. ▤

TUESDAY

SURVIVING THE CRASH, making it through the surgery and an endless batteries of tests, and then going through therapy forever wasn't even the worst part for Kim and Krickitt. After her memory loss, Kim's wife didn't know who he was, and there were times when she didn't especially like him. Rejected, humiliated, brokenhearted, Kim made an important decision. He could either blow it off and walk away from the marriage, or he could hold on in the confidence that God, who had always been faithful in the past, would make a way for them; and sooner or later, he decided, God would pull them through their difficult passage.

It was in such a time as this that God said to Isaiah, "Fear not, for I am with you; be not dismayed, for I am your God. I will strengthen you, yes, I will help you, I will uphold you with My righteous right hand" (Isa. 41:10). Isn't it gratifying to know that our God does see our distress and reach out His righteous hand to hold us up when we're wounded and alone?

Thank Him for His grace and His love for you. ▤

WEDNESDAY

THROUGHOUT HIS MINISTRY, the Lord taught His disciples the vital importance of persistence. Remember this passage from Luke? And Jesus said to them, "Which of you shall have a friend, and go to him at midnight and say to him, 'Friend, lend me three loaves; for a friend of mine has come to me on his journey, and I have nothing to set before him;' and he will answer from within and say, 'Do not trouble me; the door is now shut, and my children are with me in bed; I cannot rise and give to you'? I say to you, though he will not rise and give to him because he is his friend, yet because of his persistence he will rise and give him as many as he needs. So I say to you, *ask,* and it will be given to you; *seek,* and you will find; *knock,* and it will be opened to you" (Luke 11:5–9).

Perhaps no other Scripture makes the point so well: Ask . . . seek . . . knock . . . and it will be opened to you. We all must make the commitment to persist in the confidence that God will keep His Word.

Pray that God will strengthen your resolve for life's journey. ▤

THURSDAY

LIFE IN THE early church was often difficult, and by the end of the first century the Roman emperors unleashed fierce persecutions against the followers of Christ. Knowing what was in store for them, and having suffered many torments because of their faithful ministry, the apostles and preachers of that day made persistence and endurance a recurrent theme of their teaching.

The writer of Hebrews offers godly counsel, citing the words of the Law, "Therefore do not cast away your confidence, which has great reward. For you have need of endurance, so that after you have done the will of God, you may receive the promise: 'For yet a little while, and He who is coming will come and will not tarry. Now the just shall live by faith; but if anyone draws back, My soul has no pleasure in him'" (Heb. 10:35–38).

Let us take this lesson to heart. God delights in those who persist, against all odds, to do that which faith requires. Pray that you may make this teaching a part of your life. ▤

FRIDAY

WHEN DAVID CONSIDERED the nature of God and all the answers to prayer he had received in his adventurous life, his immediate reaction was to praise the Lord of heaven. "Oh, love the Lord, all you His saints!" he shouts. "For the Lord preserves the faithful, and fully repays the proud person. Be of good courage, and He shall strengthen your heart, all you who hope in the Lord" (Ps. 31:23–24).

David had fallen more than once, and he knew that any man who becomes vain and proud will have to answer to the Lord for his misdeeds. But those who remain faithful through adversity, who persist against all the odds in the confidence that God will provide an answer, will surely receive an eternal reward.

Kim and Krickitt struggled for years, fighting their emotions but holding onto the promises until the pieces finally began to fall into place. Today their tragedy is far from over, but they have a new life and new hope. They have renewed faith that has grown from Kim's persistent spirit.

Praise Him today as you consider the mercy of our God and King. ▤

WEEKEND

FOR EVERY ONE of us there will come a final day of reckoning. The Bible tells us that those who have been redeemed by the blood of the Lamb will receive their reward—the gift of eternal life. For those who rejected that free gift, however, there will also come a day of judgment and condemnation. "And behold," says the

Lamb in the Book of Revelation, "I am coming quickly, and My reward is with Me, to give to every one according to his work" (Rev. 22:12). There is great hope in those words. We all look forward to that day. But there is also great concern. In light of the judgment to come, how can we rest until we have shared the gospel with those who have not yet come forward to kneel at the cross?

As you think about God's unfailing mercy and faithfulness, let this be your calling: that you may reach others with the Good News, and that other lives will be saved because of your persistent witness.

Pray that God will show you how you can touch someone else with His love. And pray that He will empower you to serve. ▤

FOURTH

◀┄┄┄┄┄┄┄┄┄▶

QUARTER

Week 1
WORSHIP

I WAS INTRIGUED by a very strange fish in the aquarium in Pretoria, South Africa. I said, "Lord, that's the ugliest fish I have ever seen!" In a flash these words came to mind: *I didn't create it for you.* I thought of the words of Revelation 4:11: "Thou art worthy, O Lord, to receive glory and honor and power: for thou hast created all things, and for thy pleasure they are and were created" (KJV).

That insight has affected the way I think about my relationship to my Creator. I often remember the words of the Scottish runner, Eric Liddel, in the movie, *Chariots of Fire:* "When God made me, He made me fast. And when I run, I feel His pleasure." When a man grasps this beautiful insight, all of life becomes filled with meaning.

Another such insight came in a prayer seminar at our church in Pittsburgh. Every session began with two quotations: "Man's chief end is to glorify God and to enjoy Him forever," and less theological but just as basic, "The main thing is to keep the main thing the main thing." I like to relate these statements to worship. First, worshiping God ought to produce the purest and highest form of enjoyment. And second, it must always be the mainspring of a life lived in eternal relevancy—it *is* the main thing.

What is a worship service? What constitutes an act of worship? A review of Abraham's life reveals five important perspectives on true worship.

1. *Abraham recognized that God was in charge.*

238

He settled the question of who would be the focus of his worship and lived in that relationship.

2. *Abraham relinquished his own desires and demonstrated his willingness to do whatever the Lord called him to do.*

3. *Abraham ran to meet God (Gen. 18:2).* The scriptures refer to Abraham as the "friend of God," and this was the response of one who was eager to greet an honored guest. A hundred-year-old man running to meet his beloved Lord speaks volumes about the nature of their relationship.

4. *Abraham revered God.* He "bowed himself to the earth." In both the Old and New Testaments, the primary meaning for the word worship is the idea of prostrating one's self on the ground before a superior. Abraham expressed his worship without holding back; but in worship services today, often the most we do is bow our heads.

5. *Abraham, who had many servants, responded to God with the spirit of a servant,* even to the point of his willingness to offer his promised son, Isaac, as a blood sacrifice. Abraham's obedience would stand as the "highest expression" of worship—pleasing God—until Jesus Christ came. Jesus not only lived to please His Father, but He was the beloved Son who died to please Him.

Now, as we walk as Jesus did, we give the greatest expression of worship. This is the offering that becomes the "sweet-smelling savor" to God.

—JOSEPH GARLINGTON

MONDAY

"THE HEAVENS DECLARE the glory of God; and the firmament shows His handiwork. Day unto day utters speech, and night unto night reveals knowledge. There is no speech nor language where their voice is not heard. Their line has gone out through all the earth, and their words to the end of the world" (Ps. 19:1–4). What wonderful words of praise!

The psalms were written between 1000 and 400 B.C., by several different authors. Seventy-three of them were composed by David, forty-nine are anonymous, and many of the rest were written either by the king's chief musician, Asaph, or by temple singers known as the sons of Korah. Some of these verses are records of David's private thoughts, which include the hard lessons he learned when he struggled with various failings. But the majority are songs of worship and praise, exalting the name of the Lord, and calling the people of Israel to humble themselves in adoration of the Creator. Altogether, they give us a mighty instrument to glorify God.

Would you use David's words to praise your God and King? ≡

TUESDAY

BECAUSE THE LORD comes near to help us in our times of need, we sometimes forget the awesome majesty and power of His presence. Moses was reminded on Mt. Sinai that the mere sight of God would destroy him. God told him, "You cannot see My face; for no man shall see Me, and live" (Exod. 33:20). When Abraham came into the presence of God in the wilderness, he fell on his face. And when Daniel was approached by the angel of the Lord, his knees buckled and he fell to the ground.

When we're tempted to think of God as our celestial

buddy, we need to remember these words: "'For My thoughts are not your thoughts, nor are your ways My ways,' says the Lord. 'For as the heavens are higher than the earth, so are My ways higher than your ways, and My thoughts than your thoughts'" (Isa. 55:8–9). Though He is merciful and kind, we're told, "For the Lord is great and greatly to be praised; He is also to be feared above all gods" (1 Chron. 16:25).

As you pray, be thankful that this awesome God is a God of love. ▤

WEDNESDAY

IF WE ARE WISE, we will glorify God whenever we achieve any victory, knowing that it is the Lord who prepares our paths. When David's army conquered the Philistines and the legions of Saul, he raised a hymn of praise: "Then David spoke to the Lord the words of this song, on the day when the Lord had delivered him from the hand of all his enemies, and from the hand of Saul. And he said: 'The Lord is my rock and my fortress and my deliverer; the God of my strength, in whom I will trust; my shield and the horn of my salvation, my stronghold and my refuge; my Savior, You save me from violence. I will call upon the Lord, who is worthy to be praised'" (2 Sam. 22:1–4).

We need to be reminded that it is God, not man, for whom all things are created. It is God's glory, not ours, that should motivate us. To the question, "What is the chief end of man?" the Westminster Catechism says, "The chief end of man is to glorify God and enjoy Him forever." If we truly perceive God's glory, we will worship Him gladly and often. ▤

THURSDAY

TO UNDERSTAND THE nature of God, we must recognize two essential facts: First, He is a jealous God. He says,

"For I, the Lord your God, am a jealous God" (Exod. 20:5). Moses says, "For the Lord your God is a consuming fire, a jealous God" (Deut. 4:24). And Joshua warns: "You cannot serve the Lord, for He is a holy God. He is a jealous God. . . . If you forsake the Lord and serve foreign gods, then He will turn and do you harm and consume you, after He has done you good" (Josh. 24: 19–20). Our God will tolerate no competition.

But, second, He is merciful, and He desires to know us and to bless us. God assures Moses: "You will seek the Lord your God, and you will find Him if you seek Him with all your heart and with all your soul. When you are in distress, and all these things come upon you in the latter days, when you turn to the Lord your God and obey His voice (for the Lord your God is a merciful God), He will not forsake you nor destroy you, nor forget the covenant of your fathers which He swore to them" (Deut. 4:29–30).

Will you praise Him? ▤

FRIDAY

Two fascinating verses offer further insight into the nature of God. First, we read: "For the eyes of the Lord run to and fro throughout the whole earth, to show Himself strong on behalf of those whose heart is loyal to Him" (2 Chron. 16:9). Then David says, "The Lord looks down from heaven upon the children of men, to see if there are any who understand, who seek God" (Ps. 14:2). Isn't it amazing that God is actively looking for those who are loyal to Him?

In our reading, Joseph Garlington outlines five attributes of worship to be observed in the life of Abraham: his recognition of God's authority; his humility before God; his enthusiasm to know God; his reverence for God; and his obedience to Him. No wonder God referred to him as "Abraham my friend." If we know, as Hebrews says, that God is a rewarder of those who diligently seek Him, shouldn't we take every opportunity to give Him love and adoration?

Won't you pause now to worship Him? ▤

WEEKEND

FOR NEARLY FOUR thousand years before the time of Christ, the only way to worship Jehovah God was for the priests to prepare a special ceremony of fasting and humiliation, and for the people to assemble together in one place. At that time, the priests would offer up the blood of sheep and oxen on a massive stone altar specially prepared and consecrated for the purpose. The sacrament was incredibly complicated, long, and very costly.

But when Jesus came, to give His life as a ransom for many, the ancient ritual of sacrifice came to an end once and for all. For Jesus, our Messiah, was the perfect Lamb of God, sacrificed for the sins of the world. Jesus foretold the changes, saying: "But the hour is coming, and now is, when the true worshipers will worship the Father in spirit and truth; for the Father is seeking such to worship Him. God is Spirit, and those who worship Him must worship in spirit and truth" (John 4:23–24).

Thanks to Christ's sacrifice, we can worship God anytime, anywhere. What a privilege! Thank Him now for His matchless gift. ▤

SENSITIVITY

■■■■ A HEAVY DRINKER who worked two jobs during a
■■■■ good part of my childhood, my dad lived too
close to the edge to do more than survive. With a wife
and five kids, he felt the burden of responsibility and far
too few of the joys that came with it. Mom was the one
who cared for our needs, who made things better in the
middle of the night.

It wasn't that my dad was abusive; he wasn't. He just
wasn't *there,* either physically or emotionally. His lack of
involvement undercut my self-image and self-confidence
as a young girl. Although I desperately longed for
Dad's approval, my fear of him loomed larger than my
timid yearnings could conquer. When I became a
Christian, a similar long-distance relationship continued
with my heavenly Father. How could I trust Him when I
didn't understand just *how* a loving father acted?

Then I married Bob, a longtime friend-turned-
boyfriend. I was attracted to his quiet self-confidence
and kindness. He seemed to get along with everyone I
knew, from my university professors to my father and
brothers. He was at ease with *himself,* secure in his
manhood and his relationship with God.

Unlike my dad, Bob didn't bully his way into a conversation; he listened and weighed what was said. I
knew we could build a life together. I didn't realize that
the Lord had also chosen Bob to bring healing into my
life. After four years of marriage we decided to have a
baby, and Michael was born. I was a little frightened of
having children because I saw them as *my* entire
responsibility.

But Bob surprised me—bowled me over, really. He was eager to participate in *every* aspect of Michael's birth—childbirth classes, labor and delivery, and even changing messy diapers! For me that was the beginning of seeing real fatherhood in action. No act seemed too small, distasteful, or insignificant for Bob.

When our second child, Laura, came along, God began to reveal His fatherly love through my husband in an even greater way. Laura was a difficult baby, but Bob didn't seem to mind. As Bob fathered Michael and Laura, God the Father began to father *me*. I began to realize that good fathers don't ignore their children; they seek them out. Most of all, a loving father never sees his child as an embarrassment or a difficulty; he points the child out with delight and proudly declares, "That's *my* child!"

Bob is not perfect—and I don't expect him to be. But Michael and Laura know their daddy loves them no matter what his mood. As I saw Bob's patience with our children, it began to dawn on me: that's how Father God acts toward *me*. He doesn't just put up with me; He loves me with an everlasting love.

I now understand and experience the delight of the Father-daughter relationship myself. I have seen God's love revealed, and experienced the healing in His wings, because my husband loves our children.

—G. L. BEAVERSON

MONDAY

LIFE IS HARD, you only go around once, so get all you can get, you deserve it! How many times have you heard that litany? A modern godless society, driven by consumerism, greed, and carnal self-indulgence, makes little place for the love of family and obedient service to God. But the price men and women pay for those things can be devastating, and costly beyond belief. It destroys the hopes and dreams of our children, alien-ates wives and friends, and can heave our eternal soul into hell for eternity. So, is it really worth it?

Our Lord taught us a much better way. Paul says: "For the grace of God that brings salvation has appeared to all men, teaching us that, denying ungodli-ness and worldly lusts, we should live soberly, righteously, and godly in the present age, looking for the blessed hope and glorious appearing of our great God and Savior Jesus Christ, who gave Himself for us, that He might redeem us from every lawless deed and purify for Himself His own special people, zealous for good works" (Titus 2:11–14).

Open your heart to Him today. ■

TUESDAY

CONSIDER WHAT AN awesome sight it must have been for Peter and the disciples to have supper with the Master, to hear of His soon approaching betrayal, tor-ture, and death, and then for their teacher, the Son of God, the Messiah, to take a basin of water and a towel and go from man to man washing their feet. Peter flipped! He shouted, "No way, Lord! You're not washing *my* feet!" Jesus scolded Peter, then He explained what was going on.

He told them, "For I have given you an example, that you should do as I have done to you. Most assuredly, I say to you, a servant is not greater than his master; nor is he who is sent greater than he who sent him. If you know these things, blessed are you if you do them" (John 13:15–17). Jesus washed the men's feet to show them that every caring act, no matter how common, is an act of love approved by God. Yes, it's important that we earn a living, that we care for our families. But how much more important that we lead by our acts of love.

Pray that God will make you a model of love and

selfless devotion to your family. ▰

WEDNESDAY

THE WRITER OF this week's meditation made a life-changing discovery. Men of God care, and they share gladly in the joys, the daily dramas, and the duties of the home. What made Bill's example so different wasn't just the difference in behavior but in attitude. Bill had put his trust in God and celebrated each day as God's gift.

John says, "I have written to you, fathers, because you have known Him who is from the beginning. I have written to you, young men, because you are strong, and the word of God abides in you, and you have overcome the wicked one. Do not love the world or the things in the world. If anyone loves the world, the love of the Father is not in him. For all that is in the world—the lust of the flesh, the lust of the eyes, and the pride of life—is not of the Father but is of the world. And the world is passing away, and the lust of it; but he who does the will of God abides forever" (1 John 2:14–17).

As you speak to the Lord today, will you pledge to be a man of God to your family? ▰

THURSDAY

THERE ARE A few people around who worship statues and icons and man-made idols of various kinds. But the most dangerous idol men serve these days rides around in their hip pocket. Money, and the things it can buy, has become the god and the motivating principle of life for millions—to their own despair and eternal damnation. How very clever of Satan to lure us away from the one true God with such petty baubles. But it happens every day.

"We know that we are of God," John says, "and the whole world lies under the sway of the wicked one.

And we know that the Son of God has come and has given us an understanding, that we may know Him who is true; and we are in Him who is true, in His Son Jesus Christ. This is the true God and eternal life." And then the apostle declares with fatherly passion: "Little children, keep yourselves from idols" (1 John 5:19–21).

If we are truly in Christ, we know how to love; for He is love. And He promises us a crown of life if we overcome the world. Let's recommit ourselves to love as He loved us. ■

FRIDAY

GOD CARES ABOUT attitudes as much as behaviors. The Ten Commandments were given to Moses and the Israelites to provide a standard of law and order for the nation; but God also taught the people precepts of behavior that would provide a foundation for their personal relationships. Among the most fundamental teachings in the book of Leviticus are the words: "You shall not hate your brother in your heart. You shall surely rebuke your neighbor, and not bear sin because of him. You shall not take vengeance, nor bear any grudge against the children of your people, but you shall love your neighbor as yourself: I am the Lord" (Lev. 19:17–18).

The idea that a godly man should love God with all his heart and love his neighbors as himself didn't begin with the New Testament. The scribe in Mark 12:33 knew it because the teaching goes back to the time of Moses. The problem is that today, four thousand years later, we still fail so often.

Pray that your heart will be sensitive to model Christian love. ■

WEEKEND

THE HIGH PRIESTLY prayer that Jesus prayed in the hours

before His betrayal and crucifixion, recorded in John 17, tells us so much about the heart of our Lord. He came to teach us to love and to share our love with others. We should read it often so we will never forget the passion Jesus felt for us, and the purpose for which He so willingly gave His life.

We know that "God is love," and that Jesus was the visible expression of God's caring, sensitive Spirit. But we should not forget that we receive His gift of love when we show by our lives that we belong to Him. Jesus said, "By this My Father is glorified, that you bear much fruit; so you will be My disciples. As the Father loved Me, I also have loved you; abide in My love. If you keep My commandments, you will abide in My love, just as I have kept My Father's command-ments and abide in His love. These things I have spoken to you, that My joy may remain in you, and that your joy may be full" (John 15:8–11).

Those who serve gladly have real and lasting joy. Pray that you will always have a servant's heart. ▤

Week 3
FOCUS

My GRANDPA LEANED over his hospital bed and grabbed my hand. God had softened his heart over the previous three months, and my dad had the privilege of leading him to Jesus on the last lap of his life—after years of rejecting the Good News. "If I had a chance to live life all over again," he muttered softly, "I'd have listened to your dad a long time ago." Grandpa was the epitome of the self-made man. He may have been on the wrong track most of his life, but he crossed the right finish line!

How would you like your life to be summarized? If you could write your epitaph, how would it read? In his spiritual journey, the apostle Paul consistently had an eye on how his life would look at the finish line. He wrote, "Therefore I do not run like a man running aimlessly; I do not fight like a man beating the air" (1 Cor. 9:26). In other words, he had a fixed goal and was intensely focused on the prize.

To run with no eye on the prize is as useless as getting into the ring only to box air. For Paul, everything was for the sake of the gospel, so that he, too, might share in its blessings. What will you receive when your life is over? Will it be the prize God has prepared for you in Christ or something else?

Christian maturity (Christlikeness) is the result of passing the tests, the trials, and temptations of life by leaning into Jesus when we stumble. Christian growth is a process. We must give ourselves space and grace. But we must also run the race with a desire to win, focused on the prize.

The seven promises of Promise Keepers summarize our values and raise the standard for what it means to be a godly man. They're meant to guide us toward the life of Christ so that He, in a lifelong process, might transform us from the inside out. Promise keeping is a process, and it's vitally connected to a man's relationship with Jesus Christ.

What might happen if you focus on the prize and run the race with unswerving passion to win? What might happen if I make the same commitment? What might happen if thousands of other men join us? What about millions? What might happen if we all go the distance? I'll tell you one way to find out: Let's start with you and me.

Together, let's determine, by God's grace and strength, to go the distance and end well. With a clear conscience, I want to be able to instruct those who make my tombstone to have it read, like that of the Rev. Bunker Gay who died in 1815,

- Be thou faithful unto death
- And I will give thee a crown of gold.
- I have fought a good fight,
- I have finished my course.

—PETE RICHARDSON

MONDAY

IN THOSE FAMOUS verses in Romans 12, Paul calls believers to be transformed, and to let the reality of Christ living in our hearts make us into new men, with new hearts and new minds. As that process takes place, the focus of our hopes begins to change. We learn the value of each day, each person, and each opportunity to do a good deed. We begin to see the beauty of the creation with new eyes, and to feel new joy in the presence of our wives, children, and loved ones as we've never felt before. The old "pride of life" cannot possess our hearts any longer once we perceive the prize that's waiting ahead for the believer.

In Christ, we've had a total change of direction. Paul says, "Now we have received, not the spirit of the world, but the Spirit who is from God, that we might know the things that have been freely given to us by God. These things we also speak, not in words which man's wisdom teaches but which the Holy Spirit teaches, comparing spiritual things with spiritual" (1 Cor. 2:12–13).

Thank God for the miracle He has performed in your heart. ▤

TUESDAY

A RUNNER KNOWS he can't look over his shoulder without losing pace. If a running back keeps looking around, he'll never break free of the line. One of the most basic rules for any athlete is to "keep your eye on the goal, and don't look back." The one who wins the contest will be the one who stays in control, keeps his focus, and races for the prize.

This is the image Paul has in mind when he says, "Do you not know that those who run in a race all run, but one receives the prize? Run in such a way that you may obtain it. And everyone who competes for the prize is temperate in all things. Now they do it to obtain a perishable crown, but we for an imperishable crown. Therefore I run thus: not with uncertainty. Thus I fight: not as one who beats the air. But I discipline my body and bring it into subjection, lest, when I have preached to others, I myself should become disqualified" (1 Cor. 9:24–27).

If the Christian life is a lifelong process as Pete Richardson says, then pray that you will have the focus and the self-discipline to run the race with endurance.▤

WEDNESDAY

WE'VE ALL KNOWN someone who's hard as a rock. Maybe it was your dad, your grandfather, or some other person who lived a hard life and built a rock-hard shell around his heart. It happens to mothers sometimes. Loss, pain, and sorrow do that. Abuse can do it, too. For, as tough as we seem on the outside, we're fragile on the inside. And sometimes we let calluses form on our souls, as if that could protect us from the harsh realities of life.

But the harshest reality of all is an eternity in hell. If we have love in our hearts, it should be our greatest hope to share the love of Jesus with those who are perishing. The love of God can heal those old wounds, and believers have a mandate to be the hands and feet of Christ. When we focus on loving, and saving souls, we are the best evidence that God is love. Peter said, "Therefore, beloved, looking forward to these things, be diligent to be found by Him in peace, without spot and blameless; and consider that the longsuffering of our Lord is salvation" (2 Pet. 3:14–15). Pray for someone who needs Jesus today. ▤

THURSDAY

WALKING THROUGH A cemetery can be an eye-opening experience. Row after row of headstones and monuments mark the final resting place of those who've come and gone before us. For centuries, graveyards were commonly referred to as churchyards because people who were dying often asked to be buried close to the house of God so they'd be among the first to rise when the final trumpet sounds. As men and women walked by those cold, stone markers each week, they would be reminded of the realities of life and death. They would remember the sorrow of loss; but they were also taught to remember the hope of salvation and the resurrection of the dead. Inscriptions on the headstones, as this week's reading points out, often taught some important lessons. Too bad that old tradition has died.

Reflecting on such life lessons, Paul says, "For godly sorrow produces repentance leading to salvation, not to be regretted; but the sorrow of the world produces death" (2 Cor. 7:10).

Thank God today for the eternal joy that surpasses the brief sorrows of this life. ▤

FRIDAY

MATURITY IS NOT an overnight process. You don't go to sleep stupid one night and wake up wise the next morning! Rather, as Pete Richardson says, maturity comes through passing tests, trials, and temptations, then leaning into Jesus whenever we stumble. The good news is that our Lord is always there beside us to teach us, to challenge us, and to pat us on the back when we get it right. It was this companionship of God that David focuses on in Psalm 107.

"Oh, that men would give thanks to the Lord for His goodness," he sings, "and for His wonderful works to the children of men! Let them exalt Him also in the assembly of the people, and praise Him in the company of the elders. He turns rivers into a wilderness, and the watersprings into dry ground; a fruitful land into barrenness, for the wickedness of those who dwell in it. He turns a wilderness into pools of water, and dry land into watersprings" (Ps. 107:31–35).

God is good and greatly to be praised, correcting the foolish and blessing the faithful. As you focus on Him today, ask Him to guide you in the way you should go.▤

WEEKEND

SATAN IS ALWAYS lurking about, anxious to steal your joy and convince you of how bad things really are. The devil and his demons are never far away whenever a Christian man is beginning to make some important changes in his life. They bring up the old temptations; the old anger, bitterness, and jealousy; they bash you with bad memories of those who may have abused you or hurt you in some way. But we know this: "God is faithful, who will not allow you to be tempted beyond what you are able, but with the temptation will also make the way of escape, that you may be able to bear it" (1 Cor. 10:13).

The contest of wills between God and Satan will continue until the deceiver is finally cast into the lake of fire. In the meantime, we can focus on the prize and defeat the taunts of Satan through praise and worship of our Lord. In Revelation we read: "Do not fear any of those things which you are about to suffer. . . . Be faithful until death, and I will give you the crown of life" (Rev. 2:10).

As you pray, focus your heart on Christ who strengthens you. ▤

Week 4
PASSION

In 1958, AT twenty-three years old, Luis Palau was a rising executive in the Bank of London's Cordoba, Argentina, branch. His salary supported his mother and five sisters, but banking could never satisfy his passion to change the world. As he committed time to the Lord in the hope of following in his father's footsteps as an evangelist, nothing gave him more joy than telling people about Jesus.

Since then, about twelve million people have sat in stadiums, bullrings, and arenas around the world to hear Luis proclaim the gospel. In 1960 Luis came to America, thanks to the persistence of Ray Stedman, a California pastor who met the aspiring evangelist during a mission trip to Argentina. Stedman insisted that Luis receive formal theological study. Too impatient for four years of seminary, Luis enrolled in the one-year graduate program at Portland's Multnomah School of the Bible.

It was there that he met his wife Pat. Their oldest sons, twins Kevin and Keith, now thirty-four, were born in California less than a year before Luis and Pat were off to Latin America as missionaries with Overseas Crusades. Andrew, thirty-one, was born in Colombia, and Stephen, twenty-seven, in Mexico. Constant travel for the cause of Christ could have made Luis an absentee father, but all four sons say that wasn't the case.

Their father cultivated their ministry mind-set by taking at least one of them with him on most of his trips. Not surprisingly, all four Palau boys encountered typical teenage temptations to reject their father's example and go their own way. The twins and Stephen were saved as children and have hung onto their faith in Christ. But Andrew was another story. For several years, as Luis stood to preach to crowds of thousands, his heart was a caldron of emotions, knowing that one of his own sons was still not a believer.

The prodigal son returned in 1993. His parents had invited him to Jamaica during a crusade on the island. Andrew had come to fish for marlin; Luis had other fishing in mind. A businessman's testimony at the final meeting in Kingston reeled in the young man. Luis says those years of yearning gave him greater understanding of God's heart.

When Andrew returned, Luis shared with him a promise he claimed from the Lord twenty-five years before, when Kevin and Keith were five, Andrew two, and Stephen was on the way. In October 1968, Luis was preaching in Medellin, Colombia, but he felt loneliness and regret that he wasn't home in Mexico City with his family. The Lord gave him a Scripture verse to hold on to: "All your sons shall be taught by the Lord, and great shall be the prosperity of your sons" (Isa. 54:13, RSV).

Looking back on thirty years of evangelism, Luis says, "There is nothing more fulfilling . . . than doing the one thing that counts for eternity." And it's even better now that all four Palau sons share their dad's passion.

—MIKE UMLANDT

MONDAY

WHEN GOD PUTS a calling in a man's heart, He first gives him a passion for it. He prepares the way, ordains a spiritual anointing, then directs each step to lead him into his area of ministry. Think about this: More than seven hundred years before Christ, God prepared the heart of Isaiah as a prophet to the nations to prepare the way for Messiah. In one of many prophetic utterances, Isaiah declares: "The Spirit of the Lord God is upon Me, because the Lord has anointed Me to preach good tidings to the poor; He has sent Me to heal the broken-hearted, to proclaim liberty to the captives, and the opening of the prison to those who are bound; to proclaim the acceptable year of the Lord, and the day of vengeance of our God; to comfort all who mourn" (Isa. 61:1–2).

Though spoken by the prophet, these are the words of Christ, announcing the calling God ordained for His Son—bringing good news, healing, liberty, compassion, and repentance. If you truly want to know the heart of God, pray that He will give you a passion for the lost. ▤

TUESDAY

"WHATEVER I TELL you in the dark, speak in the light; and what you hear in the ear, preach on the housetops. And do not fear those who kill the body but cannot kill the soul. But rather fear Him who is able to destroy both soul and body in hell" (Matt. 10:27–28). When Jesus spoke these words to the disciples, He was preparing them for ministry. In fact, everything He taught them was designed to prepare them to carry the gospel to the ends of the earth. Peter wondered how much that Jesus taught was for the disciples' ears only, and how much of it was to be shared publicly. One time he said, "Lord, do You speak this parable only to us, or to all people?" (Luke 12:41). Jesus pronounced a blessing on everyone who obeys the will of God.

Most of us will never fill a stadium as Luis Palau has done so many times. Most will never speak to millions around the world or lead tens of thousands to Christ. But does that mean we only get a small part of the Great Commission? Not at all. We get it all, with the knowledge that Christ will bless our faithful obedience. Ask Him to help you to be faithful. ▣

WEDNESDAY

THE FACT THAT we are here, reading these words, and thinking about our walk with the Lord, is a tribute to all the saints and teachers who have gone on before us. Long before we were ever born—before our parents and grandparents or the founding of the nation—godly men and women, obedient to Christ's commands spread the gospel, one heart at a time.

We are their spiritual offspring. It is their faithful service, long forgotten, that made it possible for us to inherit eternal life. Today, they are our witnesses, observing our efforts to spread the Word. We get a sense of this spectacle in the challenge: "Therefore we also, since we are surrounded by so great a cloud of witnesses, let us lay aside every weight, and the sin which so easily ensnares us, and let us run with endurance the race that is set before us, looking unto Jesus, the author and finisher of our faith, who for the joy that was set before Him endured the cross, despising the shame, and has sat down at the right hand of the throne of God" (Heb. 12:1–2).

Let us thank God for our incredible inheritance! ▣

THURSDAY

THE ROOTS OF our faith don't go back to Sunday school, or to the Puritans who came to these shores from England and Holland. They go all the way through the Middle Ages to the foot of a cross on a hill called Golgotha. And, yes, they go even further, to the time and place in ages unknown when God determined to make a way to redeem mankind from the fallen world. The lust of the flesh and the wiles of Satan work against us.

The forces of darkness are eager to snatch us out of God's hands, but Paul offers the "blessed hope" that Satan can do nothing to take away our salvation. In one of the greatest chapters ever written, Paul asks, "Who shall separate us from the love of Christ? Shall tribulation, or distress, or persecution, or famine, or nakedness, or peril, or sword? As it is written: 'For Your sake we are killed all day long; We are accounted as sheep for the slaughter.' Yet in all these things we are more than conquerors through Him who loved us" (Rom. 8:35–37).

If our passion is great, God's is so much greater! Thank Him for His love. ■

FRIDAY

As MUCH AS he wants to destroy us, Satan wants our children too. He has spread his net in the schools, the media, the popular culture, and even our homes; and he poisons the very air our children breathe with wicked seductions. Just as Luis Palau did with his wayward son, we can claim the promises of God: "Believe on the Lord Jesus Christ, and you will be saved, you and your household" (Acts 16:31). We can trust Him for our children.

But Paul also warns us to be strong in the Lord, saying, "Now we exhort you, brethren, warn those who are unruly, comfort the fainthearted, uphold the weak, be patient with all. See that no one renders evil for evil to anyone, but always pursue what is good both for yourselves and for all. Rejoice always, pray without ceasing, in everything give thanks; for this is the will of God in Christ Jesus for you" (1 Thess. 5:14–18).

Then, having done all, we can stand "in the power of His might" (Eph. 6:10). That should be our godly passion.

Pray now that Christ will empower you to *stand.* ■

WEEKEND

THE LIFE OF FAITH is always challenging, always compelling, always stretching us to new limits. When we have mastered the basics of the faith, we discover other tests that call us back to the Word and to our knees. Consider, for example, the godly evangelists and teachers whose sons and daughters strayed from the faith, looking for answers. No doubt there are moments when even the strongest are weak and uncertain.

Paul knew moments of testing, but he determined to persevere. He says, "Brothers, I do not consider myself yet to have taken hold of it. But one thing I do: Forgetting what is behind and straining toward what is ahead, I press on toward the goal to win the prize for which God has called me heavenward in Christ Jesus. All of us who are mature should take such a view of things. And if on some point you think differently, that too God will make clear to you. Only let us live up to what we have already attained" (Phil. 3:13–16, NIV).

Thank Him now for all you've attained, and ask Him for renewed passion to go on.▤

Week 5
GENTLENESS

EVERY CHRISTIAN HUSBAND knows he should love his wife. But few really understand that it takes a radical kind of love to enjoy a truly healthy, happy marriage. Loving as Christ loves *is* radical. Picture it this way: Radical love is a finely-cut diamond with many sparkling facets. Let's consider four of these facets:

1. *Radical love is sacrificial.* Unlike the Hollywood image based on lust and selfishness, Christ's love is rooted in selflessness and sacrifice. We cannot love sacrificially in our own strength. By nature, we are jealous, envious, and boastful. We are proud, haughty, selfish, and rude, and we demand our own way. How long has it been since you showed sacrificial love to your wife? Think of ways you can "give yourself up" to her. Make a list. Then ask God by faith to help you love her sacrificially as Christ loved the church.

2. *Radical love takes the initiative.* Radical love is aggressive. It follows God's precept of "first love" (1 John 4:19). It reaches out in reconciliation even when she is least deserving. When Jesus sacrificed Himself on the cross for our sins, He did so by faith that we would respond to His redeeming love. He didn't wait until we were good—He loved first. If you are experiencing conflict, take the first step in reconciliation. Pray for her. Talk to her. And watch God work through you to calm the storm.

3. *Radical love is considerate.* Many couples

suffer needless turmoil because the husband is inconsiderate of his wife. The apostle Peter admonishes, "Husbands . . . be considerate as you live with your wives, and treat them with respect as the weaker partner and as heirs with you of the gracious gift of life, so that nothing will hinder your prayers" (1 Pet. 3:7, NIV). Over the years, I have learned to talk to my wife about our differences and to be more understanding of her needs and temperament. I have realized the Lord often speaks through her, so I listen to her viewpoint. Sometimes it's the little things that count most in being considerate. Like coming home from the office on time, or picking up after yourself. Going shopping with her also shows consideration.

4. *Radical love encourages development.* A considerate husband will encourage his wife to develop spiritually, personally, socially, and vocationally. A man who makes his wife his partner will find that they can achieve more together than either could separately. The only way to love as Christ did is to walk in the power of the Holy Spirit moment by moment as He did. Only He can enable you to have supernatural, unconditional, unshakable love for your wife.

If you forget everything else I have written, remember this: *You, more than your wife, are responsible for a healthy, happy marriage.* Follow the counsel in this article and you'll discover that you have a new wife. Your marriage can be a happy or miserable experience. That decision is largely up to you.

—BILL BRIGHT

MONDAY

TOUGH LOVE. Most of us know the term, but what does it

really mean? Basically, it's a Christian concept, which says that the more we ignore behavior problems the worse they become. Since we love our children and family, we hold them to high standards of behavior. Without love, toughness can be cruel; but without a firm commitment, love can be passive and irresponsible. Christ's own example sets a high standard, but with tenderness and humility—a life of profound personal integrity tempered by gentleness and patience.

Paul points to Christ as our model, saying: "Let nothing be done through selfish ambition or conceit, but in lowliness of mind let each esteem others better than himself. Let each of you look out not only for his own interests, but also for the interests of others. Let this mind be in you which was also in Christ Jesus" (Phil. 2:3–5). While calling men to obey all the commandments of God, Christ gave His life to purchase our salvation. There is no better example of "radical love."

Pray that God will develop this spirit of gentleness in you. ▤

TUESDAY

BILL BRIGHT COMPARES the aspects of love to a fine diamond with many facets. The first, he says, is that love should be sacrificial. In Ephesians we read, "Husbands, love your wives, just as Christ also loved the church and gave Himself for her, that He might sanctify and cleanse her with the washing of water by the word, that He might present her to Himself a glorious church, not having spot or wrinkle or any such thing, but that she should be holy and without blemish. So husbands ought to love their own wives as their own bodies; he who loves his wife loves himself" (Eph. 5:25–28).

Do these words describe your relationship? Do you love your wife with a love so real that she shines—literally glows—in your love? It's so important that you praise your wife. Thank her for sharing her life with you, and pray with and for her daily. Try it and see what happens to your relationship as you begin to fill her spirit with sincere affection!

Pray today that God will forgive your past failings and give you a radical new love for your spouse. ▓

WEDNESDAY

WHEN PEOPLE CHALLENGE men to be more aggressive, most of the time the point is not to make us more gentle and caring. The world expects us to be hard and ruthless; but that's not God's standard. The Bible teaches us to take the first step in loving others, taking no concern for our own well-being. It's not, "Do unto others *before* they do unto you." Christ teaches: "Do not seek what you should eat or what you should drink, nor have an anxious mind. For all these things the nations of the world seek after, and your Father knows that you need these things. But seek the kingdom of God, and all these things shall be added to you" (Luke 12:29–31). Or as Solomon advised, "*Be zealous* for the fear of the Lord all the day; for surely there is a hereafter, and your hope will not be cut off. Hear, my son, and be wise; and guide your heart in the way" (Prov. 23:17–19).

Loving others with a heart that is gentle is always a good idea; "for surely there is a hereafter." As you kneel before Him today, ask God to give you a kind and gentle spirit. ▓

THURSDAY

IN THE GREAT love chapter of 1 Corinthians 13, Paul sets a high standard regarding the nature of Christian love. He says, "Love suffers long and is kind; love does not envy; love does not parade itself, is not puffed up; does not behave rudely, does not seek its own, is not provoked, thinks no evil; does not rejoice in iniquity, but rejoices in the truth" (1 Cor. 13:4–6). If we learn to love like that, we will surely achieve Bill Bright's third facet: being considerate toward others. The only problem is human nature—sacrificial love can go to our heads, and before long we may slip back into some rather selfish thoughts.

Maybe that's why, in another famous chapter, it says, "Let love be without hypocrisy. Abhor what is evil. Cling to what is good. Be kindly affectionate to one another with brotherly love, in honor giving preference to one another; not lagging in diligence, fervent in spirit, serving the Lord; rejoicing in hope, patient in tribulation, continuing steadfastly in prayer" (Rom. 12:9–12).

Pray for a heart that is gentle and considerate. ▤

FRIDAY

DESPITE HIS bull-in-a-china-shop demeanor and his tendency to put his foot in his mouth, Peter was a compassionate husband who apparently understood the principle of encouraging our wives. He is one of the few disciples who was married during Christ's earthly ministry, and his home was always open, not only to Jesus but to others as well.

In his first letter, Peter instructed men to show respect for their wives as partners and fellow believers. "Husbands, likewise," he says, "dwell with them with understanding, giving honor to the wife, as to the weaker vessel, and as being heirs together of the grace of life, that your prayers may not be hindered" (1 Pet. 3:7). Peter was growing in knowledge, and we can be sure he was careful to see that his wife was too. In fact, the final words of his second epistle encourages all men to "grow in the grace and knowledge of our Lord and Savior Jesus Christ" (2 Pet. 3:18).

If you're not married, pray that you may see how

these principles apply to all your other relationships. But if you are married, pray for your wife. ▇

WEEKEND

IT HAS BEEN said before, but bears repeating: God created the institution of the family. It was, in fact, the first institution He created, and the one He designed as the cornerstone of society. If Christian families fall apart, then society will suffer. And if society is falling apart, it's probably because Christian families are not exerting appropriate influence.

In this light, the role of the husband and father is vital to the future of our nation. Men of God are called as leaders in their homes, with their children, in the church, and in the culture at large. That means, as some have loosely interpreted it, that charity should begin at home. Paul says, "But if anyone does not provide for his own, and especially for those of his household, he has denied the faith and is worse than an unbeliever" (1 Tim. 5:8). We are to provide material goods (as we are able), but also love, encouragement, and spiritual nourishment. Each family, then, will influence its neighborhood, community, and nation.

For this country to be all it can be, men of God must pray to become all we should be. ▇

Week 6

STEADFASTNESS

I'LL NEVER FORGET the phone call that shattered my world. "Rev. Lundstrom," the officer said, "I'd like to meet with you at the police station. Your daughter is under arrest for prostitution." My hands were trembling as I put down the receiver. I knew Lisa had been going through a spiritual struggle, but I never dreamed my seventeen-year-old would become a prostitute.

Ever since my wife and I enrolled in Bible college in the late 1950s, we had been singing and evangelizing. Our radio broadcasts, TV specials, and crusades led thousands to Christ. But somehow in the midst of the ministry activities I failed to see that Lisa was hurting. She felt "sandwiched" between her sister and brother. She was academically inclined and our audiences seldom applauded for her songs as they did for Londa's and Tiny's. But her inner anxieties were ticking away like a time bomb.

After appearing in court, I was given jurisdiction over her activities, but the situation was so explosive that almost immediately she was placed in a halfway house. And she soon escaped in the company of her pimp. To think that my daughter had chosen a pimp as her mentor, and rejected her father, was devastating.

Years earlier I made a deal with God. I said, "Lord, I'll give my life to help Your lost children get saved, but You must watch over my children and protect them from Satan." Now Lisa was gone, and I felt God had double-crossed me. Despite all this, I kept traveling and preaching three hundred nights a year, as I had for the previous twenty-six years.

One dark day when the demons of hell must have expected me to throw in the towel, the Holy Spirit spoke to my heart and said, "What did God do wrong, that the devil went bad?" Suddenly, a ray of hope burst through the darkness. Even though I had made mistakes as a father, I wasn't totally responsible for Lisa's actions. That revealing moment helped steady me, and my wife, Connie, encouraged me to keep going.

We maintained a tenuous link to Lisa through cards and gifts. She even came home one Christmas, but we knew her life was in danger. Then one night she made a call on a "customer" and discovered he was a serial killer who had already murdered eighteen women— Lisa was to be number nineteen. Silently, Lisa cried out, "O God, don't let me die like this!" The presence of God filled the room; then, in an amazing turn of events, the killer set her free and committed suicide.

God has done great things in our lives since that day. Lisa is home again, on fire for Jesus, and co-host of the *Lowell-Live!* radio broadcast. Thousands have given their lives to Christ because of Lisa's testimony, and I know beyond a doubt that our Father in heaven is faithful. To dads I say: Love your children! Spend time with them! And never, never, never give up!

—Lowell Lundstrom

Monday

"The statutes of the Lord are right, rejoicing the heart; the commandment of the Lord is pure, enlightening the eyes; the fear of the Lord is clean, enduring forever; the judgments of the Lord are true and righteous altogether. More to be desired are they than gold, yea, than much fine gold; sweeter also than honey and the honeycomb. Moreover by them Your servant is warned, and in keeping them there is great reward" (Ps. 19:8–11).

When young people from Christian homes go astray, it's usually not because they fail to understand what David says here in the nineteenth psalm. In their heart, they know God's Word is true; but for many other reasons, restlessness, disappointment, or rebellion rises to the surface, and they run away from God. When Lowell Lundstrom's daughter, Lisa, turned away, she was crying for attention but never meant to break her father's heart. Rediscovering the truth that God's judgments *are* more precious than gold, and that "in keeping them there *is* great reward" led her home again.

Pray that your family will always cling to God. ▤

TUESDAY

WHEN DAVID FELL into adultery, the entire kingdom of Israel came under judgment. The king not only complicated his own sin with lying and murder, but he pretended that his act of unbridled lust was acceptable for a man in his position. How often have we heard that story from Christian leaders who fall victim to various seductions? How often have we seen national and local political leaders found guilty of the same sort of behavior?

But when confronted with his sin, David was humiliated. He didn't try to beat the rap or plead innocence. He fell on his face and wept bitterly. He cried out to God. "Against You, You only, have I sinned, and done this evil in Your sight" (Ps. 51:4). His words resound throughout the ages: "Create in me a clean heart, O God, and renew a steadfast spirit within me. Do not cast me away from Your presence, and do not take Your Holy Spirit from me. Restore to me the joy of Your salvation, and uphold me by Your generous Spirit" (vv. 10–12).

Pray today for a steadfast spirit and the courage to avoid every appearance of evil. ▤

WEDNESDAY

NO ONE LIVES above sin. Though some pious saints are quick to point the finger at those who fall into sin, Romans 3 makes it clear that everybody has sinned. There, and in Psalm 14, we are told that there is *none righteous.* No, not one. But God is faithful and just, and offers a way of escape; and He hears our prayers of sincere repentance when we fall.

To silence any sanctimonious protests, Paul says, "And you, who once were alienated and enemies in your mind by wicked works, yet now He has reconciled in the body of His flesh through death, to present you holy, and blameless, and above reproach in His sight—if indeed you continue in the faith, grounded and steadfast, and are not moved away from the hope of the gospel which you heard" (Col. 1:21–23). Despite our failings, Christ has perfected the work of reconciliation. But when we've been restored, we are to be steadfast and unmovable in the faith. We aren't held to Christ's standard of righteousness; but through Christ we can be made new.

Pray that you may be steadfast and unmovable. ▤

THURSDAY

AS LOWELL LUNDSTROM sat alone in his study one evening, he felt the cold breath of Satan telling him what a miserable failure he was. A man of the cloth, and his own daughter had fallen into sin! But just as suddenly a voice from heaven said, "What did God do wrong, that the devil went bad?" The words didn't take away the responsibility he felt for his daughter's rebellion. They didn't change his anxiety to bring Lisa home for healing and restoration; but they did restore his confidence and help him to see the bigger picture.

The apostle John says that we can have confidence in our heavenly Father, knowing that He stands with us in our storms and stresses. "Beloved," he says, "if our heart does not condemn us, we have confidence toward God. And whatever we ask we receive from Him, because we keep His commandments and do those things that are pleasing in His sight" (1 John 3:21–22). After that night, the healing began for both Lowell and Lisa. And since that time, both have grown closer to each other and to the Lord. Praise God for healing words. ■

FRIDAY

DESPITE HER CHRISTMAS visit and infrequent phone calls, it was years before Lisa finally came home to stay. Lowell and Connie struggled with their fears and reached a point of almost giving up on their wayward child. Then God intervened.

No father would ever want his daughter held hostage by a crazed killer. Exploited, abused, threatened, and bound, Lisa was only moments away from a gruesome death when she cried out to God. Ever faithful, ever near, He heard that cry and sent strong delusion upon the mind of her would-be murderer. This is the assurance that we have of Him: "The Lord is near to all who call upon Him, to all who call upon Him in truth. He will fulfill the desire of those who fear Him; He also will hear their cry and save them. The Lord preserves all who love Him, but all the wicked He will destroy" (Ps. 145:18–20).

Do you know someone who has wandered away from God? Or have you faltered in your walk and need restoration and healing? Call upon Him in truth and He will hear you. ■

WEEKEND

HOW MANY THOUSANDS, ten of thousands, even millions of young men and women have taken the prodigal's path and walked away from family and friends? All over this land, at this very hour, millions are running away from the truth they once cherished. But take hope in this fact: Restored, renewed, cleansed from within, and reborn through repentance and obedience to God, Lisa came home to her fathers—the biological and the heavenly.

God hears our prayers and longs to grant our petitions. Sometimes, however, He uses our sorrows to heal old wounds. Sometimes He teaches us hard lessons that only years of pain and stress can instill. But He wants us to know that He is always there, and His truth has not changed. In Revelation, the spotless Lamb of God declares, "But hold fast what you have till I come" (Rev. 2:25). Despite the allure of the material world and the despair the devil uses to shake our resolve, our Redeemer has overcome sin, death, and Satan's power.

Oh, that men would give thanks for His wonderful works to the children of men! ▤

PRAISE

IN RESEARCHING MY BOOK, *Men in Search of Work and the Women Who Love Them,* I learned how common it is for a man to place his job at the center of his identity. But when the job is gone—when he's been downsized, asked to accept early retirement, or terminated—he is often devastated. But a Promise Keeper does not place his identity solely on his job. He is foremost a man of God. He has a clear sense of purpose for his life.

My husband is a true partner who puts his family before his job or his own pleasure. But I know plenty of women who aren't in the same boat. They try to manage in spite of a husband who hasn't a clue what's really going on in the lives of his family.

A man who is committed to leading and loving his family brings freedom and life. One medical student told his wife, "God is first in my life. I will not sacrifice my relationship with Him or with you for medical school, even though what I want most is to become a physician. If I can't make it God's way, I will drop out. There is no eternal value in medical school."

In fact, this man did quit medical school; the cost for him and his family was too great. Though his dream died, he has great peace about the decision. His wife and new baby will reap the rewards for years to come.

We have seen the effects of absentee fathers and irresponsible men on our society. But what will happen as this trend is reversed, as men take up the mantle of responsibility and loving leadership that God intends? Knowing our God of grace who is so eager to bless and reward faithfulness, I imagine homes that nurture children who will know right from wrong, who will love themselves, and know how to reach out to others.

I envision wives being freed to use their gifts to reach out to a dying world instead of frantically trying to be both mother *and* father to their children. I see girls who don't need to look for "love" through promiscuous behavior, but who possess self-respect and a clear vision of a future. I see boys who will learn what it means to be a man through daily contact with a father, rather than media images of violent cartoon caricatures. And I see a culture that can rebuild itself on a foundation that will not collapse when storms hit.

In our secular culture, the women's movement has been trying to convince men that women don't need them. Don't believe it. We women need our men. Our children need our men. Our culture needs our men. We need men who hear and heed the call of God. I praise God for the men who vow before Him to be men of integrity. If anything contains the power to turn our culture around, this is it.

—DIANE EBLE

MONDAY

IT IS OFTEN TRUE that men take their sense of self-worth from their jobs. Unlike their wives, who tend to find fulfillment through their husbands, families, and other personal relationships, men identify with their work and ride a crest of emotion that parallels closely their level of success or failure on the job. Perhaps it's little wonder that a lost job can crush a man's confidence; but shouldn't we be looking elsewhere for meaning in life?

Realizing that our emotions can suffer through failure, trials, and persecutions, Peter says, "In this you greatly rejoice, though now for a little while you may

275

have had to suffer grief in all kinds of trials. These have come so that your faith—of greater worth than gold, which perishes even though refined by fire—may be proved genuine and may result in praise, glory and honor when Jesus Christ is revealed" (1 Pet. 1:6–7, NIV).

Whether you've been threatened for sharing your faith on the job, fired, or downsized, God promises to uphold you through every trial. Would you thank Him for being there in your time of need? ■

TUESDAY

KEEPING A BUSY schedule, taking care of all your work and church commitments, or simply staying ahead of the tax man can sometimes be more than a guy can handle. Throw in a dose of self-pity or pride, and you become impossible to live with. Children need their fathers all the time; our wives look to us for understanding, love, and communication; and friends and family also need what we have to offer—including time and attention. Suddenly the old attitude starts acting up; and, unless something breaks the cycle, we can explode.

That's why you need a daily walk with the Savior. Talk to Him as a friend, share your heart, tell Him your hopes and fears, and get some help. Paul admonishes: "Be kindly affectionate to one another with brotherly love, in honor giving preference to one another; not lagging in diligence, fervent in spirit, serving the Lord; rejoicing in hope, patient in tribulation, continuing steadfastly in prayer; distributing to the needs of the saints, given to hospitality" (Rom. 12:10–13).

Practice patience. Practice praise. Pray for inner peace. ■

WEDNESDAY

YOUR FRIENDS DRIVE beautiful cars, and those who get ahead all have beautiful homes. They all dress right, wear the right jewelry, and jet off to exotic vacations in all the right places. But there you are. Time for a reality check? God says you're to be responsible for the welfare of your family, but He never asks you to be rich! "A faithful man will abound with blessings," the Bible says, "but he who hastens to be rich will not go unpunished" (Prov. 28:20). So why are you chasing material success and neglecting the important stuff?

"And this I pray, that your love may abound still more and more in knowledge and all discernment, that you may approve the things that are excellent, that you may be sincere and without offense till the day of Christ, being filled with the fruits of righteousness which are by Jesus Christ, to the glory and praise of God" (Phil. 1:9–11).

When you see God, He won't check your bank account. He cares for your soul. Is that your priority? Are you after the right stuff? Praise Him, and pray that you may be focused on the fruits of righteousness. ▤

THURSDAY

WHAT IMPACT COULD you have on your family if you were truly God's man? What could your children become if they had your undivided attention at those important times when they really need Dad? What changes would take place in your wife's heart and mind if you made it a priority to encourage and love her— despite her weaknesses, and yours!—and if you made a solemn pledge to build the confidence and esteem of each of these loved ones that God has given you? What would it do to your home? What would it do to you?

The apostle says that honor is a two-way street. "'Honor your father and mother,' which is the first commandment with promise: 'that it may be well with you and you may live long on the earth.' And you, fathers, do not provoke your children to wrath, but bring them up in the training and admonition of the Lord" (Eph. 6:2–4). More than any other responsibility you have, your family deserves your honor.

As a father, you're to be honored; but you also need to give honor and praise to others. Pray for the wisdom to live like that. ▨

FRIDAY

MOST OF US don't need any help creating tensions in this world. There seem to be armies of people whose only goal is stirring up trouble. Take the women's movement . . . please! For decades militant feminists have been shaking up the traditional family, beating up on men, preying on women, and sowing seeds of dissension. Unfortunately, we don't need any help breaking up homes; the numbers say we do that pretty well ourselves! What we do need is love and reconciliation. And, fortunately, that's what God wants too.

The writer of Ecclesiastes says, "Live joyfully with the wife whom you love all the days of your vain life which He has given you under the sun" (Eccl. 9:9). With God's help and a commitment to keep your marriage and family intact, even life's hardships and curses can be turned into blessings. God says, "The Lord your God turned the curse into a blessing for you, because the Lord your God loves you" (Deut. 23:5).

If we can learn the lesson of praise, and continually seek the face of God, our homes will begin to flourish with love. ▨

WEEKEND

PRAISE BEGINS IN the heart. David sang, "Make a joyful shout to God, all the earth! Sing out the honor of His name; make His praise glorious. Say to God, 'How awesome are Your works! Through the greatness of Your power Your enemies shall submit themselves to You. All the earth shall worship You and sing praises to You; they shall sing praises to Your name.' Come and see the works of God; He is awesome in His doing toward the sons of men" (Ps. 66:1–5).

The psalmist had seen God's faithfulness, His forgiveness, His hand of blessing, and he could not restrain his praise. David had felt the Father's hand of blessing so many times, how could he help but trust Him? But isn't that our story as well? He always comes through. And if we know that, shouldn't we extend a father's hand of blessing to those we love? For God not only makes men accountable, but He gives us the privilege of blessing others in His name.

Bless your wife, your children, and your family. Pray for them, and receive a blessing. ▤

CAUTION

As a man, you make mistakes. You can't avoid them all, but you don't have to make the most costly ones. If you wish to succeed in life, you need to know that "mistakes of the heart" can be deadly and should be avoided at all costs.

1. *Blind ambition.* The blindly ambitious are isolated, trapped in self-involvement. There is nothing wrong with ambition, but when it drives you beyond the line of humane treatment and integrity, it destroys you. The only way to bring ambition into check is to become accountable to another person and listen to the truth about yourself. This is the first step to true greatness.

2. *Manipulation of people.* Manipulators produce temporary results. Instead of building a team, they have a divide-and-conquer strategy. In families, manipulative people can be abusive. In companies, they cause poor morale and disloyalty. But manipulators can become motivators. If they do, they will benefit just as much as the people they work with.

3. *Pride.* Pride stands in the way of teamwork because it alienates rather than unites. Two heads are nearly always better than one, and teams succeed where individuals fail. Today's new wave of management is not a prideful empire, but a humble system of servant leaders motivating followers to greatness.

4. *Shame.* In some families shame is used as a

means of control where children learn early in life that they are unworthy of good things. Whether our families made us overly sensitive to shame or not, all of us have things in our past we wish weren't there. The first thing we have to understand is that we aren't able to keep all the rules, but God has chosen to forgive us and love us anyway. As Christians, we believe the price of our shame was paid by Jesus. Accept God's forgiveness and move on.

5. *Fear.* No one is free from fear, but some individuals respond to it courageously. Others cower in its face and are immobilized. Much of our fear has to do with how we appear to others. And the fear of failure is far more detrimental to our careers than actual failure could ever be. Don't be afraid of failing. Instead, keep your eyes on the opportunities before you, and pray for the courage to keep moving forward.

6. *Lust.* People with major lust problems usually have major ego problems. Their self-hatred is tempered by flattering romantic or sexual involvements. They get caught in the lust trap by searching for someone to assure them they're not as unlovable as they feel. Don't fall for this old ploy that has dashed so many lives.

7. *Laziness.* Overcoming laziness involves the one thing a lazy person doesn't want: work. You need to work at finishing a job and make a plan of action to change lazy behavior so you can live up to your God-given potential.

If you are struggling in any of these areas, know that with God's help you can change and win!

—STEPHEN ARTERBURN

MONDAY

AS MEN OF GOD, we don't want to be headstrong and

cocky. That's the world's approach much of the time. On the other hand, we can't be so timid and shy that we let things slide or miss important opportunities when they come along. We need to be involved, and we need to speak out, but we also need to speak with caution. Solomon offers some sage advice, saying: "He who has knowledge spares his words, and a man of understanding is of a calm spirit." Then, humorously, he says, "Even a fool is counted wise when he holds his peace; when he shuts his lips, he is considered perceptive" (Prov. 17:27–28).

Some people think the best way to avoid mistakes is to do nothing. But experience teaches that those who are willing to risk failure are the ones most likely to achieve success. Instead of being filled with fear, they go forward in faith. Yes, we'll make mistakes along the way, but we can remember the principles of faith, to keep our emotions under control, and pray that God will give us authority over those "mistakes of the heart." ▤

TUESDAY

THE BUSINESS WORLD thrives on greed and ambition. Every Wall Street image flatters the notion that to be a real success in life you have to be ruthless, acquisitive, driving, and blindly ambitious. But, as Stephen Arterburn says in this week's reading, that's a sure-fire recipe for disaster in the kingdom of God. Paul says, "Let nothing be done through selfish ambition or conceit, but in lowliness of mind let each esteem others better than himself. Let each of you look out not only for his own interests, but also for the interests of others" (Phil. 2:3–4). What a better world it would be if we could all live like that.

As we have seen repeatedly throughout this study, a new man—a man who has experienced forgiveness and who has the love of God in his heart—knows that there's a lot more to life than personal gain. Jesus said, "Life is more than food, and the body is more than clothing" (Luke 12:23).

What matters in the long run is how we live each day, and how we honor our Savior and King. Pray that God will help you make wise choices each day. ▤

WEDNESDAY

THERE IS NOTHING less flattering to a man than pride and arrogance. Pride never looks out for others because it is focused entirely on its own goals and ambitions. Pride steps on people, abuses them, and mocks godly behavior. Pride is the sin that God condemns more passionately and more consistently than any other, for it was Satan's sin. Pride and shame go hand in hand. Solomon says, "When pride comes, then comes shame; but with the humble is wisdom. The integrity of the upright will guide them, but the perversity of the unfaithful will destroy them" (Prov. 11:2–3).

When you think of the men you admire most, chances are it will be those who were gentle, kind, humble, and considerate of others. It's not the powerful and ambitious we most admire, but those with quiet dignity. They're the ones who really make a difference in people's lives.

As you consider your Christian walk in light of the "mistakes of the heart," pray that you will be a man after God's heart and not just another power-hungry hustler. ▤

THURSDAY

THE MAN WHO falls for the world's values will constantly be chasing after illusions. There will always be something bigger, better, more exciting, and more fulfilling that what he already possesses. His possessions will not satisfy him; his job will never be good enough; and his wife will lose her appeal. Sooner or later, he'll be looking for a fill-in, and then a trade-in, until the process of systematic self-destruction becomes unavoidable.

The New Testament stresses the importance of faithfulness, saying, "Marriage is honorable among all, and the bed undefiled; but fornicators and adulterers God will judge. Let your conduct be without covetousness; be content with such things as you have. For He Himself has said, 'I will never leave you nor forsake you.' So we may boldly say: 'The Lord is my helper; I will not fear. What can man do to me?'" (Heb. 13:4–6).

With God on our side, there is no need to fear. We can have peace with God, and love that lasts forever. Pray that the Lord will make you grateful for what you have. ▤

FRIDAY

DILIGENCE AND PERSISTENCE are habits that require thought and determination. We know they're important characteristics of the Christian life, not just because we've studied them in this devotional, but because they're recommended in many places in Scripture. What we may not realize, however, is that laziness is also a habit that requires persistence. It's an attitude some people cultivate over many years, not because it leads to success, but because it allows them to avoid making choices or doing anything that involves work.

The Bible condemns sloth and laziness from beginning to end. Solomon says, "The soul of a lazy man desires, and has nothing; but the soul of the diligent shall be made rich" (Prov. 13:4). Further, "Laziness casts one into a deep sleep, and an idle person will suffer hunger. He who keeps the commandment keeps his soul, but he who is careless of his ways will die"

(Prov. 19:15–16). And Paul says, "If anyone will not work, neither shall he eat" (2 Thess. 3:10).

One of the "seven deadly sins," laziness destroys lives. Pray you may avoid it. ▤

WEEKEND

A NEW MAN IS one who understands the risks of life in this modern age and has made a conscious effort to be prepared and girded with spiritual armor to defend what God has given him. He knows the wisdom in Paul's teaching: "See then that you walk circumspectly, not as fools but as wise, redeeming the time, because the days are evil" (Eph. 5:15–16). And he treasures the personal relationships in his life.

Whether married or single, and whether or not he is a father, a new man has taken precautions to avoid the "mistakes of the heart" that can wreck our relationship with God and those we love. And he receives this counsel: "Above all else, guard your heart, for it is the wellspring of life. Put away perversity from your mouth; keep corrupt talk far from your lips. Let your eyes look straight ahead, fix your gaze directly before you. Make level paths for your feet and take only ways that are firm. Do not swerve to the right or the left; keep your foot from evil" (Prov. 4:23–27, NIV).

Pray that in God you will be a new man in Christ. ▤

IT WAS SUNDAY, March 5, 1938. President Roosevelt had attended services at St. John's Episcopal Church, seeking divine guidance as head of the nation. With a country recovering from a terrible depression and standing at the brink of another world war, he opened his press conference in a way that startled reporters: "I ask that every newspaper in the country print the text of the fifteenth psalm. There could be no better lead for your story."

Historians may argue whether FDR's politics and his New Deal were right for America, but his proposal on that spring day was right on. God's message, crafted by King David in Psalm 15, isn't just a nice quote—it's a blueprint for living a godly, rock-solid life in difficult times. It begins with a crucial question, then offers ten key principles for the man of God. If you have ever wondered what a Promise Keeper should look like, here it is.

The psalm begins with the question: "O Lord, who may abide in Thy tent?" (v. 1, NAS). An amplified translation might say, "Lord, who can pitch his tent and dwell with You, day by day, here on earth?" In the second question, the psalmist asks, "Lord, who can dwell with You in heaven as well?" We know, of course, that the one who can dwell with God on earth and in heaven is someone who has made a personal commitment to Jesus Christ, asking God to forgive them of sin, cleanse their hearts, and be their Savior and Master all the days of their life. Once you have answered that question for yourself, you can look at David's ten principles for a godly, rock-solid life.

The first three are challenges: "He who walks with integrity, and works righteousness, and speaks truth in his heart" (v. 2, NAS). Walking with integrity means we are men who refuse to compromise or cut ethical corners under stress. Integrity, righteousness, and truth are the key traits of a rock-solid foundation. The next three traits in the passage call us to refrain from slander, from doing evil against our neighbors, or reproaching others with our tongue (v. 3). Then, the last four reflections instruct us on whom we should honor, and how we're to treat others in the way we make commitments and use our money (vv. 4–5).

David begins by challenging us to honor those worthy of honor: High respect should go to those whose lives reflect godly conduct and commitments. Sports or business figures who may light up the scoreboard—but who have godless characters—are to be counted as worthless in comparison with God's leaders.

Listen to David's closing words: "He who does these things will never be shaken" (v. 5, NAS). What a promise! No lawyer language here—it's backed with the full force of almighty God. Looking for a life-changing challenge? Now that you have been introduced to Psalm 15, why not dig into it yourself? You can waste time on a hundred things, but you'll never waste one minute learning and practicing God's blueprint for an unshakable life.

—JOHN TRENT

MONDAY

THROUGHOUT HIS LIFE, David trusted God completely and never wavered in that hope. It was his courage and confidence that gave him victory over Goliath when Saul's brawny warriors cowered in fear. Yes, he suffered at the hands of his enemies, and we can virtually feel his anguish in his psalms and prayers whenever God was silent for long periods of time. But David had a heart fully committed to God, and God, in turn, had a heart for him.

Hear the words of his first psalm: "Blessed is the man who walks not in the counsel of the ungodly, nor stands in the path of sinners, nor sits in the seat of the scornful; but his delight is in the law of the Lord, and in His law he meditates day and night. He shall be like a tree planted by the rivers of water, that brings forth its fruit in its season, whose leaf also shall not wither; and whatever he does shall prosper" (Ps. 1:1–3). What a great word of hope for a new man! If Psalm 15 offers rock-solid counsel for times of stress, David's first psalm gives a profound sense of security and trust. Thank the Lord your security is in Him. ▤

TUESDAY

IT'S EASY ENOUGH to be a godly man when everything's going your way, and when all your battles result in victories. And it's easy to preach at others when, through no merit of your own, you've managed to dodge the really hard blows. But the test of a man is how he behaves when the going gets tough. How does he react when his job gets axed? What does he say when his cherished hopes and plans fall through? What words come from his lips when the car breaks down or he bangs his shin on the coffee table? Or, even more to the point, how does he react when death claims someone he loved more than life itself?

David prays, "Keep my soul, and deliver me; let me not be ashamed, for I put my trust in You. Let integrity and uprightness preserve me, for I wait for You" (Ps. 25:20–21). Those words say a lot about what life can do to a man. David had seen his share of sorrow by that point, but he decided to wait upon the Lord. When integrity and honesty were all he could muster, still he trusted God. Praise God that He is always trustworthy.▤

WEDNESDAY

AS SHEPHERD, SOLDIER, WARRIOR, and king, David witnessed every trick the mind of man can conceive. His own sons turned against him. Absolom tried to kill him. The king he sang to sleep night after night, whom he had faithfully served for years, sent thugs to take his life. David wept over such treachery, and he begged for relief from his sorrows.

In one prophetic utterance, David cries, "My God, My God, why have You forsaken Me? Why are You so far from helping Me, and from the words of My groaning? O My God, I cry in the daytime, but You do not hear; and in the night season, and am not silent" (Ps. 22:1–2). Yet, in the very next verse, David says, "But You are holy, enthroned in the praises of Israel." And before the end of the psalm, he says: "I will declare Your name to My brethren; in the midst of the assembly I will praise You. You who fear the Lord, praise Him!" (vv. 22–23). His opening words—which, a thousand years later, would become the last words of Christ on the cross—echo down the ages. Would you worship this God and King? ▤

THURSDAY

THE PRICE OF INTEGRITY is high. Any man who has paid his taxes faithfully, admitted his mistakes, or apologized for hurtful words knows how costly it can be to always do the right thing. So costly, in fact, that a growing majority of people no longer consider honesty and integrity worth the effort. After much debate, the national consensus seems to be that character does *not* count. But morality and integrity before God aren't determined by opinion polls or popularity contests. We can only imagine what today's pundits and false prophets will say for themselves when they give an account for their lives to a holy God.

Samuel records David's victory song in which he says, "With the merciful You will show Yourself merciful; with a blameless man You will show Yourself blameless; with the pure You will show Yourself pure; and with the devious You will show Yourself shrewd. You will save the humble people, but Your eyes are on the haughty, that You may bring them down" (2 Sam. 22:26–27). Character *does* count with God, and men of God will always strive to please Him. ≣

FRIDAY

THROUGHOUT SCRIPTURE we are advised not to worry or to fear what the future may bring. Jesus said, "Do not worry about tomorrow, for tomorrow will worry about its own things" (Matt. 6:34). There will be more than enough to concern you when tomorrow comes, He said, so live in peace. Thanks to modern science, we now know how true that is. Seventy years ago the number-one cause of disease in this country was bacterial infection. Today, however, the leading cause of disease is emotional stress.

Dr. David Larson, M.D., has chronicled in great detail the fact that mature faith in God really is the best medicine. More than pharmaceuticals, surgery, psycho-analysis, or rest in bed, faith brings healing and peace of mind. Isaiah says, "The work of righteousness will be peace, and the effect of righteousness, quietness and assurance forever. My people will dwell in a peaceful habitation, in secure dwellings, and in quiet resting places" (Isa. 32:17–18). Even when stress seems unavoidable, God gives security to those who trust in Him. ≣

WEEKEND

NO MATTER HOW HARD we try, sooner or later we all stumble. God doesn't disown us when we do, but, like any father, He uses punishment to teach us lessons we can't learn any other way. In a *Saturday Evening Post* interview, former coach Lou Holtz talked about the uses of discipline at Notre Dame. "We ask three questions," he said. "Will it make him a better man? A better student? A better athlete? If the answer is yes, we make him do it."

But the next step, Holtz says, is up to the player: Either he can get bitter or he can get better. Hebrews offers a similar word: "If you endure chastening, God deals with you as with sons; for what son is there whom a father does not chasten? But if you are without chastening, of which all have become partakers, then you are illegitimate and not sons. Furthermore, we have had human fathers who corrected us, and we paid them respect. Shall we not much more readily be in subjection to the Father of spirits and live?" (Heb. 12:7–9).

As you speak to Him today, thank the Father for the security of His unbending love. ▰

Week 10
Fun

CREATIVITY MEANS PUTTING THINGS together with imagination and skill to produce newness. A guy who's striving for maturity in his character brings creativity to work and play. He holds onto his boyish enthusiasm, encouraging and motivating others. At the same time, he's diligent, working hard and playing hard, not just at the stuff he enjoys but at the stuff that's important. A creative joy finds the fun in what needs to be done.

During our first tour of potty training, my wife read somewhere to use Cheerios to potty train little boys. That made little sense to me, and I suggested candy would make a better bribe. Beth informed me that the Cheerios weren't to eat: They were to motivate little boys to "hit the target," making potty training a fun game instead of a battle of wills. The solution worked wonderfully until the day our youngest started eating the Cheerios!

Creativity's power to combine enthusiasm and diligence isn't limited to parenting, however. It can liven up a marriage, too. Shortly after we moved into our first house, we were confronted with the task of waxing our wooden floors. After applying the wax, we found the instructions about buffing. We didn't have an electric buffer, so we got four or five old T-shirts and started to rub. Then it hit me. I went into the next room and turned on some upbeat music, jumped back into the kitchen, and invited my Cinderella to her feet. I offered her two T-shirt slippers and we started to dance. We have an electric buffer now, but sometimes we get the

292

T-shirts out and do some touch up whether the floor needs it or not.

When Jesus was faced with the task of feeding the five thousand, He creatively showed how diligence and enthusiasm can be combined. He went about it almost playfully. He sent His diligent, task-oriented disciples into the crowd to find an enthusiastic, fun-loving boy. What fun there must have been in seeing that boy's lunch multiply!

It's a creative approach to our work and play that gives the boy in us enthusiasm for what the man in us diligently needs to do. Finding that fun in what needs to be done is the key to demonstrating maturity in this most public character area, and anyone who sees or shares in our work or our play will benefit when we do.

Don't just take my word for it. Jesus said to His disciples, "The kings of the Gentiles exercise lordship over them, and those who exercise authority over them are called 'benefactors.' But not so among you; on the contrary, he who is greatest among you, let him be as the younger, and he who governs as he who serves" (Luke 22:25–26).

Creativity can balance enthusiasm and diligence in work and play. "Whatever you do, work at it with all your heart, as working for the Lord . . . It is the Lord Christ you are serving" (Col. 3:23–24, NIV).

—NATE ADAMS

MONDAY

NOTHING COULD BE better than a good laugh to take the edge off a tense situation. Maybe that's why so many comedians come from tough neighborhoods: They learned early on that sometimes a sense of humor can be a lifesaver. But, as Nate Adams points out, humor, joy, and a little creative fun are always welcome in our harried and over-stressed lives. Given that fact, how refreshing to know that God, our Creator and the very essence of creativity, touches us from time to time with His own Spirit of creative joy.

In the midst of his prophecies, Isaiah declares, "The Lord God has given Me the tongue of the learned, that I should know how to speak a word in season to him who is weary. He awakens Me morning by morning, He awakens My ear to hear as the learned" (Isa. 50:4). Even when the message was dark or frightening, imagine the prophet's joy to be taking dictation from God Himself. Surely a God who inspires our hearts and imaginations and gives us the impulse to bless others, deserves our praise! Would you praise Him now? ▤

TUESDAY

WE KNOW THAT GOD delights in our worship. David says God is enthroned in the praises of His people. And through Isaiah, the Lord says, "Be glad; rejoice forever in my creation! And look! I will create Jerusalem as a place of happiness. Her people will be a source of joy" (Isa. 65:18, NLT). The idea that Christians are all sad and dreary people walking around with long faces is a false stereotype. Who has a greater right to rejoice and sing for joy than those who are redeemed, who've been given the keys of the kingdom?

In one of the most challenging psalms ever written, David exults, "Sing to Him a new song; play skillfully with a shout of joy. For the word of the Lord is right, And all His work is done in truth. He loves righteousness and justice; the earth is full of the goodness of the Lord. By the word of the Lord the heavens were made, and all the host of them by the breath of His mouth" (Ps. 33:3–6).

Pause now to thank Him for the work of creation, and for His creative work in you. ▤

WEDNESDAY

JUST THINK OF all the marvels of creation that fill the pages of Scripture. God started things off with a bang, creating a universe from nothing at all, simply by speaking the Word. He created angels by the millions, the first man and woman, and animals of every size and description. He seeded the forests, the seas, and the rivers, set the geological time clock in motion, and designed the seasons and climates to foster life and regeneration from nature. The incredible originality and diversity of God's creatures overwhelms our imaginations.

No wonder the prophet cried out: "Sing a new song to the Lord! Sing his praises from the ends of the earth! Sing, all you who sail the seas, all you who live in distant coastlands. Join in the chorus, you desert towns; let the villages of Kedar rejoice! Let the people of Sela sing for joy; shout praises from the mountaintops! Let the coastlands glorify the Lord; let them sing his praise" (Isa. 42:10–12, NLT). Even in times of stress, the hand of the Creator fills our hearts with awe and wonder. Thank Him for the splendor of it all. ▤

THURSDAY

MORE AWESOME even than the creation is God's plan of salvation for mankind. He gave us minds and bodies remarkably adapted to life on earth. David says, "I am fearfully and wonderfully made; marvelous are Your works, and that my soul knows very well" (Ps. 139:14). He gave us souls, designed for fellowship with Him. He could have devised any other system. He might have been a cruel and angry god, like the deities of the pagans. He could have been a capricious and evil god, or a silent and invisible one, making no provision for man's salvation. Instead, He sent His only Son to die in our place—humbled, rejected, and betrayed by those He came to save. He called us His children, and equipped us to live with Him forever. "Eye has not seen, nor ear heard, nor have entered into the heart of man the things which God has prepared for those who love Him" (1 Cor. 2:9).

As you meditate on His Word today, think of the ways He has blessed you. Consider His remarkable creativity, joy, and love. Ask Him to open your eyes to all His wonders. ▤

FRIDAY

A LESS IMAGINATIVE God might have created a world with safe, trouble-free beings who'd never get out of line. He could have made us zombies or androids who would obey every command without thinking. Surely such creatures would have given Him a lot less grief. But our creative, joyful, incredibly wise God made us as we are, with all our capacity for sin and deceit, so we'd have the freedom to choose Him over life's distractions.

When the disciples returned from their first evangelistic excursion, they were elated. Wherever they went, they were received gladly by the people. They had preached the Word, cast out demons, and healed the sick. When they reported back, Jesus danced for joy and prayed aloud, "I praise you, Father, Lord of heaven and earth, because you have hidden these things from the wise and learned, and revealed them to little children. Yes, Father, for this was your good pleasure'" (Luke 10:21, NIV). If even the Son of God was awed by His Father's masterful touch, shouldn't we exalt Him with praise? ▤

WEEKEND

THE THINGS THIS WORLD thinks of as fun have a pretty hefty price tag attached. And the harder men work to get it, the less fun they have. The problem is that Satan has corrupted the whole idea of fun, and the average person is chasing things that will break his heart and fill him with remorse. Knowing that joy comes through faith, Paul says, "Finally, brethren, whatever things are true, whatever things are noble, whatever things are just, whatever things are pure, whatever things are lovely, whatever things are of good report, if there is any virtue and if there is anything praiseworthy—meditate on these things" (Phil. 4:8).

We can, indeed, have real and lasting joy through faith in Christ. Just before He ascended, Jesus knew that His followers would be sad to see Him go, so He said, "You now have sorrow; but I will see you again and your heart will rejoice, and your joy no one will take from you" (John 16:22). *That* is the joy we should feel today. Those who are redeemed have the blessed hope of spending eternity in His presence. Thank God for His gift of life. ▤

Week 11

ACCEPTANCE

DO YOU KNOW ANYBODY who's HIV-positive? Most Christians would answer, "No, I don't hang around that type of individual." The facts are that one out of every hundred adult males in America is now infected with HIV—which means you quite likely do know such a person. And there are a fair number of born-again, seriously committed Christian men living this very day with HIV.

Herb Hall went to church with his mom every Sunday and, at age seven, answered the pastor's altar call. Throughout high school and college in Southern California, he kept battling homosexual urges. Then one night when he was twenty-one, he finally walked into an adult bookstore. By the end of the evening, a guy had picked him up and given him his first gay experience.

Herb's spiritual conflict came to a head with a 1987 suicide attempt. Three years of pastoral counseling followed. "God healed me gradually," he says. "At the end of that period I was finally free." His sins were forgiven but the HIV he had contracted did not go away. Herb is now vice president of a ministry called "HIV—He Intends Victory" and works with churches and individuals to start groups all across the country for people with AIDS.

As a boy, Charles Linares did a good job of avoiding drugs. After college, he enlisted in the navy and that's when the trouble began. "I went from being Momma's little boy to mainlining heroin and chasing women." For years he had just one thing in mind: getting money for drugs. In time his armed robberies landed him in Sing Sing. "I gave the state twelve to thirteen years of my life," he says.

Along the way, a fellow prisoner talked to Charles about Christ, and he made a confession of faith. Today you'll find him working as a counselor at a place called Nuestra Clinica. Some of his clients don't know he's HIV-infected. "I don't give much thought to my condition," he says. "I'm more focused on getting to share some truth with somebody who needs it. Christ still goes where the prostitutes and alcoholics and thieves are," Charles says. "He still suffers with them."

Mike Hylton spends much of his days in a recliner. He contracted AIDS from a blood transfusion. Prior to 1985, the nation's blood supply was polluted with HIV. Blood banks were buying blood from virtually any donor—drug addicts, alcoholics, active homosexuals. The tragic result is that out of America's twenty thousand hemophiliacs like Mike, ten thousand were infected with HIV. When Mike joined the group that meets at Herb Hall's church, he needed to work on his attitude toward gay men and drug abusers. "Friends like Herb helped me . . . realize that we all need God's help," Mike says. "God is saying, 'Tell them I love them . . . I sent My Son to die for all of you.'"

If Mike's vision will be embraced by thousands of other Christian men, Mike says, then he can rest in peace.

—DEAN MERRILL

MONDAY

GOD'S PLAN OF SALVATION wasn't designed for perfect people. Jesus had to remind the Pharisees, "Those who are well have no need of a physician" (Matt. 9:12). He had come for those who would turn from their sin and ask for forgiveness. The plan of redemption was not complete until Jesus came, of course, but ages before Messiah's birth, David had said, "Blessed is he whose transgression is forgiven, whose sin is covered. Blessed is the man to whom the Lord does not impute iniquity, and in whose spirit there is no deceit" (Ps. 32:1–2). The model of forgiveness for our sins had been established before the beginning of time.

That's why David could say, "I acknowledged my sin to You, and my iniquity I have not hidden. I said, 'I will confess my transgressions to the Lord,' and You forgave the iniquity of my sin" (v. 5). God forgives those who confess and turn away from sin. And Jesus taught, "If your brother sins against you, rebuke him; and if he repents, forgive him" (Luke 17:3).

Pray that God will help you understand and apply His principle of acceptance. ■

TUESDAY

NOW AND THEN Christians are guilty as charged. We are quick to condemn sinners, and we're the first to point the finger at those who do wrong. Imagine the nods and shouts of accusation when Paul said, "Do you not know that the unrighteous will not inherit the kingdom of God? Do not be deceived. Neither fornicators, nor idolaters, nor adulterers, nor homosexuals, nor sodomites, nor thieves, nor covetous, nor drunkards, nor revilers, nor extortioners will inherit the kingdom of God." But imagine the deafening silence that ensued when he went on to say, "And such were some of you. But you were washed, but you were sanctified, but you were justified in the name of the Lord Jesus and by the Spirit of our God" (1 Cor. 6:9–11).

Remember Peter's lesson on forgiveness in Matthew 18? No matter how often our brother may fail, we're obliged to accept his sincere apology and leave judgment to God. Pray today that you may learn to accept those who come to Christ in humble repentance. ≣

WEDNESDAY

PAUL DIDN'T STOP at reminding the Corinthian Christians of their less-than-virtuous past. With complete honesty, he accepted responsibility for his own past, saying, "Here is a trustworthy saying that deserves full acceptance: Christ Jesus came into the world to save sinners—of whom I am the worst. But for that very reason I was shown mercy so that in me, the worst of sinners, Christ Jesus might display his unlimited patience as an example for those who would believe on him and receive eternal life" (1 Tim. 1:15–16, NIV).

The message of the gospel is that *Christ came to save sinners.* To accomplish that goal, He has prepared you and me to be His emissaries, to go into all the world and make disciples. He has entrusted us to recruit for the kingdom of God, and to welcome all who believe in Him, and turn away from their enslavement to sin and the idols of materialism. In the end, Christ Himself will judge the hearts of those who come, and will separate the sheep from the goats. In the meantime, would you ask Him to give you a passion for the lost? ≣

THURSDAY

WHEN PAUL WROTE to the Romans, he laid it on the line. "You, therefore, have no excuse, you who pass judgment on someone else, for at whatever point you judge the other, you are condemning yourself, because you who pass judgment do the same things. Now we know that God's judgment against those who do such things is based on truth. So when you, a mere man, pass judgment on them and yet do the same things, do you think you will escape God's judgment? Or do you show contempt for the riches of his kindness, tolerance and patience, not realizing that God's kindness leads you toward repentance?" (Rom. 2:1–4, NIV). In light of such strong words, maybe it shouldn't be surprising that so few churches will deal with these issues from the pulpit. But that doesn't make them less important.

The lesson Mike Hylton learned from Herb Hall and Charles Linares, as described in this week's reading, was that only God can judge a man's heart. To condemn those whom God has forgiven is an act of supreme disrespect. Pray today for a trusting, forgiving heart. ▤

FRIDAY

THE ACRONYM HIV has become a death sentence in more ways than one. Anyone who admits to being HIV-positive these days automatically becomes *persona non grata* in every group. They are the lepers of our day. Despite our mission of love and compassion, too often Christians are the least accepting of those who have received this sentence. We draw back, smile politely, then walk away, when Christ would have us reach out in love.

"It is written: 'As surely as I live,' says the Lord, 'every knee will bow before me; every tongue will confess to God.' So then, each of us will give an account of himself to God. Therefore let us stop passing judgment on one another. Instead, make up your mind not to put any stumbling block or obstacle in your brother's way" (Rom. 14:11–13, NIV). It would be wrong to accept a sinner who continues to sin without restraint; but it's just as wrong to condemn those who have renounced their sin and come to Christ.

Would you pray today that God will give you a new compassion for each of these? ▤

WEEKEND

WHEN WE ADMIT our sins of intolerance and our tendency to reject certain groups of people, we may wonder if God can rebuild what our arrogance has torn down. Perhaps we need to hear Nehemiah's prayer, before he returned from the Babylonian captivity to rebuild the walls of Jerusalem. "We have acted very corruptly against You," he said, "and have not kept the commandments, the statutes, nor the ordinances which You commanded Your servant Moses. Remember, I pray, the word that You commanded Your servant Moses, saying, 'If you are unfaithful, I will scatter you among the nations; but if you return to Me, and keep My commandments and do them, though some of you were cast out to the farthest part of the heavens, yet I will gather them from there, and bring them to the place which I have chosen as a dwelling for My name'" (Neh. 1:7–9).

God heard Nehemiah's prayer and touched the heart of the king, who paid the bills to rebuild the ancient city. Pray that He will touch your heart as well and teach you to love. ▤

Week 12
HOPE

COURT TV BRINGS America face-to-face with some of the best-known prisoners in our land. In televised courtroom scenes, the accused may appear to be as free as anybody else. But outside it, they are completely at the disposal of the penal system. What they eat, how they dress, where they sleep, are controlled by forces beyond themselves.

The same may be said of Christians. Zechariah says, "Because of the blood of My covenant with you, I have set your prisoners free from the waterless pit. Return to the stronghold, O prisoners who have the hope. This very day I am declaring that I will restore double to you" (Zech. 9:11–12). Because of Christ's cross, God is forever transforming prisoners of waterless pits into "prisoners of hope." Not just any hope either, but the supreme hope of both personal and widespread revival.

But what is revival? J. I. Packer has defined revival as "a work of God by His Spirit through His Word bringing the spiritually dead to living faith in Christ and renewing the inner life of Christians who have grown slack and sleepy. In revival God makes old things new . . . Revival reanimates churches and Christian groups to make a spiritual and moral impact on communities."

A witness of the Second Great Awakening in the 1700s said, "When the Redeemer comes in the triumphs of His grace to visit His churches, then His true followers are seen waking from their apathy, and going forth to welcome the King of Zion with an energy and earnestness and ardor of affection greatly surpassing their first love." We can conclude that what God has done before, He is very willing to do again—and ever more.

The cry for hope has never been greater. Our nation is deeply torn over the role of religion in society. Spiritual pursuits are increasingly excluded from public life, while our troubled nation is beset by violent crime, broken families, deteriorating cities, and racism. No wonder that researcher George Barna recently concluded that in the next five to ten years America will experience one of two revolutions: anarchy or revival.

What should be our response to the spiritual decline in our country? In the words of James Dobson, "Every great revival has been accompanied by social reform . . . We seek the Lord in earnest prayer that He would once again grant revival to His church in the United States and around the world."

Among the signs of revival that make us prisoners of hope are the National Day of Prayer, denominational prayer strategies, national youth prayer initiatives, city-wide prayer gatherings, the multiplication of local and national prayer-training ministries, the linkage of millions by radio and TV, the increase in congregational initiatives, and the individual prayer bands that dot the land.

As God impresses this hope upon us, it will make us even more hungry for revival. Praying and preparing *makes* us hungry. The hope is at hand. Know that God wants revival for us far more than we want it for ourselves.

—DAVID BRYANT

MONDAY

HOPE. Such a small but powerful word. It contains the disappointment of "not just yet" and the joyful expectation of the "not long now!" It separates the flimsy optimism of the secular man from the radiant confidence of the believer. For the world, hope is waiting for some man-made vista, some earth-bound consumerist dream. But for the man of God, our hope is the absolute certainty of a breath-taking reunion with the King of kings! "For yet a little while, and He who is coming will come and will not tarry" (Heb. 10:37). In this hope we put our trust, because we know that "the just shall live by faith" (v. 38).

David says, "My soul, wait silently for God alone, for my expectation is from Him. He only is my rock and my salvation; He is my defense; I shall not be moved. In God is my salvation and my glory; the rock of my strength, and my refuge, is in God" (Ps. 62:5–7). Anticipation of the fulfillment of our hope draws us onward, despite the frustrations along the way, knowing what's ahead. Thank the Lord today that you have that hope within you. ■

TUESDAY

A VISITOR TO ALASKA stepped off the train to a vista like nothing he had ever seen. Mountains soaring toward the heavens through ice caps and banks of pink and golden clouds illuminated by the morning sun. Deep purple rivers, vibrant green forests, and cool, crisp air that filled his lungs with a sudden rush of new life. "My God!" he exclaimed. "That's right!" whispered the old porter beside him. "That's right. And if God can do that with a little ol' mountain, just imagine what He can do with you and me!"

Aren't you glad that God hasn't given us the best part yet? Just imagine what's coming next! Paul says, "Therefore, having been justified by faith, we have peace with God through our Lord Jesus Christ, through whom also we have access by faith into this grace in which we stand, and rejoice in hope of the glory of

God. And not only that, but we also glory in tribulations, knowing that tribulation produces perseverance;
and perseverance, character; and character, hope"
(Rom. 5:1–4). Pray that you may live each day in that
hope. ▤

WEDNESDAY

THE WORLD OFTEN LOOKS at us with disbelief. They
shake their heads at Christians and laugh that we've
given up so much for our religion. "What, no wild par-
ties?" they say. "No adulterous flings? No cheating,
lying, stealing, or getting even with those you hate?
What is it with you guys?" The reason is very simple.
We're waiting for something so much better.

"For the grace of God that brings salvation has
appeared to all men, teaching us that, denying ungodli-
ness and worldly lusts, we should live soberly,
righteously, and godly in the present age, looking for
the blessed hope and glorious appearing of our great
God and Savior Jesus Christ, who gave Himself for us,
that He might redeem us from every lawless deed and
purify for Himself His own special people, zealous for
good works" (Titus 2:11–14). The fact that we have a
blessed hope doesn't mean we're waiting on some
magic-carpet escape. There's tons to be done while we
wait, and that's why the apostle says we're to be
"zealous for good works." Let us rejoice and praise
God today for our radiant hope. ▤

THURSDAY

AS DAVID BRYANT points out, the fabric of our nation is
being torn apart. Many would like to separate church
and state once and for all. But the more they try, the less
influence the virtues of faith can have on society. But
we must also admit that, had the church been more
visible in the past, and had our leaders not compro-

mised with the illusions of this life, things might not have fallen so far so fast. At least a part of our problem is our own doing.

Long ago, Ezra wrote, "Since the days of our fathers to this day we have been very guilty, and for our iniquities we, our kings, and our priests have been delivered into the hand of the kings of the lands, to the sword, to captivity, to plunder, and to humiliation, as it is this day. And now for a little while grace has been shown from the Lord our God, to leave us a remnant to escape . . . that our God may enlighten our eyes and give us a measure of revival in our bondage" (Ezra 9:7–8). We, too, live in the hope of revival, so that many may share our eternal hope. As you confess your failings today, pray for revival in America. ■

FRIDAY

BY ALL RIGHTS, eternal life and the joys of heaven could have been God's little secret. He could have kept it all for Himself and a few close friends; but, instead, He chose to share eternity with "whosoever will." Jesus said, "For God so loved the world that He gave His only begotten Son, that *whoever* believes in Him should not perish but have everlasting life" (John 3:16). J. I. Packer says revival is a sovereign work of God through the Holy Spirit, "bringing the spiritually dead to living faith in Christ." Why God would do it, and why He would send His Son to redeem us from our sin, is the greatest mystery of all time.

Paul says, "God willed to make known what are the riches of the glory of this mystery among the Gentiles: which is *Christ in you, the hope of glory.* Him we preach, warning every man and teaching every man in all wisdom, that we may present every man perfect in Christ Jesus" (Col. 1:27–28). If God went to such incredible lengths to share His home with us, shouldn't we pray today for the skill to share the Good News with others? ▤

WEEKEND

THROUGHOUT HIS ministry, Jesus taught parables that warned believers to be faithful and longsuffering. The parables of the foolish virgins, the fig tree, the two sons, the wicked vinedressers, the talents, and the women grinding at the mill all teach us not to lose hope, to be steadfast and unmovable, to be found serving faithfully when the Landlord returns. We should make it our pledge of faith to be constantly in prayer for those who are lost, to minister to and care for those in need of a healing touch, and to shepherd our loved ones.

Even in the midst of flight from Saul's wrath, David sang, "My heart is steadfast, O God, my heart is steadfast; I will sing and give praise. Awake, my glory! Awake, lute and harp! I will awaken the dawn. I will praise You, O Lord, among the peoples; I will sing to You among the nations. For Your mercy reaches unto the heavens, and Your truth unto the clouds. Be exalted, O God, above the heavens; let Your glory be above all the earth" (Ps. 57:7–11). Can you share that song? Thank the Lord today, and praise Him in song. ▤

WATCHFULNESS

▰▰▰ TWO THOUSAND YEARS AGO in the turbulent
▰▰▰ Middle East, the most deadly battle of all time
was fought. Not between two armies, but a life-and-
death struggle between two generals. At stake was the
eternal destiny of the human race. As Jesus launched
His public ministry, He withdrew to the Judean wilderness for a time of prayer and fasting—only to face
Satan in the spiritual battle of the ages. By studying
Satan's attack, we can discover his *modus operandi* and
understand when he is most likely to ambush us.

The final verse of Christ's temptation in the wilderness concludes: "And when the devil had finished every
temptation, he departed from Him until an opportune
time" (Luke 4:13, NAS). An "opportune time" means a
moment when the conditions are more favorable for
attack. Here are six elements of this "danger zone:"

1. *After a spiritual victory.* It was after one of
   Jesus' greatest victories—the moment of His
   baptism—that Satan launched his attack. This
   was the moment when Christ stepped out of
   obscurity to begin His ministry. God thundered,
   "This is My beloved Son," and Satan coun-
   tered, "If you are the Son of God . . . " We can
   expect no less. After every spiritual victory in
   our lives, Satan will be lurking in the shadows.
   Are you riding a spiritual high? Then watch
   out! Satan has you in his cross hairs.

2. *When you're all alone.* In the wilderness, Jesus
   was all alone and perceived to be vulnerable by
   Satan. Men: A time of isolation is a danger

zone for all of us. Christ sent out His disciples
two by two; so remember, there's strength in
numbers.

3. *When you're physically drained.* For forty days,
Jesus ate nothing while in the rugged Judean
terrain. This is precisely when Satan fired his
three temptations. Lack of sleep, sickness,
fatigue, hard work—that's when Satan moves
in to clobber us.

4. *When you're waiting on God.* Waiting on God
seems to be especially hard for men. The
earthly kingdoms had already been promised to
Christ by His Father; but God's plan required
that Jesus die for our sins. Only then would He
receive His reward. Are you waiting on God for
something that's important to you? Then you're
in the danger zone.

5. *When you're in God's house.* We tend to think
all temptations are in the world, not in church
gatherings. But Satan's temptations are more
dangerous in church—they're unexpected
because our hearts are open and unguarded, and
even normal people can go berserk if the music
or the order of service should change!

6. *When you're starting something great for God.*
Whenever a great work for God is about to
begin, Satan will be there to stop it. If you're
beginning a new phase in your ministry,
beware. You have entered another danger zone.

How many of these apply to you right now? Be alert,
put on your spiritual armor, and arm yourself with the
Word of God.

—STEVEN J. LAWSON

MONDAY

HE IS A MASTER of disguise. He can appear gentle and

compassionate in moments of weakness, or daring and carefree when you're riding the crest of success. But in his natural state, Satan is a destroyer who crushes the hearts of the careless and inattentive in a vicelike grip. Peter warns, "Be sober, be vigilant; because your adversary the devil walks about like a roaring lion, seeking whom he may devour. Resist him, steadfast in the faith, knowing that the same sufferings are experienced by your brotherhood in the world" (1 Pet. 5:8–9).

If he were some slapstick character in a red suit, with a long tail and a pitchfork as he's often portrayed in cartoons, the serpent wouldn't stand a chance. But he's a smooth operator, masquerading as an angel of light, laying traps for unsuspecting victims. Steven Lawson's list of *danger zones* should give us a clue that our adversary really means business and he's looking, even now, for ways to sneak up on you. As you consider the battle before you, be watchful, and pray that you can always keep your eyes on the prize. ■

TUESDAY

THERE'S NOTHING LIKE a little success to defeat a guy's Christian walk. We struggle to overcome some long-term problem and, just when we begin to see victory ahead, we throw back our heads and gloat just a little too much. It's not a Christian thing; it's a *human* thing, and Satan knows it. That's why we're warned in this week's reading to be especially careful when we've gained any kind of spiritual victory.

Paul had plenty of reason to be proud of his accomplishments. He had been taken in the spirit into the very presence of Christ and shown the mysteries of salvation. He founded churches throughout Judea, Asia Minor, Greece, and Rome, and multitudes came to faith under his teaching. Yet, he says, "God forbid that I should boast except in the cross of our Lord Jesus

Christ, by whom the world has been crucified to me, and I to the world" (Gal. 6:14). In the hope of receiving the crown of life that Christ will award to the faithful, pray today that you will be able to crucify the pride of life and boast only in the cross of Christ. ▤

WEDNESDAY

WHAT AN INCREDIBLE battle must be raging in the heavenlies, in a dimension of time and space no mortal eye can see. We are given brief hints in several verses of Scripture, but few men have had even a glimpse of that parallel universe where the battle of the ages is being waged. God could strike down Satan's forces in a heartbeat, and someday He will. But He is so certain we'll choose heaven over hell—siding with Christ instead of the enemy—that He has given us absolute freedom to choose where we will spend eternity.

Satan, however, is betting he can bluff us out. What pride! The same sin that got him into hot water in the first place! Paul says, "Therefore let him who thinks he stands take heed lest he fall. No temptation has overtaken you except such as is common to man; but God is faithful, who will not allow you to be tempted beyond what you are able, but with the temptation will also make the way of escape, that you may be able to bear it" (1 Cor. 10:12–13). Pray for vision and perception, to see Satan's lies for what they really are. ▤

THURSDAY

A CHILD DIES, a mother takes her life, a priest molests a little boy, or a father deserts his family and disappears without a trace. Everyday, it seems, we hear news like that, news that breaks our hearts. And in the aftermath, someone turns away from God because they're convinced that either He doesn't care or He isn't there. Harold Kushner, who wrote *When Bad Things Happen to Good People,* reached the conclusion that God is out of control. He would like things to be different, but He's a victim of circumstance like everybody else. If that were true (which it isn't), then why not shake your fist at God and live as you please?

Anger, bitterness, and deception are tools of Satan to rob us of our hope. But if we fill our hearts with the Word of God, we can rise above such things. Isaiah says, "Surely God is my salvation; I will trust and not be afraid. The Lord, the Lord, is my strength and my song; he has become my salvation" (Isa. 12:2, NIV). Ask the Lord today for the courage to overcome all your doubts, and then to help others find hope in His faithfulness. ▤

FRIDAY

IF IT WEREN'T SO TRUE it might be funny. But as Steven Lawson observes, one of the places where Satan and his demons do their best work is in church on Sunday mornings. If there's any danger that you might learn something, he'll lull you to sleep. If there's a chance you might be offended, he'll tweak your anger by pointing out everything that's wrong with the service. If you're inattentive, he'll let something really important slide by. Or, most of all, he'll get you to worrying about all those things you can't do anything about.

If you've ever experienced any of that, don't blame God. James says, "Let no one say when he is tempted, 'I am tempted by God'; for God cannot be tempted by evil, nor does He Himself tempt anyone. But each one is tempted when he is drawn away by his own desires and enticed. Then, when desire has conceived, it gives birth to sin; and sin, when it is full-grown, brings forth death" (James 1:13–15). Satan knows what he's doing: he's been at it for centuries! But you can take back your Sundays, and defeat him with prayer and praise. ▤

WEEKEND

WHENEVER YOU DECIDE to serve God in an active way, whether in full-time ministry or a more active roll in your church, Satan will lay traps for you as never before. Not only with doubts and fears, but especially with jealousy, pride, and envy. At one point, David began to think he wasn't getting his fair share. He says, "But as for me, my feet had almost stumbled; my steps had nearly slipped. For I was envious of the boastful, when I saw the prosperity of the wicked" (Ps. 73:2–3). But no sooner had the thought formed in his mind than he cast it out through confession, prayer, and thanksgiving.

As you reflect on all you've read in these pages, pray that you'll always be watchful, holding fast to this truth: "Put on the whole armor of God, that you may be able to stand against the wiles of the devil. For we do not wrestle against flesh and blood, but against principalities, against powers, against the rulers of the darkness of this age, against spiritual hosts of wickedness in the heavenly places" (Eph. 6:11–12). In Christ, you are a *new man!* ▤

Sources

First Quarter

Week 1: Promise Keepers, "Raising the Standard," *New Man*, January/February 1995.

Week 2: Gary Rosberg, "We're in This Together," *New Man*, November/December 1995.

Week 3: Ken Davis, "Love in a Vacuum," *New Man*, May 1997.

Week 4: Warren Wiersbe, "The Journey of Faith," *New Man*, January/February 1997. Originally published in Warren W. Wiersbe, *Being a Child of God: Your Guide for the Adventure* (Nashville, TN: Thomas Nelson, 1996).

Week 5: Ken R. Canfield, "When It's Hard to Honor Dad," *New Man*, June 1997.

Week 6: Greg Johnson, "Best Friends Once Again," *New Man*, July/August 1996. Originally published in Greg Johnson, *We're Finally Alone. Now What Do We Do?* (Wheaton, IL: Tyndale, 1996).

Week 7: Randy T. Phillips, "God's Calculated Risk," *New Man*, March/April 1996.

Week 8: Lynette Blair Mitchell, "Takin' It Home," *New Man*, June 1997.

Week 9: Randy Alcorn, "Investing for Eternity," *New Man*, June 1997.

Week 10: John C. Maxwell, "Helping Your Child Climb Higher," *New Man*, November/December 1996. Originally published in John C. Maxwell, *Breakthrough Parenting* (Colorado Springs, CO: Focus on the Family, 1996).

Week 11: Gary J. Oliver, "Living in a Gray-Area World," *New Man*, May/June 1995.

Week 12: David Stiebel, "Keeping Peace at the Office," *New Man*, March/April 1997. Originally published in David Stiebel, *When Talking Makes Things Worse! Resolving Problems When Communication Fails* (Whitehall & Nolton, 1997).

WEEK 13: Brian Peterson, "The Stuff of Life," *New Man,* May 1996.

SECOND QUARTER

WEEK 1: Gary D. Chapman, "Are You Speaking the Right Language?" *New Man,* March/April 1997.

WEEK 2: Jim Nelson Black, "The Heart of the New Man," *New Man,* November/December 1994.

WEEK 3: Robert Jeffress, "When the Task Is Never Finished," *New Man,* September 1996.

WEEK 4: Ken R. Canfield, "The Heart of a Forgiver," *New Man,* March/April 1997.

WEEK 5: Ken Ruettgers, "Taking the Home-Field Advantage," *New Man,* October 1996. Originally published in Ken Ruettgers, *Home Field Advantage* (Portland, OR: Multnomah, 1996).

WEEK 6: J. Allan Petersen, "Temptation, Traps & Triumphs," *New Man,* July/August 1995.

WEEK 7: Greg Laurie, "Mr. Nice God," *New Man,* May/June 1995. Originally published in Greg Laurie, *The Great Compromise* (Dallas, TX: Word Publishing, 1994).

WEEK 8: Edward Gilbreath, "Adopted by Love," *New Man,* June 1996.

WEEK 9: Patrick Morley, "An Open Letter to Men of Color," *New Man,* June 1997. Originally published in Patrick Morley, *Seven Seasons of a Man's Life* (Nashville, TN: Thomas Nelson, 1995).

WEEK 10: Larry Kreider, "Yield Control Without Giving Up," *New Man,* September 1996. Originally published in Larry Kreider, *Bottom Line Faith* (Wheaton, IL: Tyndale, 1995).

WEEK 11: James Sandell, "Dad's Video Toolbox," *New Man,* June 1996.

WEEK 12: Ken R. Canfield, "Treat Him Like a Best Friend," *New Man,* November/December 1995.

WEEK 13: Edward Gilbreath, "The 2nd Chapter of Matthew," *New Man,* January/February 1997.

Third Quarter

WEEK 1: Bob Buford, "What's in the Box?" *New Man,* July/August 1996. Originally published in Bob Buford, *Halftime* (Grand Rapids, MI: Zondervan, 1995).

WEEK 2: Neil T. Anderson, "God's Way to Freedom," *New Man,* May 1997.

WEEK 3: Joe Maxwell, "Treasures From the Galilee," *New Man,* September/October 1994.

WEEK 4: George Barna, "The Battle for the Hearts of Men," *New Man,* January/February 1997. Originally published in George Barna, *The Index of Spiritual Indicators* (Dallas, TX: Word Publishing, 1996).

WEEK 5: Wellington Boone, "Have Mercy," *New Man,* January/February 1997.

WEEK 6: David Culp, "A Global Awakening of Men," *New Man,* January/February 1995.

WEEK 7: Kip Burke, "Do As I Don't, Don't As I Do," *New Man,* September/October 1995.

WEEK 8: Mike Yorkey, "Comeback Kid," *New Man,* October 1996.

WEEK 9: Jennifer Ferranti, "Hijacked!" *New Man,* March/April 1997.

WEEK 10: Bill McCartney, "The Power of a Promise," *New Man,* March/April 1995.

WEEK 11: Steve Sjogren, "Real Men Clean Bathrooms," *New Man,* November/December 1994.

WEEK 12: Jack and Jerry Schreur, "Adaptable Dads," *New Man,* November/December 1996. Originally published in Jack and Jerry Schreur, *Fathers & Sons* (Wheaton, IL: Victor, 1995).

WEEK 13: Kim J. Carpenter with Dean Merrill, "Stolen Memories," *New Man,* January/February 1997.

Fourth Quarter

WEEK 1: Joseph Garlington, "The Pleasure of Worshiping God," *New Man,* June 1997.

WEEK 2: G. L. Beaverson, "The Father I Never Knew," *New Man*, June 1996.

WEEK 3: Pete Richardson, "What Will Your Tombstone Say?" *New Man*, October 1996.

WEEK 4: Mike Umlandt, "A Father's Passion," *New Man*, June 1997.

WEEK 5: Bill Bright, "Radical Lover," *New Man,* May/June 1995. Originally published in Bill Bright, *Building a Home in a Pull-Apart World* (Orlando, FL: NewLife Publications, 1995).

WEEK 6: Lowell Lundstrom, "My Precious Prodigal," *New Man*, November/December 1996.

WEEK 7: Diane Eble, "Reason to Rejoice," *New Man*, March/April 1995.

WEEK 8: Stephen Arterburn, "Seven Big Mistakes Men Make," *New Man*, November/December 1995.

WEEK 9: John Trent, "Unshakable Men," *New Man*, November/December 1995.

WEEK 10: Nate Adams, "Finding the Fun in What Needs to Be Done," *New Man*, November/December 1994.

WEEK 11: Dean Merrill, "Living With a Killer," *New Man*, June 1997.

WEEK 12: David Bryant, "Prisoners of Hope," *New Man*, September 1996.

WEEK 13: Steven J. Lawson, "In the Line of Fire," *New Man*, October 1996. Originally published in Steven J. Lawson, *Faith Under Fire* (Nashville, TN: Crossway, 1995).